there's more to the Story

Using Literature to Teach Diversity and Social-Emotional Skills in the Elementary Classroom

Gwendolyn **Cartledge**

Amanda L. **Yurick**

Alana **Oif Telesman**

Solution Tree | Press
a division of Solution Tree

Copyright © 2022 by Solution Tree Press

Materials appearing here are copyrighted. With one exception, all rights are reserved. Readers may reproduce only those pages marked "Reproducible." Otherwise, no part of this book may be reproduced or transmitted in any form or by any means (electronic, photocopying, recording, or otherwise) without prior written permission of the publisher.

555 North Morton Street
Bloomington, IN 47404
800.733.6786 (toll free) / 812.336.7700
FAX: 812.336.7790

email: info@SolutionTree.com
SolutionTree.com

Visit **go.SolutionTree.com/diversityandequity** to download the free reproducibles in this book.

Printed in the United States of America

Library of Congress Cataloging-in-Publication Data

Names: Cartledge, Gwendolyn, 1943- author. | Yurick, Amanda L., author. | Telesman, Alana Oif, author.
Title: There's more to the story : using literature to teach diversity and social-emotional skills in the elementary classroom / Gwendolyn Cartledge, Amanda L. Yurick, Alana Oif Telesman.
Other titles: There is more to the story
Description: Bloomington, IN : Solution Tree Press, [2022] | Includes bibliographical references and index.
Identifiers: LCCN 2021053452 (print) | LCCN 2021053453 (ebook) | ISBN 9781952812675 (Paperback) | ISBN 9781952812682 (eBook)
Subjects: LCSH: Literature--Study and teaching (Elementary)--United States. | Multicultural education--United States. | Social skills--Study and teaching (Elementary)--United States. | Emotions--Study and teaching (Elementary)--United States. | Social skills in children. | Emotions in children.
Classification: LCC LB1575.5.U5 C37 2022 (print) | LCC LB1575.5.U5 (ebook) | DDC 372.64/044--dc23/eng/20211213
LC record available at https://lccn.loc.gov/2021053452
LC ebook record available at https://lccn.loc.gov/2021053453

Solution Tree
Jeffrey C. Jones, CEO
Edmund M. Ackerman, President

Solution Tree Press
President and Publisher: Douglas M. Rife
Associate Publisher: Sarah Payne-Mills
Managing Production Editor: Kendra Slayton
Editorial Director: Todd Brakke
Art Director: Rian Anderson
Copy Chief: Jessi Finn
Senior Production Editor: Christine Hood
Content Development Specialist: Amy Rubenstein
Acquisitions Editor: Sarah Jubar
Copy Editor: Evie Madsen
Proofreader: Jessi Finn
Editorial Assistants: Charlotte Jones, Sarah Ludwig, and Elijah Oates

Acknowledgments

We are grateful to Solution Tree for its interest in our work and willingness to publish this manuscript. We extend special thanks to Amy Rubenstein for the many hours spent in reviewing, editing, and structuring the text of this book. We also appreciate the valuable reviews and input of Christine Hood and other Solution Tree staff. Their suggestions and the assistance of many nameless others helped to greatly strengthen this product.

We thank our families for their endless support and all the young people in our lives (progeny and students) who served as willing or unwitting subjects for our social-emotional learning studies, materials, and activities.

We want to recognize a friend and colleague, Rudine Sims Bishop, who is indeed an icon in the area of culturally diverse children's literature. Her scholarship in promoting literature for racially and ethnically diverse children has had a tremendous impact on the field and greatly aided this undertaking.

Finally, we would like for this book to honor the memory of two outstanding teachers, scholars, and mentors who were pioneers in the field of social-emotional learning and to whom we are deeply indebted: Thomas M. Stephens and JoAnne Fellows Milburn.

Solution Tree Press would like to thank the following reviewers:

Dean Armstrong
High School ELA
Melfort & Unit Comp Collegiate
Melfort, Saskatchewan

Kimberly Freiley
ELA Teacher
Ingersoll Middle School
Canton, Illinois

Rosemarie Nodine Swallow
Social Studies
Lava Ridge Intermediate
Santa Clara, Utah

Nancy Petolick
Instructional Coach
Savannah Elementary
Aubrey, Texas

David Pillar
Assistant Director
Hoosier Hills Career Center
Bloomington, Indiana

Table of Contents

About the Authors ix

Introduction 1
    Purpose of This Book 2
    What's in This Book 3
    How to Use This Book 6
    Conclusion 8

Part I
Promoting Social-Emotional Development Through Diverse and Culturally Relevant Children's Literature 11

1   Developing Social-Emotional Skills in Young Children 13
    Self-Related Skills 14
    Interpersonal Skills 16
    Social Awareness 19
    Presence or Absence of Social-Emotional Learning in Young Children 21
    Conclusion 23
    Chapter Reflections 23

2   Using Diverse and Culturally Relevant Literature 25
    Diverse and Culturally Relevant Literature Selection for Social-Emotional Learning 27
    Model for Using Diverse and Culturally Relevant Literature for Social-Emotional Learning 30
    Literature Formats for Social-Emotional Learning 33
    Student Engagement With Books 34
    Conclusion 36
    Chapter Reflections 36

Part II
Affirming Others and Self and Asserting Self Through Diverse and Culturally Relevant Children's Literature............37

3 Affirming Others..39
- Being Kind and Affirming Others 39
- Affirming Others in Poverty 42
- Literature on Affirming Others in Poverty. 42
- Affirming Others With Ability Differences 49
- Literature on Affirming Others With Ability Differences 50
- Affirming Others From Different Religious or Cultural Groups 57
- Literature on Affirming Others From Different Religious or Cultural Groups 58
- Books on Affirming Others 67
- Conclusion 69
- Chapter Reflections 69

4 Affirming Self..71
- Affirming Self With Regard to Race 72
- Literature on Affirming Self With Regard to Race 73
- Affirming Self With Regard to Gender Differences. 82
- Literature on Affirming Self With Regard to Gender Differences 83
- Books on Affirming Self 93
- Conclusion 93
- Chapter Reflections 95

5 Asserting Self..97
- Asserting Self With Regard to Ethnic and Cultural Differences 98
- Literature on Asserting Self With Regard to Ethnic and Cultural Differences. 98
- Asserting Self Across Immigrant and Migrant Groups 107
- Literature on Asserting Self Across Immigrant and Migrant Groups 107
- Books on Asserting Self 115
- Conclusion 115
- Chapter Reflections 117

Part III
Dealing With Aggression and Conflict Through Diverse and Culturally Relevant Children's Literature 119

6 Responding to Aggression 121
Responding to Physical Aggression. 122
Literature on Responding to Physical Aggression 123
Responding to Verbal Aggression. 133
Literature on Responding to Verbal Aggression 134
Books on Responding to Aggression 145
Conclusion 145
Chapter Reflections 147

7 Playing and Working Cooperatively With Others 149
Playing and Working Cooperatively Across Age Groups. 150
Literature on Playing and Working Cooperatively Across Age Groups 151
Playing and Working Cooperatively Across Racial and Ethnic Groups 158
Literature on Playing and Working Cooperatively Across Racial and Ethnic Groups 158
Books on Playing and Working Cooperatively With Others 166
Conclusion 167
Chapter Reflections 168

8 Questioning Unfair Practices. 169
Questioning Unfair Practices With Regard to Race. 172
Literature on Questioning Unfair Practices With Regard to Race 173
Questioning Unfair Practices With Regard to Poverty 183
Literature on Questioning Unfair Practices With Regard to Poverty. 184
Books on Questioning Unfair Practices 192
Conclusion 193
Chapter Reflections 193

Epilogue 195

References and Resources 199

Index 213

About the Authors

Gwendolyn Cartledge, PhD, is a professor emerita at The Ohio State University, College of Education and Human Ecology. She began her career as a preschool and elementary public school teacher, continuing with youth with learning and behavior disorders, but she taught most extensively in higher education. Her professional research and writings center on the social and academic skills of children with and without disabilities, particularly those from culturally and linguistically diverse backgrounds. She extensively researches literacy and social development interventions for these populations, as documented in over one hundred publications, including four books and four curricula on social and emotional skills.

Gwen obtained competitive national and state grants to support her research and writings. In addition to her university teaching and mentoring over fifty dissertation and thesis students, she has made over 180 state, national, and international professional presentations. She also has conducted numerous local in-service and professional development sessions for teachers on students' social and literacy development. Over the course of her career, Gwen has been a member of nine professional organizations and continues to maintain membership and affiliation with the Council for Exceptional Children and the American Education Research Association.

Among her various awards, Gwen was recognized for Leadership and Distinguished Service by her state professional organization in 1996, received the Distinguished Teaching Award from The Ohio State University in 2003, and received the Educator of the Year Award from the Ohio Council for Exceptional Children in 2006 and the Distinguished Alumni Award from the University of Pittsburgh in 2010. Gwen earned undergraduate and master's degrees from the University of Pittsburgh and a doctorate in education from The Ohio State University.

To learn more about Gwen's work, visit her Google Images site (shorturl.at/qEHQS) or Google Scholar site (shorturl.at/lGLQT).

Amanda L. Yurick, PhD, is an associate professor in special education at Cleveland State University (CSU). She teaches graduate and undergraduate students pursuing licensure in special education and applied behavior analysis. Amanda has been an educator since 1999 and began her career working with adjudicated youth in a private facility in Northeast Ohio. Following this work, she served as a consultant for educational and behavioral initiatives with the Ohio State Department of Youth Services, which works with individuals in the juvenile justice system. Additionally, Amanda worked on various projects with the Nisonger Center at The Ohio State University, including federally funded technology innovation grants with the Office of Special Education Programs, which developed a transition, career-readiness curriculum and an e-mentoring program that facilitates partnerships with industry leaders to mentor youth. Her other work has included reading intervention research with English learners and students with and at risk for disabilities.

Amanda is director of the Community Learning Center for Children and Youth (CLC). This year-round instructional facility serves both CSU College of Education students and faculty, as well as K–12 learners from across greater Cleveland. Through her work with the CLC, Amanda has led initiatives to provide in-person and remote learning opportunities in after-school programs across the region that provide individualized tutoring services for more than two hundred K–12 learners.

Amanda received a bachelor's degree in music from Kent State University. She received her master's degree and doctorate in special education and applied behavior analysis from The Ohio State University. She is a member of the Association for Behavior Analysis International and the Council for Exceptional Children.

To learn more about Amanda's work, visit shorturl.at/giquE to view her faculty profile.

Alana Oif Telesman, PhD, is the director of the First Education Experience Program at The Ohio State University. This program provides field experiences to college students considering careers in education while also focusing on areas of inequity, social justice, and diversity within schools. She also teaches several undergraduate and graduate courses in special education and applied behavior analysis. Alana was formerly a special education teacher in Chicago Public Schools, where she taught culturally and linguistically diverse students with wide-ranging academic and behavioral needs. She was also a reading specialist for the past decade and has seen significant progress for her students with reading challenges. Her research interests focus on reading and behavioral interventions for students in high-poverty areas.

Alana is a member of the Council for Exceptional Children, and in 2020, she was selected as a doctoral research scholar. She has written more than seven research publications, including a study published in the esteemed *Journal of Special Education*. She has also cowritten several chapters for education textbooks about evidence-based practices for diverse populations of students with exceptionalities. Alana has presented her research on reading and behavior interventions at local, national, and international conferences. She has also provided professional development and coaching to school districts in the areas of reading and behavioral interventions, specifically for elementary-aged students.

Alana received a bachelor's, master's, and doctoral degree in special education and applied behavior analysis from The Ohio State University.

To book Gwendolyn Cartledge, Amanda L. Yurick, or Alana Oif Telesman for professional development, contact pd@SolutionTree.com.

Introduction

When Gwen Cartledge attended fifth grade in a Midwest suburban elementary school, she was the only African American student in a class of approximately thirty White students. In addition to the race difference, she was the only student from the lower-income Black section of town. This class was a novel experience for Gwen, and she wasn't sure if the other students would accept her. One day during indoor recess, she stood watching other students play a simple card game when one of the boys, Jimmy, noticed her standing near him; he immediately made a noise of repulsion and jumped to get away.

Gwen was very hurt. She moved to a corner in the classroom, and began to cry. When her teacher, Ms. Conner, asked her about her tears, Gwen shared Jimmy's reaction to her and said she didn't think the students wanted her in the class. Ms. Conner was visibly moved, and Gwen knew she would take some action. This also frightened Gwen because she did not want the teacher to say or do anything that would offend the other students.

From Gwen's current perspective, it is obvious that Ms. Conner was presented with several challenges. First, she wanted to affirm Gwen as a valued student in her class. Second, she wanted to create a classroom environment so all her students, especially those in the majority group, learned to embrace other students from diverse backgrounds or who presented differences of any sort. Ms. Conner was White and had the special challenge of presenting issues of another race in honest, non-stereotypical ways. Ms. Conner did respond to the moment. We will discuss Ms. Conner's successes and weaknesses in handling this situation later in this book.

Diversity in our schools and the larger society has grown exponentially in the decades since Gwen was an elementary student. These changes are projected to continue; so by midcentury, the United States will not have a single racial or ethnic majority (Cohn & Caumont, 2016). A report from the National Center for Education Statistics (NCES, 2019) provides an even shorter timeline for the disappearing racial majority. It points out that since 2000, White students decreased 14 percent, while in the same period, Hispanic students increased 10 percent, with relatively small changes for Black and Asian students, indicating that by 2031, U.S. schools will be 45 percent White with the remaining student population being Hispanic (29 percent), Black (15 percent), Asian or Pacific Islander (6 percent), Native American (1.3 percent), and students reporting two or more races (4 percent).

These changes are driven largely by immigration, an international phenomenon observed in many other countries. Canada, for example, in 2019, noted the highest ever immigration population, with the greatest number of immigrants coming from China, India, and the Philippines. Immigrants to Canada tend to settle in urban areas; so by 2019, cities like Toronto and Vancouver were majority-minority (Norris, 2020). Similarly, immigration has changed the face of populations in countries such as Germany, the United Kingdom, France, Australia, South Africa, and Israel (Cilluffo & Cohn, 2019).

Purpose of This Book

The purpose of this book is to weave together the development of social-emotional and culturally diverse competencies for elementary-aged students. A critical focus for the developing child is the ability to systematically grow in the understanding of self and others. Authorities in the field contend that social-emotional learning is an effective means for developing competencies such as managing emotions, showing empathy for others, maintaining positive relationships, and so on (for example, Domitrovich, Durlak, Staley, & Weissberg, 2017). Ideally, this process would help children learn to value themselves as well as appreciate others, especially those who present distinct differences from themselves. We have included a wide range of diversity, such as disability, gender, race, religion, ethnicity, socioeconomic status, and so on. In the elementary grades, no later than kindergarten, children need to begin viewing themselves as global citizens, acquiring a worldview of their respective connectedness and reciprocal responsibilities.

The activities are designed to teach direct and explicit social-emotional skills related to how to affirm peers who might be impoverished or of a different group, such as ethnic, cultural, gender, or religious. These activities will help students learn not only how to welcome a new student into the class but also, and more important, how to welcome a student who looks, speaks, or acts different from them. The activities also help students who represent cultural and racial differences affirm and validate themselves, even in settings where their differences are stark. The goal is for students to become self-aware, affirm themselves, and learn how they can empower themselves and others to achieve socially appropriate goals. Educators want them to become socially aware, so they learn to act in ways that value others, including those who do not share their backgrounds. The activities on social-emotional development address interpersonal and self-related skills. Thus, teachers encourage students to value others, value themselves, and assert themselves and manage conflict situations with others.

Although you could teach these skills and concepts using a variety of materials, this book stresses the importance of incorporating culturally diverse literature. Additionally, we will address other forms of diversity, which are gaining in importance. These include differences in religion, gender, socioeconomics, (dis)ability, and age. Educators should teach students from books that reflect the entirety of society, not just an increasingly smaller, albeit dominant, slice of it. All students should have access to a full array of diverse books in their classrooms, libraries, and homes. Further, students who come from diverse backgrounds need to find books that represent themselves and others as commonplace in their environment, not the exception. Finally, we hope using culturally diverse books in teaching these skills enables students to focus on their commonalities with others rather than their differences.

Clinical psychologist Beverly Daniel Tatum (2017) endorses the use of children's books and other media for this purpose and points out that educators can help children develop critical consciousness relative to bigotries such as racism, sexism, and classism, even from their earliest ages (such as preschool, or three to five years old). It is to students' advantage to have wholesome, healthy relationships with others. Social competence not only enhances the self-worth of the individual but also enables the individual to contribute to the well-being of the immediate and larger environment. Thus, the overall purpose of this book is to support teachers in helping young students become, to the extent possible, emotionally and socially accomplished individuals in a pluralistic society.

What's in This Book

This book is divided into three major parts: (1) an explanation of children's literature and social development, (2) information and activities on affirming and asserting self and others through diverse and culturally relevant children's literature, and (3) information and activities on dealing with aggression and conflict through diverse and culturally relevant children's literature. Part I contains two chapters, which provide basic information on social-emotional skills and children's literature. Social-emotional development, the topic of chapter 1, is an important part of the school curriculum. This instruction must be explicit, so students do not misperceive social expectations and, more important, learn critical behaviors that empower themselves and others. This means in addition to presenting and discussing a skill concept, educators must help students relate the skill to their lives, act out the learned behavior in socially appropriate ways, and use this skill in real-life situations.

The research on school-based social-emotional learning clearly documents these components to be most important for effective social-emotional learning (Domitrovich et al., 2017). Chapter 2, on literature, emphasizes the importance of diverse and culturally relevant children's literature for all young students and how this literature can contribute to the overall love of literature, the appreciation of other cultures, and ways to act to promote harmony and goodwill across and within cultures. We showcase high-quality, authentic stories that depict all groups in wholesome, constructive ways.

Parts II and III provide activities that teach social-emotional skills through the use of diverse and culturally relevant children's literature. Embedded in these activities is the important understanding of how people relate to and embrace the diversity in others and themselves. We feature specific culturally diverse books in chapters 3 through 8. All chapters feature at least two books and two concepts focused on different aspects of diversity. Additionally, the selected books cover a range of elementary grade levels, from primary (grades K–3) through upper elementary (grades 4–5). The overlapping nature of social-emotional skills and cultural diversity is such that we use several of the same books for the principal discussion or as a reference in more than one activity. (Teachers might consider replacing the hard copies of these children's books with digital sources such as YouTube channel readings.)

Part II focuses on affirming and asserting self and others. Chapter 3 highlights specific ways to engage and affirm others within the context of poverty, exceptionality (ability or disability), religion, or culture. The children's books we selected to address these issues, respectively, are *Each Kindness* by Jacqueline Woodson (2012), *Louie* by Ezra Keats (1975), *Under My Hijab* by Hena Khan (2019), and *Mrs. Greenberg's Messy Hanukkah* by Linda Glaser (2004). Although the stories and activities differ for each concept, we encourage students to think about why it is important to affirm others and the specific things they can do to value and affirm others.

Chapter 4 addresses affirming self. At a very young age (grades K–3), children must learn to deal with their differences and ways to value themselves, even if others are disparaging. We use *Amazing Grace* by Mary Hoffman (2007) to teach two concepts: (1) affirming self with regard to race and (2) affirming self with regard to gender. We treat race and gender separately, offering activities for students to focus on self-affirmation under each or combined conditions. We extend the activities on gender a bit not only to address male and female differences but also to acknowledge that differences may occur within this binary context as well as across the spectrum of nonbinary gender identities. We view gender issues in a medical and historical context, not as a recent phenomenon.

Closely aligned to self-affirmation is self-assertion, which we cover in chapter 5. Within the context of immigration and migration (*Dreamers* by Yuyi Morales, 2018) and ethnicity (*The Name Jar* by Yangsook Choi, 2001), students engage in specific actions to show they value themselves. We also encourage students to be bold and make changes in their social environment in new and exciting ways. Students learn they don't have to be like everyone else to be accepted; being different is OK and can have special advantages.

Part III discusses helping children deal with aggression and conflict. This part also has three chapters, each devoted to a specific topic: (1) responding to aggression, (2) playing cooperatively with others, and (3) questioning unfair practices. In chapter 6, we use children's literature to address how to respond to physical aggression (*Angel Child, Dragon Child* by Michele Maria Surat, 1989) and verbal aggression (*The First Strawberries* by Joseph Bruchac, 1993). In these activities, the issue is not the absence of conflict, but how to manage and resolve the inevitable presence of conflict.

Playing cooperatively with others, an important means for minimizing conflict, is the theme of chapter 7. We use the Jackie Robinson and Hank Greenberg story *When Jackie and Hank Met* (Fishman, 2012) to show cooperation between two professional baseball players despite age and racial differences. We highlight cooperation across race and ethnicity through the book *Angel Child, Dragon Child* (Surat, 1989). This discussion extends the previous activity showing how children can enjoy and benefit from cooperative play rather than endure the negative effects resulting from physical and verbal aggression.

Unfair practices, the topic of chapter 8, are commonplace, and students must learn appropriate ways to question them when they occur. Sometimes people treat others unfairly about things over which they have no control. It was unfair that Jackie Robinson could not play in the major leagues because of his race (as discussed in *When Jackie and Hank Met* [Fishman, 2012]) or that the children had no place to play because they were poor in *The Streets Are Free* [Kurusa 1995]). Learning to be fair to others is part of kindness and overall social competence. These activities focus on learning to be fair to others and recognizing when others are not being treated fairly. In addition to learning how to question unfair practices that occur to themselves, students must learn to advocate for those who others treat unfairly.

There's More to the Story highlights culturally diverse children's literature that is appropriate for elementary grades. The highly recognized, award-winning authors of these commercial books offer authentic and insightful presentations of their topic. The beautiful illustrations enhance the attractiveness of these books, making them good picture books for group readings, and students will likely gravitate to them for independent reading. We use each book to introduce one or more concepts.

Visit **go.SolutionTree.com/diversityandequity** to find the "Integration of Digital Media for Diverse and Culturally Relevant Children's Literature" document, which provides additional resources to support and extend the content covered in each chapter of this book. It offers some of the more ubiquitous platforms, such as video streaming and services, podcasts, social media, and ebooks. We briefly discuss each platform and then highlight resources that address all kinds of diversity in children's literature. In many cases, you can find corresponding digital content (for example, book trailers on YouTube) for the books we use in the activities, as well as in the recommended additional readings. You may choose to use these aspects of digital media integration as a hook to capture initial interest, as integrated supports for use within the context of the activities, or as a means of maintaining or enriching the skills you are teaching. This document will be updated frequently.

How to Use This Book

Each of the social-emotional skills and the related culturally diverse concepts are presented in the same format. The chapters begin with a reading and discussion of a culturally diverse book. We intend for the discussion section of each chapter to clarify the events of the story and the specific targeted social-emotional skills. To increase skill understanding, we direct students to act out the behavior in skill-building activities or scenarios and generate their own responses to social situations. We then provide simple ways to apply the behavior with real-life applications. We encourage you to provide brief but realistic discussions of the addressed type of diversity. Additionally, we propose other literature activities to reinforce literacy as well as increase students' cultural and social-emotional understandings. We recommend action projects to help extend this learning into each student's everyday school and community environment. We provide a more detailed discussion of this format in chapter 2 (page 25).

The time you spend on each social-emotional skill and related culturally diverse literature piece will vary according to the amount of time available and the developmental level of your students. We anticipate each instructional concept taking place over several blocks (for example, thirty minutes), allocating one session for each of five to seven components for each activity. Students' needs as well as the teacher's discretion also dictate the amount of time spent. For example, you might choose to spend more time on activities relative to accepting culturally diverse students in the classroom or on managing conflict if the student population shows greater need in these areas. The book sequences well into a nine-week grading period, either as a cross-disciplinary global diversity course or within a literacy block, as roughly one session per week.

Additionally, schools that engage in the International Baccalaureate curriculum may find this book well-suited to their program. Students' interest also might be a factor in how much time you spend on a particular topic. Your students might be especially interested in reading more books about different religious practices or about different refugee groups in their community. These are good and legitimate reasons for devoting more time to particular concepts. You should present all the material kindly and nonjudgmentally with no harshness toward anyone. In the unfortunate situation in which a student might express a negative view of another student or group, you should help the student think through his or her statement while pointing out that in this environment, everyone is welcomed.

Present these materials in the most positive, upbeat manner. Invoke as much excitement as possible about this literature and reading in general. Permit students to read these books as a group and individually. You can use your school or community library to find the recommended books as well as other similar books you or others identify. We provide a list of additional books at the end of each chapter. Praise students who do additional readings on their own, and give them a two-minute stage in the classroom to share their independent reading. This practice could encourage others in the class to read more.

Depending on the setting, you could teach the activities in small or large groups. We designed this book to avoid technical jargon to make the activities user friendly and, thus, easy to deliver for teachers, clinicians (for example, school psychologists, guidance counselors, social workers, specialized tutors), as well as paraprofessionals. It's completely ready to go for the practitioner. It effectively integrates social-emotional skill instruction within the framework of global diversity and literature activities. Note that several of the activities throughout the book require advanced preparation, so be sure to read the instructions ahead of time.

Teaching for and with cultural competence can be a challenge for all teachers, especially under conditions of racial and cultural discontinuity. That is, despite the ongoing increases of the racially and culturally diverse student population, the U.S. teaching workforce remains primarily White (Billingsley, Bettini, & Williams, 2019). Even though there has been some growth in teachers of color to nearly 20 percent, the U.S. workforce remains 80 percent White and predominantly female (Carver-Thomas, 2018). Further, Carver-Thomas (2018) points out this growth is mainly among Hispanic and Asian teachers, with declines among African American and Native American teachers. Other Carver-Thomas (2018) findings punctuate these statistics, indicating teachers of color appear to positively impact the academic and social-emotional growth of diverse students, further underscoring the critical nature of cultural competence for all teachers.

In addition to this book, we recommend researching further, especially if you are teaching about diversity that is not part of your background. Do not assume you are well-informed about other groups; you want to avoid stereotypes and misinformation. Also, it is important to understand that no identity group is a monolith, and natural variations exist. A broad, multifocal perspective on any group dynamic can bring depth and context to the educational experience; thus, further investigations are advantageous. To aid in this pursuit, we strongly recommend the book *"Why Are All the Black Kids Sitting Together in the Cafeteria?" And Other Conversations About Race* by Tatum (2017). This very readable source provides an excellent primer on race and culturally diverse groups, which is extremely useful for teachers, regardless of teaching assignment or class diversity. Another recommendation is *Anti-Bias Education for Young Children and Ourselves* (Derman-Sparks, Edwards, & Goins, 2020). This book also provides basic information about the issues of cultural diversity plus offers applied examples of handling these issues in the classroom.

Although we target students in elementary grades K–5, you can adjust the book for all age groups. Throughout the book, we refer to students in various ways, according to age or grade level. *Primary* or *younger students* refers to learners in grades K–3. *Older* or *upper elementary students* refers to learners in grades 4–5. However, we encourage you to use the book in the way that works best for your students and your classroom.

Conclusion

The concepts and related activities in this book center on young children's social-emotional development within a context of diversity: race, religion, gender, socioeconomics, language, ethnicity, disability, and age. The concepts are for all classrooms, whether the class composition is highly diverse, moderately diverse, or fairly monolithic. This book is for all races or ethnic groups: White and non-White. The shrinking of the planet means diversity will continue to grow throughout the world, so more diverse classrooms are inevitable.

All children need to learn the behaviors that enable them to affirm themselves and others, work and play cooperatively with others, and question unfair practices. Accordingly, we urge teachers to present these activities positively and nonjudgmentally. All students are welcomed and valued. Favor is based on one's actions, not one's group membership or some immutable characteristic. It is human nature to prefer the known and comfortable, but as people explore and invest in every aspect of the universe, all environments become more complex. Orderly and prosperous societies will demand everyone recognize, respect, and indeed, celebrate the "others." These understandings and acquisitions begin with, but are not limited to, students in grades K–5.

Part I

Promoting Social-Emotional Development Through Diverse and Culturally Relevant Children's Literature

Part I includes two chapters and discusses the two main components of learning in this book: (1) the social-emotional learning essential within a culturally diverse context and (2) the rationale for using culturally diverse children's literature as a means for this learning. As noted previously, our intent is not to be exhaustive in all that we want students to acquire within the realm of social-emotional learning. We are aware, however, of some of the special contemporary challenges that teachers and parents encounter within the changing face of the United States and around the world.

Thus, our focus is two-fold: (1) the key learnings elementary students need to value and affirm themselves, and (2) how students learn to affirm and value others in order to contribute to the common good. The categories and skills listed will help you understand the learning expectations. Further, each skill reflects that two-fold focus.

Our previous research and writings (for example, Cartledge, Bennett, Gallant, Ramnath, & Keesey, 2015; Cartledge, Keesey, Bennett, Ramnath, & Council, 2015; Robinson-Ervin, Cartledge, Musti-Rao, Gibson, & Keyes, 2016) support the use of culturally diverse literature in teaching social-emotional learning as well as reading. We emphasize the importance of using culturally diverse stories for learning within a diverse context. Although stories can be an excellent vehicle for learning, we do not want to leave the impression that stories alone can bring about the desired effects. Many students may not fully grasp the most salient understandings or may focus instead on some unsavory tidbit. Thus, we provide specific guidelines for the readings and related activities. We discuss stories relative to specific social-emotional understandings and the actions that best reflect this learning. These stories give students the opportunities to practice, discuss, and display this learning under various conditions to ensure they truly understand and acquire this learning.

chapter one

Developing Social-Emotional Skills in Young Children

Social-emotional development is an educator's key focus for young children. It is during the preschool and elementary grades that students learn to share, play nicely with others, greet others positively, follow directions, develop critical social and communication skills, and so forth. Indeed, some preschool settings concentrate almost exclusively on social-emotional development, recognizing this critical period for building the foundation for current and future social competence. Much of this learning is informal, conveyed through a variety of sources such as parent and teacher prompting, peer play, media, and observations of others in one's environment. Teachers and parents know socially skilled children have certain advantages. Social-emotional skills not only help children get along with others but also facilitate academic learning, contribute to healthy school and home environments, support positive self-regard, empower goal achievement in socially appropriate ways, lead to self-discipline, and contribute to school and adult success. Analyses of over a decade of studies repeatedly show these short- and long-term gains resulting from school-based social-emotional interventions (Taylor, Oberle, Durlak, & Weissberg, 2017).

Many of the social-emotional skills will occur almost automatically as long as children have good models, and the conditions exist to help these skills occur and persist. The young children who regularly have adults smile and greet them with a friendly "hello" will eventually begin to imitate the behavior when they see that adult on subsequent occasions. Similarly, when children see those adults warmly greet other children in the setting, they are likely to imitate that behavior toward other children. Some children will pick up this behavior quickly; others will need slight prompting, and still others, especially those with special needs, may need physical prompting and praise to produce these behaviors. This latter step (prompting and praise) falls within the realm of direct instruction in which a child's face and eyes must be oriented toward the recipient of the greeting, and the teacher encourages the child to smile and say "hello." This instruction should be repeated regularly (daily, if needed) until the greeting is within the child's repertoire. We recommend this more deliberate instruction. That is, we recommend classroom activities designed to help students make real-life associations with the events in the literature and perform the related social and prosocial behaviors.

In addition to being disciplined and socially appropriate, we want young children to acquire a set of prosocial skills that enable them to become more empathic and caring toward others. *Empathy*, the ability to understand and identify with the feelings of others, is essential for being helpful and caring toward others. Empathic or prosocial behaviors are especially important in settings where individuals are from diverse backgrounds. Because differences are so pervasive in many societies, the challenge is to not just tolerate but also celebrate and possibly embrace the other; that is, the one who doesn't look, speak, or act like you.

The books we read to young children vary a great deal, but we want to emphasize books designed to help children to celebrate themselves, celebrate others, and celebrate and find awe in their surroundings. Celebrating and taking pride in oneself is a universal goal among parents and teachers for the young people in their lives. This goal takes on even more importance if young people find themselves to be unique and shunned because of their special differences from a larger group. Whether these differences are obvious (for example, racial) or minor (for example, poor athlete), there is excellent literature to help children affirm themselves regardless of differences.

This book focuses on the former type of difference (racial, cultural, linguistic) and literature useful in addressing those types of differences. Accordingly, we organize the social-emotional concepts and related activities into three major categories: (1) self-related skills, (2) interpersonal skills, and (3) social awareness. We do not intend these categories and related skills to be inclusive of all social-emotional skills elementary-aged students need. Indeed, other social-emotional learning materials exist for that purpose (for example, Durlak, Domitrovich, Weissberg, & Gullotta, 2015; Gresham, 2018). Instead, we focus on some of the most important skills that aid the social-emotional learning of elementary students within the context of diversity.

Self-Related Skills

Self-related skills enable people to affirm themselves while simultaneously respecting and valuing others. These skills help people appropriately understand and express emotions resulting from various events. Self-related skills help people acquire the personal self-control requisite for overall social competence. These skills are important for all children, but they are especially important for children who find themselves marginalized or singled out for ridicule because of some immutable difference. All children must learn that differences are not inherently bad or inferior. In some ways, people are all different, and that not only is OK but also creates value to embrace those differences.

There are some key skills relative to these understandings. The following is not an exhaustive list for elementary-aged students; we could identify many more (for example, Gresham, 2018). We determine these are the most important for racially and culturally different students to learn to affirm themselves and others (Cartledge & Milburn, 1995, 1996). Showing respect and appreciation for others helps these behaviors become reciprocal.

- Making positive self-statements
- Expressing feelings
- Speaking assertively
- Controlling temper
- Respecting others and accepting individual differences

Making Positive Self-Statements

Children who are racially or culturally different from the majority of other children around them should learn to make positive self-statements. For example, books that tell young girls with an array of skin colors and hairstyles they are pretty are affirming and help these girls make positive self-statements, even if they don't see the media glamorizing their image.

Expressing Feelings

Children who others taunt will undoubtedly have lots of negative feelings. They need to learn how to label and express those feelings. They must be able to express those feelings to a kind, caring adult, who will help them tell others how they feel in the most appropriate ways. Literature that depicts children experiencing and expressing similar emotions is helpful for this purpose. Children will learn to express these feelings to not only adults but also their peers—those who are empathic as well as those who are being unkind.

Speaking Assertively

We want children to speak assertively when expressing their feelings, especially to peers who are being unkind. Children can learn to say things like,

"I like my name. I don't like it when you purposefully miscall my name. This is the way to say my name."

Controlling Temper

An important aspect of speaking assertively is being able to control one's temper while speaking in a firm, calm manner. You can help children become more comfortable with who they are. The stories in these books help children discover that anger expressed aggressively only makes things worse, but they can often make things better by sharing how they feel.

Respecting Others and Accepting Individual Differences

Learning to respect others and accept individual differences helps children refrain from making unkind statements or actions toward individuals who present those differences. Literature on racially and culturally diverse groups emphasizes the special gifts of these children. For instance, children can learn and speak one another's language, which can be a lot of fun. Learning about other countries and cultures can be exciting. Teachers and other responsible adults can direct this learning, helping children to respect and appreciate other cultures.

Interpersonal Skills

Everyone needs interpersonal skills to get along with others, regardless of age. At the most rudimentary level, children should learn to make eye contact, employ a pleasant affect, and use kind words of greeting. We recognize that making eye contact is not universally valued across all cultures, especially relative to adults. Nevertheless, we advise teachers to prompt the skills that are important for success within the school setting, and then, advise children to switch, if necessary, with other authority figures. Early on, children learn that social skills are reciprocal and emitting positive behaviors toward others will likely elicit similar actions from them. This understanding can lead to the realization that unkind acts toward others are more likely to result in a series of punishing (rather than rewarding) consequences (Mize, 1995). The following list of social-emotional skills is not comprehensive, but it does make up some of the most basic behaviors children need to effect positive and consistent interactions with others.

- Making positive statements to others
- Sharing materials
- Joining group activities

- Following play rules
- Helping others participate
- Asking for help
- Managing conflict

Making Positive Statements to Others

Many children will have little or no difficulty making positive statements to others. In many cases, even though they know how to say kind things to peers and others, they may need prompting to make these statements more frequently, or they may need directions on when to make these statements at the right time. For example, it's unwise to compliment a peer about winning a board game when the teacher is trying to teach the entire class a new mathematics concept. Some children might know the appropriate words and have a keen understanding of timing but may be too shy or inhibited to make the desired utterance. These children need not only prompting and encouragement but also lots of reinforcement when they do respond. They also need safe, comforting environments so others do not pressure or ridicule them for their shyness. Rather, they need a place where they receive gentle help to grow in their positive interactions and still feel valued for being themselves.

The children who present the greatest concern are those who frequently make unkind statements to others and seem resistant to instructions to be more positive to others. These children often value the attention they get for negativity and yet become explosive when others respond in kind. Such children benefit from lots of direct instruction on how to bring about more positive relationships with others through what they say.

Sharing Materials

Sharing with others is another key behavior that educators should teach young children. Many classroom activities tend to be either competitive or individualistic, neither of which is ideal for building cooperative or sharing behaviors. Competitive and individualistic conditions often emphasize personal ownership and being better than the other person rather than sharing or working together so everyone is successful. Further, these situations can lead to negative antagonistic interactions rather than positive ones. Children who learn to share and cooperate with one another develop harmonious relationships with others as well as positive self-regard.

Joining Group Activities

The ability to share and cooperate with others can boost a child's social confidence and the willingness to join group activities. Partner and group play are important arenas for developing critical social skills. Under these conditions, children acquire the language and behaviors to label and direct play and interpersonal activities. Children learn to give and receive. To participate in small- and large-group activities, children must learn to initiate play activities (for example, creating play activities and asking others to join), and they must be able to ask others if they can join ongoing play activities (Jung & Sainato, 2013; McIntyre, Blacher, & Baker, 2006). Some children lean more toward solitary rather than group play. Adults should respect their preferences, but the adults must ascertain if the children are playing alone by choice or because of possible rejection. Children who experience high levels of rejection need deliberate and direct instruction on ways to interact more cooperatively with peers.

Following Play Rules

Some of the explicit behaviors children must acquire include how to follow play rules. Often others reject or avoid children who refuse to follow the rules during play activities. Although everyone enjoys winning, it is more important to be fair in play, so everyone has the same chance to win and enjoy games. Children who insist on conducting games and other activities simply to advantage themselves are not well regarded by others. Children who fail to follow the rules because they don't know them or can't remember them need someone to teach them the rules. Teachers must teach those who fail to follow the rules *just because they don't like them* how to respect the rights of others.

Helping Others Participate

Another important skill for children to learn to promote positive interactions is helping others participate. Children who have not learned to respect the rights of others are not inclined to help them be successful in an activity. Children must learn that activities are much more enjoyable when everyone knows how to perform and can participate fully. This means they should spend time teaching peers the rules and helping them in some way. These peers are then likely to want to play with them and are more willing to help them when needed.

Asking for Help

Children who are good at helping others must also learn to ask for help. However, they need to learn the appropriate ways to ask for help. Children should not be too shy to ask for help; neither should they demand help from others in offensive ways or ask for help too often, especially if they are able to manage the situation themselves. There are times when everyone needs help.

Children should learn how to ask for help appropriately, so others are willing to respond to and support them.

Managing Conflict

Conflict is a constant in life; people cannot totally eliminate or avoid it. It is possible, however, to manage it, and the ability to manage conflict is a major factor in overall social competence. Knowing whether to ignore, negotiate, or seek help regarding a particular event may mean the difference between managing and escalating a conflict. Responding in kind to an aggressor typically makes the aggression worse. Learning self-control, to respond positively and cooperatively to others (as appropriate), and to act wisely to manage the unwise acts of others is a simplified formula for social competence.

Social Awareness

Social awareness (or *social perception*) pertains to how people perceive or read their environment. Every social situation involves myriad cues of how to interpret it. There are *nonverbal cues* such as facial expressions, physical gestures, voice tone, as well as verbal statements and paralanguage (for example, grunts, groans, yawns, and so on). People must process this information, along with the social context, to get an accurate reading of the social situation. Obviously, social awareness, like social competence, is developmental. Educators should not expect primary students or those with cognitive disorders to be fully aware of all the nuances that make up a social situation, but through observations, adult labeling, coaching, and direct instruction, they gradually but steadily learn the meaning of these various cues in their environment. Children will learn to use this information to respond competently to these situations, including reading others' body language (for example, facial expressions, gestures, and posture) to connect the observed expressions and corresponding actions of others. Further, children must understand the effect of their own actions on others' behaviors—for example, noting how a classmate acts when another student follows the rules during a board game and how the classmate reacts when the student doesn't follow the rules.

Spatial relations are another important area of learning. For example, standing too close to another person may be offensive or intimidating to that person. On the other hand, distancing oneself too far from others may signal indifference or dislike. Children also should be aware of auditory cues such as voice tones. An unusually loud voice may suggest anger, fear, or surprise, while a soft tone may be trying to convey a more positive effect. Additionally, children should make associations with appearance (for example, formal or informal dress, uniforms that indicate authority, clothes characteristic of another country, and so on). Becoming socially aware helps enable students to avoid hostile situations and to respond to others empathically.

Avoid Hostile Situations

Accurately interpreting these verbal and nonverbal cues enables children to identify friendly and unfriendly conditions. If correctly detected, children can learn ways to defuse or prevent a hostile situation. Children can learn steps to take to get away from a bad situation; make an assertive, nonaggressive statement; go for help; or simply ignore the microaggression. A *microaggression* is "a comment or action that subtly and often unconsciously or unintentionally expresses a prejudiced attitude toward a member of a marginalized group (such as a racial minority)" ("Microaggression," n.d.). Children can also learn how to help those who others are treating unfairly. For example, they can leave with the child another is taunting, change the subject or activity, go get help, or perform some other action that will prevent psychological or physical harm to the child.

Respond Empathetically to Others

Most children acquire these understandings at a rather steady pace as they move through the primary grades. What is not so obvious is the extent to which children use this information to foster good interpersonal relationships, and, equally important, aid the well-being of others. For example, does Louis recognize that Juan is sitting alone at the lunch table because he is new to the class and not yet fluent in English, which is the language of all the other children in the class? Further, is Louis sufficiently caring and self-assured to sit with Juan during lunch or ask Juan to join him and his buddies for lunch? If so, Louis is responding empathically to Juan. Responding with empathy to others is a skill we feel undergirds one's ability to care about others and interact kindly toward them.

Typically, *empathy* is the process of recognizing an event that someone is experiencing and responding emotionally in kind. For example, a child who rushes to the aid of and expresses concern for a sibling or classmate who falls, gashes his or her knee, and is crying in pain is displaying empathy. Revisiting the previous example of Louis and Juan, Louis is showing empathy because he sees Juan's loneliness, suspects Juan is feeling bad, and this makes Louis feel bad, accordingly. These caring feelings toward others lead Louis to reach out and attempt to befriend Juan. In addition to possibly finding a good friend in Juan, Louis is helping many others in his immediate environment. He is potentially helping his teacher and school because he is helping a new student adjust to a different school. He is helping his classmates because they are learning how to welcome a new student to the class. He is helping Juan's family because a friendly classmate will ease Juan's adjustment and contribute to his school success. And, of course, Louis is helping Juan.

Empathy is the basis for prosocial skills, such as helping others, inviting others to play, welcoming others, and so on, noted earlier in this chapter; we present how to teach these skills throughout this book. Empathy is increasingly important as children encounter more individuals in school and in their immediate environment who have a slightly different appearance or culture than their own. Responding to others in humane and respectful ways and expecting that type of response in turn is essential to an orderly and healthy society.

Another aspect of feelings is labeling and understanding feelings within oneself. Initially, young children tend to describe themselves as feeling *good* or *bad*, but as they grow, they begin to refine those feelings. Losing a ball game, for example, is feeling not just bad but also disappointed. The disappointment may be with yourself and with other members of the team, but this labeling may help in how you direct your feelings and respond appropriately. Disappointment may help you think about mistakes made and how to avoid them in the next game. On the other hand, if you label those feelings as *anger*, you might then begin looking for someone to blame, turning that anger inward or outward in nonconstructive ways. Labeling and managing feelings are key to fostering positive interpersonal relations, as well as helping affirm oneself and others.

Presence or Absence of Social-Emotional Learning in Young Children

There are many social skill–assessment instruments educators can use to evaluate children's level of social-emotional learning. However, for children with significant behavior disorders, we recommend a certified school psychologist or guidance counselor conduct this assessment. For the purposes of these social-emotional learning activities, however, we advise teachers to make this assessment an ongoing process rather than a single event. The preceding targeted self-related, interpersonal, and social-awareness skills align closely with the major themes of this book: affirming self and others and dealing with conflict. Important subthemes are positive interactions across race and culture.

We recommend informal observations of students prior to initiating these social-emotional learning activities, noting which behaviors you feel need the most attention. During instruction, continue observing for behavioral improvements and areas for additional prompting or instruction. Use a record-keeping system, such as the one in figure 1.1, to assess students' competence in these skills. You can find a more comprehensive list of skills, along with detailed activity plans in *Taking Part: Introducing Social Skills to Children, PreK–Grade 3* (Cartledge & Kleefeld, 2009).

Social-Emotional Skill (or Desired Behavior)	Description	Performance		
		Needs Improvement	Improving	Mastery
Makes positive self-statements	Says something he or she does well without bragging Takes pride in self			
Expresses feelings	Labels feelings and says how he or she feels			
Speaks assertively	Tells others to stop or what he or she would like without using aggressive words			
Controls temper	Stays calm and does not overreact to difficult situations			
Respects others	Acknowledges the differences of others without negative judgment			
Accepts individual differences	Shows kindness and is welcoming to those who are different			
Makes positive statements to others	Regularly compliments and makes kind statements to others			
Shares materials	Shares materials with others			
Joins group activities	Asks others to join group activities			
Follows play rules	Follows the rules when participating in group activities			
Helps others participate	Offers to help others participate in class activities, as appropriate			
Asks for help	Asks for help when needed			
Manages conflict	Defuses or avoids conflict with others			
Avoids hostile situations	Knows how to get away from hostile situations			
Responds empathetically to others	Understands and responds appropriately to the feelings of others			

Source: Adapted from Cartledge & Kleefeld, 2009.

Figure 1.1: Tracking individual social-emotional skills checklist.

*Visit **go.SolutionTree.com/diversityandequity** for a free reproducible version of this figure.*

Conclusion

Whether or not the instruction is explicit, schools have long been key for children's social-emotional learning. Confronted with a rapidly changing immediate and larger society, especially as it pertains to racial and ethnic diversity, school professionals are now commissioned to equip students with the skills needed for success within a markedly diverse environment. In this book, we broadly describe social-emotional learning as self-related, interpersonal, and social awareness or perception. Although there is considerable overlap across categories, we analyzed these categories into relatively discrete skills for clearer understanding of what needs to be taught and when it has been learned. This is important for both the teacher and learner. An informal assessment instrument is provided at the end of the chapter for this assessment purpose.

Chapter Reflections

Individually or with a collaborative group, review and discuss the following questions to reflect on your learning in this chapter.

1. Why is social-emotional learning important to the well-being of students and the larger society?
2. Why is explicit instruction preferred over informal or casual learning?
3. Why is empathy important to prosocial behavior?
4. Is it more important for students to be able to affirm others than to affirm themselves?
5. How might informal assessment be useful in social-emotional learning?
6. Do educators need to include social-emotional learning within a context of diversity? Why or why not?
7. Beyond the skills listed in this chapter, what else might you add for social-emotional learning within a context of diversity?

chapter two

Using Diverse and Culturally Relevant Literature

Culture is defined in various ways, but generally one thinks of culture as the ways of doing things (Mironenko & Sorokin, 2018). For example, culture dictates the way people dress, the food they eat, and the language they speak. Further, culture influences, to various degrees, the ways people think, act, and ultimately develop. Culture is dynamic. For example, think about the changes in one's diet resulting from the introduction of many different foods from other countries. Because society and the world are dynamic, cultural understanding is important for the appropriate interpretations and understandings of others with cultural differences. As a teacher and education professional, you should assess a child's social competence within the context of that child's culture and, in turn, help the child gain critical cultural knowledge to enable him or her to become socially competent as well as affirm him- or herself and others. Some basic cultural principles adhere to (1) the internal coherence and integrity of every culture; (2) the idea that no culture is inherently better or worse than another; and (3) the idea that all people, to some extent, are culturally bound (Cartledge & Milburn, 1996). One way to help elementary students gain critical cultural knowledge is through culturally diverse literature (McKeown, Williams, & Pauker, 2017).

According to Gwen Cartledge and Mary W. Kiarie (2001):

> Children's literature is an extremely important aspect of the childhood experience. Children should be encouraged and permitted to enjoy books for a variety of reasons, including adventure, the love of words and reading, the beauty of the books, excitement, humor, increased knowledge, personal interest, and so forth. (p. 40)

Of course, lessons on social learning should not dominate children's literature exposure, but we are suggesting that professionals and parents capitalize on the inherent attractiveness and messages of literature to help elementary-aged students develop. In addition to a positive effect on academic performance, a general consensus among authorities in the field is that culturally relevant literature will improve cultural competence and raise social consciousness (Bishop, 2007; Fleming, Catapano, Thompson, & Carrillo, 2016).

Some of our work helps support these positions. For example, we measured the fluency of first- and second-grade African American students in an urban school reading culturally relevant and non-culturally relevant passages and found statistically significant more fluency for the culturally relevant passages. Although not significant, the students also indicated a greater preference for the culturally relevant passages (Cartledge, Bennett, et al., 2015).

Children who read books that reflect people who look like them with shared language and experiences are undoubtedly empowered, resulting from self-affirmations and connections with others. Non-minority and minority readers alike can benefit greatly from reading culturally diverse literature (Bishop, 2007). Research and professional authorities document the importance of literature in students' personal and social lives. Author, child psychiatrist, and Harvard University professor emeritus Robert Coles (1992), for example, expresses his faith in the power of literature to change lives, stating, "Stories and pictures address the fundamental basis of who we are, and they're in that sense the most existentially penetrating aspect of teaching" (p. 21). Researchers Shelley McKeown, Amanda Williams, and Kristin Pauker (2017) use stories to increase the interaction among primary-aged, racially diverse students, and Porsha Robinson-Ervin, Gwendolyn Cartledge, Shobana Musti-Rao, Lenwood Gibson Jr., and Starr E. Keyes (2016) use culturally relevant literature to increase the social-emotional skills of adolescent males with behavior disorders.

Unfortunately, most of the literature in schools and classrooms is that with White or animal characters (Sharma & Christ, 2017). Further, the increasing diversity and accompanying school segregation in society sets the occasion for greater social tension and misunderstandings (Garcia, 2020). Nevertheless, with a focused effort, building on the existing research evidence (McKeown et al., 2017; Robinson-Ervin et al., 2016; Sridhar & Vaughn, 2000), educators can build empathy and foster a positive worldview by recognizing connections with others through literature, helping children take the perspective of those who look and sound different from themselves. Children can identify with and respond to individuals from vastly different demographics. Indeed, as The Ohio State University professor emerita and renowned children's literature researcher Rudine Sims Bishop (2007) states, "Reading such literature has the potential to help all students understand who we are today as a society and how we might become a better society" (p. xiv).

Diverse and Culturally Relevant Literature Selection for Social-Emotional Learning

Many children's books provide valuable lessons about social-emotional learning (Venegas, 2019), but some are easier to use for this purpose than others. There are some especially important considerations in selecting culturally relevant literature. We recommend the following set of guidelines.

- Choose culturally diverse stories from cultures throughout the world (Henderson & May, 2005; Sharma & Christ, 2017), especially those representing the five major ethnic or racial groups specified by the U.S. Census Bureau (2019): Asian American, Black, White, Latino/Hispanic, American Indian/Alaska Native. Diversity is increasing in U.S. society as well as throughout the world (Frey, 2020; Poushter & Fetterolf, 2019). This underscores the need for children to learn to respect and embrace the legitimacy of all groups. Furthermore, identity issues should not be used to undermine the social or psychological development of any group. Culturally diverse children's literature can be a viable means whereby children can see themselves valued and embraced within this society (Bishop, 2007).

- Children from dominant or majority groups should begin to see others from all groups in wholesome and equitable ways. All classrooms, especially homogeneous classrooms with few students from diverse backgrounds, should include literature representing all ethnic and cultural groups. The availability of literature that includes diverse characters and ideas is equally, if not more, germane in these settings.

- Books on diverse or underrepresented populations must be authentic, realistic, positive, and, if possible, authored by a member of the targeted population. Books authored by members of the targeted group are most desired (Bishop, 2007). Exceptions, however, might be when the book is highly affirming and valued (for example, *Amazing Grace* [Hoffman, 2007] and *Louie* [Keats, 1975]).

- Culturally diverse books should avoid stereotypes and caricatures that present any group in negative, demeaning ways. Emphasize stories that involve real-life contemporary events (Bishop, 2007).

Book awards, especially those given for specific cultural groups, can help validate the authenticity of some culturally diverse books (Sharma & Christ, 2017). Examples are the Coretta Scott King Book Awards for African Americans and the Tomás Rivera Mexican American Children's Book Awards.

- Observe students and notice the books to which they naturally gravitate. For example, one teacher in an urban classroom told us her female students love the book *I Love My Hair!* by Natasha Anastasia Tarpley (2001). That book is a mainstay in her classroom. Also, learn about the lives of your students (Sharma & Christ, 2017). A direct approach we use in our work is to interview children and observe them in the classroom and during recess. Our interviews, for example, reveal the importance of grandmothers in the lives of the African American students in urban schools. In presenting various passages to students, we find that students love the passages presenting grandmothers positively, but they are likely to reject passages where the grandmother is harmed, even though the passage centers on helping her when she falls (Cartledge, Keesey, et al., 2015).

- Select books with characters in the story with whom students can identify. Students tell us they like the passages best when story characters are doing things they have done (for example, making pancakes with a grandma) or things they want to do (for example, fishing with an uncle; Cartledge, Keesey, et al., 2015). Students will identify with the character's activities, ethnicity, language, age, religion, travel experiences, and so on. The students do not need to match all these markers to enjoy the book or story; the book just needs to be relevant to students. In some cases, as noted previously, students will read books of totally different ethnic groups for cultural knowledge and understanding.

- Consider gender issues, taking steps to select stories that present females and males in empowered, non-stereotypical ways.

- Make sure the stories you present closely reflect the social-emotional learning you are trying to develop in students. Many children's books advertise social-emotional learning but only indirectly address the desired skills or include too many skills or ideas in one story, possibly leading the learner to miss the main idea. *The Quarreling Book* by Charlotte Zolotow (1991) is an excellent book for teaching primary students the effects of positive and negative statements on others. In this book, the author presents one idea repeatedly, so the reader clearly sees the statement or act and its direct positive or negative effect. Similarly, *The Rainbow Fish* by Marcus Pfister (1995) has one consistent theme, making the positive and negative effects of sharing obvious to readers.

- These books address diversity, but they are not culturally relevant. In many books for elementary-aged students, the characters are either non-minority or animals (Sharma & Christ, 2017). *Each Kindness* by Woodson (2012), however, also focuses on kindness toward others and has special advantages—the story is set in the classroom, the students are racially diverse, and the problem is a common one (dealing with poverty). We discuss this book further in a learning activity later in this chapter.

- Violence or physical aggression is an important consideration when using children's books for social-emotional learning. Many children's books, including classic fairy tales, contain violent acts. These books are pervasive in students' lives, and we also know that it is easy for students to glamorize the unsavory (for example, the killing of the old witch) and overlook the desired social skill of using brain over brawn in threatening situations. Thus, it is important to make the desired behavior explicit, explain why it is the preferred behavior, and point out why aggression serves only as a last resort to get away from a harmful situation.

    Although you want to avoid gratuitous violence, violence does occur in life, including between ethnically- or language-different individuals. Educators want students to learn to manage conflict particularly when differences trigger or escalate the conflict. An effective story for managing conflict is *Swimmy* by Leo Lionni (1963). In this story, Swimmy, a little fish, uses social problem-solving skills to outsmart potential bullies, avoid aggression, and achieve his goals. This story can span many age groups. But *Swimmy* is about a fish and does not address racial or ethnic differences. An alternative book that depicts managing conflict is *Angel Child, Dragon Child* by Surat (1989; see page 123). This is a culturally diverse book involving an Asian girl and a White American male in a school setting.

- Give preference to well-written but easy-to-follow stories. Stories used for social-emotional learning need to have obvious themes easily deciphered by elementary-aged students. Some delightful children's books have valuable social-emotional learning understandings but are too cumbersome for social-emotional learning purposes, especially for students with cognitive disabilities.

Along the same lines, try to keep the stories brief. Longer stories are likely to present the noted comprehension problems, and they take more time, which is at a premium in most classrooms. Do not, however, abandon the well-written, exciting longer books, especially if they have social-emotional implications. These books could be great resources for independent literacy reading and reinforcing a previously taught social-emotional skill.

Figure 2.1 provides a list of guidelines for selecting diverse and culturally relevant literature for social-emotional learning.

1. Choose culturally diverse literature, representing cultures from around the world as well as the five major ethnic groups in the United States.
2. Ensure students, including those from nonminority groups, read culturally diverse books representing all groups.
3. Choose books featuring diverse groups that are authentic and devoid of stereotypes and caricatures.
4. Learn about your students' lives. Observe and interview students to determine culturally diverse books of particular interest.
5. Select books with characters and related activities with which students can identify.
6. Consider gender issues, presenting females and males in empowered, non-stereotypical ways.
7. Provide a good match between the social-emotional skill and the lessons in the story.
8. Try to use a culturally diverse book for the targeted social-emotional skill.
9. For social-emotional instruction, avoid using violence-dominated stories.
10. Select books with simple, clear story lines so students can easily understand the social-emotional skills or main ideas.
11. Keep stories brief to adhere to time limits and students' attention span.
12. Identify books that address a variety of cultural and social issues such as religion, poverty, and so on.

Figure 2.1: Guidelines for selecting diverse and culturally relevant literature for social-emotional learning.

*Visit **go.SolutionTree.com/diversityandequity** for a free reproducible version of this figure.*

Model for Using Diverse and Culturally Relevant Literature for Social-Emotional Learning

Explicit instruction for social-emotional learning consists of more than just the way you present stories. Stories can be major factors in making social lessons attractive to students; provide appropriate models and help students maintain behaviors once you teach them. This essentially involves modeling, coaching, and behavioral rehearsal (Cartledge & Kleefeld, 2010; Gresham, 2018). That is, *show* students how to perform the skill, *prompt* them to enact the skill most effectively, and then provide opportunities for them to *demonstrate* the skill independently.

The literature-based activities in this book use the following steps. We chose these specific elements (discussion, enactments, and so on) based on more than ten years of research showing these active components to have a greater overall effect than more passive methods on social-emotional learning in school interventions (Domitrovich et al., 2017). Before presenting the story, explicitly state the skills the story highlights.

1. Present the story.
2. Clarify the story concepts through discussion.
3. Clarify the features of the desired behaviors through enactments.
4. Practice the desired behaviors through real-life applications.
5. Respond appropriately to issues of diversity.
6. Provide extension activities to maintain the desired behaviors.

The following sections describe each step and provide an example of the step in action using the book *Each Kindness* by Jacqueline Woodson (2012).

Present the Story

Each activity begins with reading the story to and with the class. If students have a hard copy of the book or if they access the story online, they could follow along as you read aloud. If not, students could simply listen as you read. We include a synopsis of each story for your reference.

***Each Kindness* example:** This is an effective book to use when you focus on students being kind and positive toward one another, regardless of ethnic or personal differences. In this story, students in the class decide to reject a new student largely because she looks different, apparently due to poverty. The teacher presents a lesson about the main character's failure to be kind, despite the new student's many overtures of friendship.

Clarify the Story Concepts Through Discussion

Through discussion with students, you can make sure students understand the story, the featured social-emotional behavior, and the specific responses that make up this behavior. During the discussion, ask factual questions (such as, "What did Alex want to do?"), inferential questions (such as, "Why did Alex want to do this?"), affective questions (such as, "How do you think Alex feels, and why?" or "How does this make you feel, and why?"), and speculation and prediction questions (such as, "What else could Alex do to solve the problem?" or "What do you think Alex will do in the future?").

***Each Kindness* example:** You might ask, "Why did all the students in the class feel they should not speak to the new student?" (One reason might be that they felt the other students might tease them.) Through these kinds of questions, students not only discover what happened in the story but also realize that how they think and feel about events might affect whether they act wisely or foolishly. As with all such activities in this book, the level, type, and extent of questioning depend on students' age and abilities. Obviously, you should expect more sophisticated responses to higher-order questions, such as making inferences, from older students than primary students. During the discussion, be sure to connect the desired skill with specific actions. For example, ask, "What does it mean to be kind to a new student?" A possible response: "You could introduce yourself to the new student."

Clarify the Features of the Desired Behaviors Through Enactments

An especially effective way to use stories in social-emotional learning is to have students role-play the story using the desired social skill and related skill components that evolve from the story discussion.

***Each Kindness* example:** Students take turns introducing themselves to a new student in the class, employing whatever statements you and the class deem most appropriate. They also get many opportunities to enact related behaviors, such as inviting the new student to play or offering to help the student with some class activity. Then give students brief scenarios in which they can display their kindness. For example, a new student in your school looks like he does not have a pencil. You have an extra pencil in your book bag you do not need right now. Ask students, "What do you do?"

Practice the Desired Behaviors Through Real-Life Applications

In this step, prompt students to identify ways they have performed or can perform the skill in everyday life.

***Each Kindness* example:** Once students have the opportunity to use the story to enact desired kindness skills, encourage them to identify real-life situations in which they had the opportunity to display kindness to another person. Encourage students to list examples such as a new young person who moves into the neighborhood, a guest in their home, a substitute teacher, and so on. Look for opportunities for students to be kind to one another. Pay particular attention to situations in which students reject others because of their differences. These activities should take place over a period of several days, while you would prompt, correct, and reinforce students as needed.

Respond Appropriately to Issues of Diversity

In this step, help students understand the specifics of the diversity you are targeting. Students who can recognize, understand, and possibly embrace diversity will respond more appropriately to it.

***Each Kindness* example:** In this story, the critical difference appears in its depiction of poverty. Poverty is relative, and in the classroom it could manifest itself modestly to excessively (that is, the new student not being able to afford the most popular clothes to being homeless with food insecurity). Discuss with students what it means to have less than others and why it is not fair to be unkind to someone just because that person has less. Discuss why fancy clothes are not as important as being a good worker, friendly, helpful, kind, and so on. Discuss ways students can respond to those who ridicule classmates who have less money or things than the other students. Discuss with students how it makes them feel when they are kind to a classmate who may not have as much as others.

Provide Extension Activities to Maintain the Desired Behaviors

This step provides a variety of ways to have students practice and help maintain the desired behaviors. It includes options such as retelling the story, doing projects, reading additional stories, and more.

***Each Kindness* example:** Extend the discussion on poverty by reading a book such as *Last Stop on Market Street* by Matt de la Peña (2015) and identifying some ways your community helps those who lack basic needs. Other activities could include inviting parents or community members to come to class and share things they did to overcome poverty and things even students in elementary school can do to help those living in poverty. If possible, students could help collect items to help refugees or visit a soup kitchen to help serve those in need.

Literature Formats for Social-Emotional Learning

For students from diverse backgrounds and with special needs, authentic, contemporary books can be affirming and exceptionally valuable for social-emotional learning. This is particularly important for children who might receive negative messages from others in the larger society about their worth. For example, the story *Amazing Grace* (Hoffman, 2007) tells of a student who is told she cannot have a lead role in a class play because she is female and Black. Grace's parents affirm her and she achieves her goal. For recent immigrant children, a book such as *Angel Child, Dragon Child*

(Surat, 1989) relates how an immigrant Vietnamese girl overcomes the conflict and discomfort initially encountered with her U.S. classmates. Along the same lines is the book *Home at Last* by Susan Middleton Elya (2006), in which a young Latina tells how her mother learns English to overcome a neighborhood retailer's aggression.

Biographies also can be a valuable resource for social-emotional learning. These stories can be effective tools for helping children learn how major personalities conquered special social-emotional problems in their lives. A favorite biography written for young people is *When Jackie and Hank Met* (Fishman, 2012). Jackie Robinson lived a good life with many highly regarded accomplishments, but especially noteworthy for social-emotional learning are the first two years of his integration into the White major baseball leagues. For these two years, Robinson contracted with his manager not to respond to the aggression he experienced on the field. This story allows teachers to point out the advantage of planned ignoring, which in some cases (such as with Jackie Robinson) can be an effective counter to the aggression of others.

Student Engagement With Books

Much of the foregoing discussion is based on teacher-directed instruction. Student-directed options also have strong implications for social-emotional learning and literacy within a culturally diverse context, especially to supplement and reinforce a learning activity. One enticing student-led format is the classroom book club, which, in addition to being student led, typically rules out formal questions, quizzes, or written book reports. Instead, the focus tends to be on students' critical analysis and the enjoyment of literature.

In the article "Critical Book Clubs," Robin Jocius and Samantha Shealy (2017) emphasize that to make this format especially worthwhile and avoid chaos, teachers should structure and implement book clubs in phases. They describe this procedure using four phases in a third-grade classroom: (1) development, (2) practice, (3) independence, and (4) refinement. During the first two phases, the teacher models questioning and discussion strategies, and children practice these strategies. The last two phases, independence and refinement, involve organizing children into small groups (approximately five students each) in which they read a book of the group's choice according to the overall class theme (for example, children with disabilities). In these groups, children displayed previously taught strategies with increasing independence across the final phases. Along with gaining critical literacy skills, children made gains in their social-emotional learning, engaging in social justice activities to develop materials to advocate for children with disabilities.

Literature circles is another student-directed format useful in promoting literacy and interpersonal skills or social-emotional learning (Herrera &

Kidwell, 2018; Venegas, 2019). Literature circles are small groups of students who gather to discuss some literature in depth (Literature Circles Resource Center, n.d.). Although these circles vary greatly in practice, teachers typically group students according to literature choice or interest, and students guide discussion through insights and questions (LCRC, n.d.). Elena M. Venegas (2019) describes using literature circles in a fifth-grade class of racially and ethnically diverse (Hispanic, White, and Black) students to promote literacy and social-emotional learning.

Although literature circles often prescribe specific roles, such as the discussion leader, these roles can vary greatly or be non-existent (Herrera & Kidwell, 2018; Venegas, 2019). Venegas (2019) emphasizes the importance of providing structure, assigning roles, and establishing a class theme (for example, children with disabilities) for selected books. She also observed social-emotional growth in that one child displayed noticeable insight and empathy for children with disabilities following the reading on disabilities: *Rules* by Cynthia Lord (2007). Because they are student-directed, literacy circles give students the opportunity to exercise their own culture; but if conducted within culturally diverse groups, students have an even greater opportunity to respect and embrace the culture of others.

Although book clubs and literature circles are designated as student rather than teacher directed, as noted in the previous studies (Jocius & Shealy, 2017; Venegas, 2019), considerable teacher-directed structure is advised for these formats to eventually run smoothly and promote literacy and social-emotional learning. These and other student-directed strategies easily could be integrated into the practice segments recommended in the activities provided in the chapters of this book. For example, instead of structured book clubs or literature circles, following class instruction on one of the themes presented in this book (such as poverty), you could identify books on this topic for students to read independently. Allocate at least fifteen to twenty minutes twice per week for all the students to engage in independent reading for their selected books. After an appropriate time period (for example, one week), students can volunteer to share their books with the rest of the class. Make sure to encourage students to participate, but do not penalize them for not volunteering.

Social-emotional learning needs to be explicit, and literature is one tool for providing this learning. We recommend children's literature for this purpose because it is inherently attractive, provides high-quality models for emulation, and often contains valuable prosocial messages that can be the basis of social-emotional learning. Books lend themselves most directly for introducing and maintaining social-emotional learning (Cartledge & Kiarie, 2001). Culturally diverse literature aids in facilitating social-emotional learning within a context of a full range of differences.

Conclusion

Children and adults love stories, and stories have long served as a means of learning as well as entertainment. Children's and young adult (YA) literature are a valued part of children's lives from infancy throughout the teen years. In elementary school (grades K–5), not only do students acquire literacy, but literature can provide valuable learning about self and others. Literature for children has increased in recent years in volume and authenticity. It can help children understand the differences they observe in their immediate and larger environment and how they might most appropriately react to them. Teachers and other adults can be purposeful in selecting authentic literature that helps learners of all backgrounds see themselves in positive constructive ways. In reading this literature, teachers should use guidelines to select books for specific social-emotional learning, ensure learners understand the nature of appropriate actions toward self and others, and receive sufficient practice to achieve satisfactory performance within a diverse environment. This explicit instructional sequence is likely to produce the greatest returns. Other less structured formats, such as book clubs and allotted reading times, can be useful in reinforcing this instruction.

Chapter Reflections

Individually or with a collaborative group, review and discuss the following questions to reflect on your learning in this chapter.

1. What is the culture of the characters in the children's literature in your classroom library?

2. Does the children's literature in your classroom authentically reflect the racial and ethnic backgrounds of your students?

3. How do you think a book like *Amazing Grace* (Hoffman, 2007) might be affirming for all students?

4. What advantages or disadvantages might explicit instruction have, as described in this chapter?

5. What problems might you encounter in obtaining culturally diverse books for your students?

6. What additional strategies would you recommend to attract all your students to read culturally diverse books?

Part II

Affirming Others and Self and Asserting Self Through Diverse and Culturally Relevant Children's Literature

The importance of affirming oneself and others, and asserting oneself, cannot be overstated. Indeed, Maslow (1954), in the often referenced hierarchy of needs, includes the need to belong, the need to be valued and esteemed, and the need to be self-actualized (Huitt, 2007). According to Huitt (2007), (1) belongingness pertains to affiliating with others and being accepted; (2) self-esteem is to be competent and gain approval and recognition from others; and (3) self-actualization is to find self-fulfillment or realize one's potential. Maslow's theory is relevant, for it is through affirmation that people are able to establish or restore relationships for positive, caring interactions. These affirmations of self can lead to agency fostering self-actualization or self-assertion (Tov-Nachlieli, Shnabel, Aydin, & Ullrich, 2018).

In part II, we present two affirmation strategies focused on achieving caring relations and personal self-regard, and the related assertion strategy regarding the ability to act on one's affirmed or actualized self to become socially competent within and across culturally diverse populations.

- **Affirming others:** Learning to deliver affirmations in word or deed can promote prosocial actions toward others (Tov-Nachlieli et al., 2018). Activities in this chapter focus on learning to be kind and thoughtful through affirming others, especially those who present significant differences.
- **Affirming self:** Self-affirmations are especially beneficial when we encounter novel or threatening situations (Steele, 2010). All children need to acquire self-affirmations that lead to personal integrity and

valuing oneself. This is especially important for the student presenting significant group differences.

- **Asserting self:** Self-assertion is putting forward one's opinions or taking actions that express one's needs, rights, or wishes (APA Dictionary of Psychology, n.d.). In this chapter, we focus on instruction and classroom activities designed to help students fully embrace their affirmed self to take positive or non-aggressive actions to achieve socially appropriate goals. Assertive actions may be on behalf of oneself or a group in the interest of the common good.

chapter three

Affirming Others

It is *affirming* when students of all ages see themselves, their communities, and the people most important to them presented positively in the materials they read. It shows society values them and they can do worthwhile things. Authentic, high-quality, and affirming culturally relevant literature is especially important for students from culturally and linguistically diverse backgrounds (Bishop, 2007; Fleming et al., 2016). Cultural resources could serve as buffers to external forces that communicate directly or indirectly that students from culturally and linguistically different backgrounds are of limited value and ability. It is important to include in culturally relevant literature accomplished, successful characters who reflect the readers.

Affirming culturally relevant literature teaches learners not only to value their own culture but also to respect the cultural differences of others. Teachers should expose all children to affirming culturally relevant literature representing all cultures, not just their own. When children are affirmed, they begin to think of themselves more positively, capable of succeeding, and able to perform challenging tasks. In this chapter, we focus on learning to affirm others with a variety of differences.

Being Kind and Affirming Others

A major goal in social development is helping children learn to be kind to one another. Researchers in the field typically view kindness as a product of empathy, which involves emotional understanding, perspective taking, and prosocial behavior (for example, Malti, Chaparro, Zuffiano, & Colasante, 2016). Adults often observe young children acting kindly toward others without prompting or adult intervention. Some researchers view empathy as a natural emotion because they find aspects of empathy in children less than a year old (Campbell, Leezenbaum, Schmidt, Day, & Brownell, 2015). These and other authorities (for example, Tov-Nachlieli et al., 2018) contend that the ability to have concern for others facilitates prosocial behavior. Infants (birth to one year) and toddlers (one to four years), for example, may respond in kind to the distress of another individual, or slightly older children (four to six years) may attempt to comfort someone who is hurt or appears unhappy.

As children develop, they are increasingly able to anticipate and take the perspectives of others. Researchers consider *perspective taking* a component of empathy that helps us understand the situations of others and respond to others in socially appropriate ways (Davis, Martin-Cuellar, & Luce, 2019; Sang & Nelson, 2017). The child who observes a classmate strike out in a ball game and display a negative affect might assume his or her classmate is disappointed in him- or herself and might try to cheer him or her up with encouraging words or a simple positive touch. Socially appropriate or prosocial behaviors will vary according to age, developmental level, cultural background, and socioeconomics (Cartledge & Milburn, 1995; Gresham, 2018).

Gwen Cartledge observed an application of cognitive developmental and cultural differences several years ago while teaching second graders—with and without mild disabilities—the skill of welcoming a new child to the class. Several of the second graders, especially those with disabilities, had problems communicating socially with their peers. The more competent students served as models, and although they had a prepared script, they consistently went off script. The students were directed to say, "Hello, _____. My name is _____. Welcome to our school. Would you like to . . . (for example, play ball at recess)?" After saying, "Welcome to our school," the competent student models invariably would add, "Do you need anything?" Gwen subsequently learned that the students in this school had to provide their own school supplies. Because this was a low-socioeconomic area, many students came to school without supplies, especially those who transferred into the school later in the school year. Although their own resources were limited, these students were prepared to share what supplies they had with a new student who had even less. This unprompted act of kindness was even more impressive when you consider that being the new student in the class can result in maltreatment or neglect from classmates.

Whether this kind, caring attitude toward new students occurred in other situations or continued throughout the grades for these students is questionable. John-Tyler Binfet, Anne Gadermann, and Kimberly Schonert-Reichl (2016), for example, assessed students in fourth to eighth grades and their teachers on perceptions of student kindness in the school. They found the highest levels of perceived kindness among fourth graders with declining levels from fourth to eighth grade. They also found significant agreement between student and teacher perceptions of student kindness. Cartledge's own professional and personal experiences with students confirm acts of kindness vary greatly within and among individuals with increasing variability as they age. Further, even the most empathic individual may be challenged if there are stark personal differences among individuals.

Based on her teaching and consulting experiences in the schools, Gwen occasionally observed that generally kind and caring young students might be less likely to display caring behaviors toward classmates who presented differences in appearance, language, background, and so forth. To illustrate, within that same school district noted previously in this section, Gwen consulted with teachers about helping their fourth- and fifth-grade students affirm or be kinder to one another. One student, Lynn, experienced taunting in her class and from other students in the school. Lynn lived with her grandmother, wore her grandmother's clothes to school, and responded in awkward, profane ways when classmates teased her. Her responses amused her classmates who proceeded to tease her even more. At this point, Gwen conducted professional development sessions with the teachers on social-emotional learning interventions with their students.

The teachers taught students how to make kind statements to their peers and then practice using them with their classmates. The teachers assigned students in pairs to make kind statements, and eventually they paired each student with every other student in the class. This meant that at some point, each student in the class had to make a positive statement to Lynn. The outcome of this instruction and teacher reinforcement was students not only became more positive to one another but also became friendlier to Lynn in the classroom, prompting other students in the school to be nicer to her.

Schools are academic arenas, but a hidden social curriculum may be countering the desired positive environment educators need to help develop social competence among students. Some students display acts of kindness at higher rates than others, but all students benefit from purposefully planned positive environments, explicit instruction on prosocial behavior, and ample opportunities to demonstrate kindness toward others. Although positive school climates are critical, educators would be wise to be deliberate in making certain all students understand the nature of kind acts, and that each student has the opportunity to carry out and receive acts of kindness. Otherwise, students with anxiety, cognitive, or perception problems will miss out on this important social-emotional learning.

Evidence suggests students who get help in acting out acts of kindness make greater skill progress than those who are simply exposed to these events (Trew & Alden, 2015). Further, reductions in racial bias may result from kindness training (Stell & Farsides, 2016). To become ingrained and spontaneous, kind acts must occur frequently under a variety of conditions with a variety of people. Educators can guide upper elementary students, adolescents, and adults in devising plans where they can consistently engage in such acts. For example, you might plan to greet each student with a smile and compliment as he or she enters the classroom each morning. Because elementary students need much more structure and explicit instruction to perform such acts on a consistent basis, integrating activities with culturally diverse literature and specific literacy instruction is particularly beneficial.

People constantly encounter the opportunity to display kindness to others. Educators should coach students to take advantage of these opportunities and embrace others' differences. The activities in this chapter give explicit examples of social kindness when observing differences of affluence, language, ability, and religion or culture.

Affirming Others in Poverty

Poverty is a worldwide phenomenon, and it extensively impacts children. According to the Children's Defense Fund (2021), nearly one in seven children (birth to age 18) in the United States lives in poverty, making them the poorest age group (compared to adults and seniors) in the country. This means most children who do not live in poverty will encounter another child either directly or indirectly who does. Poverty, even if temporary, can result in significant long-term consequences. Children living in poverty are more likely to experience educational, behavioral, physical health, and emotional problems and their overall well-being is jeopardized (McLaughlin & Rank, 2018). Educators can all help children living in poverty lead better lives, and elementary students can begin to learn how too. An important first step is learning to be kind.

Literature on Affirming Others in Poverty

You could use several children's books to illustrate the significance of responding appropriately to individuals experiencing poverty. We use the book *Each Kindness* by Woodson (2012) as a model for suggested activities, but we reference other books as well throughout. We also note books particularly appropriate for primary or upper elementary students.

Book: *Each Kindness* by Jacqueline Woodson (2012)

As noted previously, the steps for introducing each book to the class include present the story, clarify story concepts through discussion, clarify the features of the desired behaviors through enactments, practice the desired behaviors through real-life applications, respond appropriately to issues of diversity, and provide extension activities to maintain the desired behaviors.

Present the Story

Read the story to and with the class. If students have a hard copy of the book or if they can access the story online, they can follow along as you read aloud. If not, students can simply listen as you read.

Story Synopsis

This book is appropriate for all elementary school students. It depicts a fairly common occurrence in many classrooms; a new student who is obviously poor and friendless comes to school. Chloe, the student narrator, and the other students, comfortable with their existing friendships, rebuff every overture the new student makes to be friendly, talk, and play with them. Throughout the school year, Chloe and the class shun the new student, Maya. One day, the teacher gives students a lesson about kindness, and Chloe regrets her past behavior and her lack of kindness toward Maya. Chloe now wishes for the opportunity to be kinder toward her, even just to smile at Maya. But Chloe does not get the opportunity to show kindness to Maya.

Discussion

Within this story are several important relational concepts but initially, you might limit discussion to (1) why Chloe was not friendly with Maya and (2) the benefits of being friendly with a new acquaintance such as Maya. For the first point, encourage students to identify reasons why Chloe chose not to welcome Maya to the class or respond positively to Maya's efforts to befriend Chloe and the other students. Among the various reasons students give, you should highlight that people often reject others because outsiders are new to the group (friendships are already established, and group members may see newcomers as threats to those friendships), and they tend not to readily accept those who look different. In Maya's case, she was not as well-groomed as the other students and reflected a lower-income group. In this initial discussion, help students understand the following.

- Chloe and her friends were happy with their group and did not want to include another student.
- Chloe and her friends did not like Maya's physical differences or poor dress.
- Chloe was probably afraid the other students would tease her if she befriended Maya.
- Chloe was probably afraid her friends would stop playing with her if she befriended Maya.

Failing to be kind or affirm someone else has consequences not always readily evident. Discuss Chloe's feelings with students. Ask questions such as: "Why do you think Chloe had trouble stating something kind she did for someone?" "How did she feel about not befriending Maya?" "Because Maya left the school permanently, what do you think Chloe would do if Maya came back to school?" Some basic student understandings might include the following.

- Being kind and affirming others makes them feel good.
- Being kind to others makes you feel good.
- Being unkind to others can make you feel bad.
- Being unkind to others can cause you to lose friends.
- Do not listen to others who tell you to be unkind.

Help students generate a list of kind and affirming acts students could do for a new student in the class. Ideas might include the following.

- Introduce yourself to the new student.
- Smile at the student and say you are happy to have him or her in your class.
- Offer to share your materials with the student.
- Invite the student to play with you at recess.
- Tour the student around the school.
- Show the student how to do things in the classroom.
- Offer to help the student with some classwork.
- Compliment something about the student, such as something he or she is wearing or doing (for example, "You are a good kickball player. We had fun at recess").

Enactments

Direct students to role-play the scenes in figure 3.1 (page 45) with classmates. Pair students and have one student act as the new student and the other as the welcoming student. Then have them switch roles. For example, you could review the ways students in the story were unkind to Maya and what the students in your class could do instead to show acts of kindness.

Real-Life Applications

Prior to a new student joining the class, review with students what you expect and the kinds of things they might say to or do for the new student. Observe when students carry out these acts. Prompt students who have difficulty doing something to welcome a new student to class. If there isn't an opportunity with a new student, practice acts of kindness with students

When Maya . . .	What Do You Say?
Smiles at you	
Says hello to you	
Asks you to play a game of jacks with her	
Asks, "What is your favorite game?"	
Comes to school with a pretty new dress and fancy shoes	
Asks you to play jump rope	

Figure 3.1: Role-play scenes for *Each Kindness*.

Visit *go.SolutionTree.com/diversityandequity* for a free reproducible version of this figure.

already in the class. Give each student the name of another student, and make sure every student is participating. Direct students to deliver an act of kindness to the student they are assigned to, such as making a compliment, inviting him or her to play a game during recess, helping carry materials, helping with a special assignment, smiling and greeting in the morning, and so on.

Tell students to think about their everyday acts of kindness within the classroom, throughout the school, and outside of school. Each student should list at least one kind thing the student did for a classmate and one kind thing the student did for or said to an adult. Ask students to list as many kind acts they performed over the past week as they remember. Allow students to share at least one of their kind acts with the class. Praise students for engaging in these acts of kindness. Repeat this activity at least once each week so students regularly think of carrying out acts of kindness.

Diversity Issues in This Story

Dealing with differences is a common human experience. It is important to understand the nature of the difference and an appropriate reaction. In this story, the children react to Maya's differences of (1) being new to the class and (2) being less well-groomed or impoverished compared to the other students. Being the "new kid on the block" often causes anxiety for a new student, and elementary school children often are not sufficiently skilled in welcoming newcomers, especially if the new student looks or acts in ways that do not fit in with the existing group. Additionally, sometimes members of the existing group are afraid the new student may disrupt their friendships. Discuss with students how it feels to be a new person in a group. How would they want others to treat them?

Discuss Maya's appearance with the class by asking questions such as the following.

- "What was Maya wearing?"
- "How did the other students feel about Maya's clothes?"

- "Was Maya's clothing her fault?"
- "How should you treat someone who has less than others?"
- "How do you think Maya felt when the other students did not speak to her or smile at her?"
- "How should you think about someone who does not have enough money to buy the clothes, food, or housing they need?"

Help students understand that having limited resources is not a reason for rejecting others. Accepting and being kind to others can help them feel better about themselves.

Extended Literature Activities

Use these literature activities to further ascertain students' understanding of the story and desired social-emotional learning skills. Students use their own words to retell the story and specify appropriate ways to respond. You also could use the annotated book list in the section Books on Affirming Others (page 67) to assign more relevant readings to individuals or groups. For each book, we provide the reading levels suggested by the publishers; but for primary students, you might also use a readability calculator such as the Spache Readability Formula (https://readable.com/readability/spache-readability-formula).

Retell the Story

Organize students into small groups to retell the story in their own words. Make sure each student gets an opportunity to participate in the retelling. During these retellings, help students identify the things about Maya her classmates did not like, what Maya did to try to make friends, who Chloe's friends were, what Ms. Albert (the teacher) did to teach the students about kindness, and how that lesson made Chloe feel. Also, get students to think about some kindnesses Chloe could have shown Maya. For older or more advanced elementary students, assign different stories from the books we describe later in this activity (see Additional Readings) to each small group, which on separate days can share its book with the rest of the class.

Extend the Story: If Maya Came to My Class

Organize students into small groups of two to four. Give each group a sheet of newsprint or large sheet of paper with the title *If Maya Came to My Class*. Direct students to work together to write two to four sentences about what they would do to be kind to Maya if she came to their class. Help students complete their thoughts, as needed. If students have not yet mastered the ability to work well in small groups, direct them to write (or draw, depending on their skill level) at least one thing they would do if Maya was a new student in their class. Give students a few minutes to complete their task, and then let them share their writings or drawings with the entire class. List students' suggestions in a chart and note the similarities of students' suggestions.

Conclude the activity by noting Chloe was very sorry that she did not get to see Maya again so she could be kind to her. Tell students to pretend Chloe did get a chance to see Maya again, and write what they think Chloe would say to Maya. If students have limited writing skills, encourage them to draw a picture of Chloe and Maya and tell the class what Chloe is saying to Maya.

Additional Readings

Explore additional readings about economic hardship, poverty, hunger, and homelessness. The more educators expose students to literature that addresses these important topics, the less taboo the issues become. Help lessen the stigma and shame surrounding poverty by sharing high-quality children's literature with students. You can use most of these stories across elementary grades, but you will need to make adjustments according to the abilities and developmental levels of your students. Beside each book, we offer a general suggestion regarding primary, elementary, or upper elementary levels, but you need not adhere rigidly to these suggestions.

Last Stop on Market Street by Matt de la Peña (2015; Primary)

Following church, young CJ's grandmother takes him by bus to the last stop on Market Street. During the trip, CJ notices things about his life and his community that are different from other children's. He asks his grandmother about the world in which they live and why he doesn't have things many of his friends have (for example, a car or access to technology). His grandmother answers each question directly and sensitively, and helps CJ see beauty in his world. CJ appreciates the sights and the journey, ending at a soup kitchen where he happily joins his grandmother in serving the less-fortunate diners.

La Frontera: El Viaje Con Papá (My Journey With Papa) by Deborah Mills and Alfredo Alva (2018; Elementary)

This is the true story of Alfredo, a young boy living in a small Mexican village. When his father is no longer able to find work to support Alfredo and his family, the father decides he and Alfredo should leave their village and travel to the United States to find work and money for the family. This story tells of difficulties Alfredo and his father have traveling to the United States. The story explains how Alfredo learns English, makes friends, becomes a U.S. citizen, overcomes poverty, and reunites with his family.

Home at Last by Susan Middleton Elya (2006; Elementary)

Ana and her family move to the United States from Mexico. Ana learns to speak English in school and Papa learns English in night school. Mama stays home to take care of the younger children, but she soon learns that she cannot master shopping or other household matters without speaking the language. Mama begins to learn English and is able to manage her daily activities without getting help from Ana or Papa.

Those Shoes by Maribeth Boelts (2007; Elementary)

Jeremy desperately wants a pair of shoes like those of his classmates, but Grandma says there is no money. Even after obtaining an affordable, albeit too-small pair, Jeremy finds more personal satisfaction in giving the coveted shoes to a classmate with an even greater need than his. For himself and others, Jeremy learns how needs supersede wants.

The Lunch Thief by Anne C. Bromley (2010; Upper Elementary)

This story examines why some people do things they know are wrong (for example, stealing) when the need is too great to bear. Kevin is caught stealing lunches, but later, his classmate Rafael finds out he is a victim of wildfires and has lost his home. In an effort to survive, Kevin resorts to stealing lunches. Rafael takes notice and invites Kevin to share his lunch so that he does not have to steal. In addition to considering the possible causes of poverty, this story gives a good example of empathy and how in even small ways, students can help others in need.

Fly Away Home by Eve Bunting (1991; Upper Elementary)

This book explores the unique challenges of homelessness. A widower and his young son with no other place to live find themselves staying in the airport and working together to navigate the logistics of this arrangement. They move from place to place within the airport, always careful not to be discovered. The boy is aware he will soon have to start school and experiences anxiety over how he will be able to, given his housing situation. The boy and his father feel hopeful by watching a trapped bird make its way to freedom.

The Streets Are Free by Kurusa (1995; Upper Elementary)

Neighborhood children living in a barrio in Venezuela wish to have a playground or some place of their own to play and enjoy the outdoors. The children, along with family members, lobby local elected officials, but they are met with empty promises. They come to understand that the change they would like to see in their community starts with them as they embark on the collective goal of developing a community park.

The Hundred Dresses by Eleanor Estes (2004; Upper Elementary)

Wanda is different from the other students in her class. She has a Polish name others have difficulty pronouncing, and she is very impoverished, wearing the same blue dress to school every day. For both her name and obvious poverty, other students ridicule Wanda daily. In a futile attempt to fit in, Wanda volunteers that she has one hundred dresses at home, setting herself up for even greater abuse from her peers. As the story develops, the students learn of Wanda's exceptional talent as an artist and begin to recognize their unkind behavior. This book has a theme consistent with *Each Kindness* (Woodson, 2012), but its length and wording are more appropriate for slightly older students. This book is especially relevant to social-emotional understanding, but the reading level is beyond the primary grades. If you use this book, we suggest you read it to students a few chapters at a time over several sessions.

Action Project: Personalities

If possible, identify a major personality in your school or local community, such as a school administrator, teacher, political figure, businessperson, and so on, who had an impoverished childhood and is willing to come to your classroom to share personal experiences of poverty and achievement. Parents and guardians may be good options for this purpose. Also, try to identify a major personality most children admire, such as a national entertainer or athlete, who had a rather modest upbringing. Discuss why students should not make negative assumptions about people simply because they did not have as much as others when they were younger.

Action Project: Field Trip

If possible, arrange for available parents to accompany the class on a field trip to a community soup kitchen. Arrange for students to take part in serving the diners. Throughout the trip, encourage students to make note of the different, attractive, and exciting things they see. Where appropriate, take photos of these things to discuss later after returning to the classroom.

Affirming Others With Ability Differences

Individuals with exceptionalities fall along a continuum, ranging from those with exceptional talents and gifts to those with severe or profound disabilities. These differences may include sensory impairments (such as hearing or vision impairment), physical differences (such as cerebral palsy or muscular dystrophy), communication challenges (such as disorders of language and thinking), emotional disabilities (such as childhood psychosis or mild behavior disorders), and cognitive disabilities (such as severe to mild intellectual disorders).

Students with gifts and talents also often warrant special considerations. These are students who have unusual abilities and are performing several grades beyond their age mates, but often do not have commensurate social-emotional skills. Peers may single out these students for either ridicule or indifference. On the other hand, exceptionally intellectually advanced children may need special attention for appropriate interactions with their age mates or interactions with higher-grade learning mates. The same considerations may apply for unusually talented students, such as music or athletic prodigies. Regardless of ability levels, all children have a legal right to a free education in U.S. public schools and should be welcomed accordingly (Cartledge, Gardner, & Ford, 2009; Heward, 2017).

Literature on Affirming Others With Ability Differences

Louie by Keats (1975) is a classic, sensitively written book about a young boy with a somewhat ambiguous difference. We chose to label that difference as a mild learning disability in the form of a communication disorder. Although the book is written for primary students, it also easily can be useful with older students. This section includes books with more explicit references to disabilities across elementary grades.

Book: *Louie* by Ezra Jack Keats (1975)

As noted previously, the steps for introducing each book to the class include present the story, clarify story concepts through discussion, clarify the features of the desired behaviors through enactments, practice the desired behaviors through real-life applications, respond appropriately to issues of diversity, and provide extension activities to maintain the desired behaviors.

Present the Story

Read the story to and with the class. If students have a hard copy of the book or if they can access the story online, they can follow along as you read aloud. If not, students can simply listen as you read.

Story Synopsis

Louie is a shy, quiet little boy who rarely talks to anyone. One day he goes to a puppet show, and the puppets fascinate him, particularly a puppet called Gussie. Louie stands up and says "hello" to the puppet, and does other things to disrupt the show. Louie sits down, enjoys the show, and goes home where he dreams about the puppet, Gussie. Louie is sad about having to leave

Gussie, but then he gets a message and goes outside to find the surprise the puppeteers have for him.

Keats's gentle treatment of Louie is special, and although the story does not specify his difference, at the very least Louie is shy and quiet. Although a disability is not specified, Louie probably has special needs, such as limited English (an English learner), autism, language delay, or a learning disability. Louie is excited with the puppets but misunderstands the social situation and initially does not respond appropriately. Nevertheless, the story suggests that regardless of Louie's differences, he deserves to be treated kindly. Two of the key points to make about this story include the following.

1. When Louie is mistaken in his actions, he is not punished but rather helped to respond appropriately.
2. The puppeteers find a way to treat Louie kindly and make him happy.

Discussion

Help students speculate why Louie acted inappropriately when the puppet show started. Some thoughts might include that Louie had never been to a puppet show before; Louie needs more help than most children to learn how to act at puppet shows; Louie is shyer than most children; Louie is extremely excited by puppets; and so on. Help students understand everyone has differences and everyone likes for others to be kind to them rather than to tease or belittle them. Note that Louie has some distinct differences, probably more than the other children at the puppet show. Help students identify specific actions the puppeteers took to help Louie act appropriately during the puppet show. These actions include letting Louie say "hello" to the puppet and using the puppet to tell Louie what he should do so he and the others enjoy the show. Emphasize that the puppeteers said these things nicely to Louie; they did not yell at Louie or punish him.

For the second key point, discuss the special acts of kindness the puppeteers perform for Louie following the puppet show. Using very kind words, the puppeteers permit Louie to hug the puppet, Gussie, but even more exciting, they later give Louie the puppet as a gift. During discussion, help students identify kind, non-offensive ways to help someone understand and correct misbehavior. For example, some kind things you could say to Louie before the show include the following.

- "The puppet show cannot begin if anyone is standing up."
- "If you stand up, other people will not be able to see around you."
- "When we sit down, everyone can see, and we can all enjoy the show."

Some kind things you say to Louie after the show include the following.

- "Thanks so much, Louie, for sitting down during the show. We all got to see and enjoy the puppet show."
- "Would you like to play with Gussie the puppet?"
- "Would you like to make up a puppet play with Gussie the puppet?"

Louie's tremendous affinity for puppets or some other toy might be a great way to help reduce his shyness and increase his speech or social communication skills. Discuss with students how much better they might feel if they befriended Louie and helped him feel better than if they yelled at or taunted him.

Enactments

Discuss with students some situations in which they befriended or helped someone with differences, such as a classmate or neighbor who is visually impaired, in a wheelchair, or cognitively impaired; or someone who has a speech impediment or health condition that limits play activities, and so on. Discuss some of the special behaviors the person with differences may have to learn and how students can help him or her. Also point out how they can be kind to the person. Help students with enactments such as the following.

- My friend Georgie likes to play kickball with the kids on the playground, but he often forgets the rules on how to take his turn. I help Georgie take his turn correctly by saying, "Georgie, . . ."
- Alicia is a good basketball player, but she often forgets to put the ball in the right basket. This upsets her team. I help Alicia remember the right basket by telling (and showing) her, "Alicia, . . ."
- Angie has trouble remembering all her spelling words each week. I help Angie by . . .
- Lorenzo has trouble putting away his materials when free time is over. I help Lorenzo by . . .

Real-Life Applications

Identify classroom situations in which students can learn to gently prompt classmates about classroom rules and routines. In each case, students should speak in a gentle, friendly voice, making sure classmates know they are being helped and not punished. Students should always frame their supportive statements from the position of helpfulness and friendship. Students also should know the prompted behavior will be to their advantage and others'. Some example prompts include the following.

- "I can help Brian learn how to put away the crayons so we will have a full box of crayons to use the next time we need them."
- "Leon has a bad leg and has to use crutches, so he can't run well. When we play softball, we will let Leon hit and Charlie will run the bases for him."
- "I'll help Ray pass out the papers, so everyone gets a sheet."
- "I can see that Martina needs help putting away her lunch tray so the whole class can get a chance to go out for recess. I'll check how she's doing."
- "LeRoy has vision problems. I can guide him as he passes out papers to the class."
- "If I share the rules for playing kickball with Mario, he can play with the other boys and girls too, and we will all have more fun."

Encourage students to show kindness to others who might be in temporary or permanent need of help. Following are some examples.

- Help your teacher collect papers at the end of class.
- Compliment Richie on the picture he painted in art class.
- Remind or help Leticia to keep her shoes tied.

Diversity Issues in This Story

Although not clearly specified in the story, the racial or cultural components associated with Louie may be twofold, including language differences resulting from a language background other than English or a communication disorder. Louie may have a mild disability. He may be a native English speaker but has a communication disorder that causes him to fail to receive or express language in the same way as typically developing children. This difference could cause him to misunderstand appropriate behavior in social situations.

According to the American Speech-Language-Hearing Association (ASHA, 1993), a *communication disorder* is an impairment in the ability to receive, send, process, and comprehend concepts or verbal, nonverbal, and graphic symbol systems. This means a communication disorder may exist in the way the individual receives or expresses language, or both. Communication disorders vary greatly in form, ranging from mild to severe, and they may start developing from birth or can be acquired later in childhood or adulthood. Problems with learning and interpersonal relations are characteristic of children with communication disorders (Heward, 2017). Social learning problems appear to be evident with Louie in the puppet show. He doesn't seem to understand the expectations of the social situation and, initially, has difficulty comprehending verbal directions from others. Without kind understanding, such events could escalate, resulting in poor social interactions.

Help students understand that some people have communication differences, and they need others to be patient with them and help them understand what people are saying to them and how they should act. Have students practice delivering information or directions to their peers in a patient, thoughtful manner and pretend they are giving directions to Louie.

Extended Literature Activities

Use these literature activities to further ascertain students' understanding of the story and desired social-emotional learning skills. Students use their own words to retell the story and specify appropriate ways to respond. You also could use the annotated book list in the section Books on Affirming Others (page 67) to assign more relevant readings to individuals or groups. For each book, we suggest general elementary reading levels.

Retell the Story

Encourage students to retell the story using their own words. Have each student offer his or her own ideas on why Louie was so excited about the puppet, Gussie. Have students imagine what they think Louie did with the puppet, Gussie, after he received it as a gift.

Extend the Story: Kind Words for Louie

For each statement in figure 3.2, ask students to check the box beside it if it was a *kind* thing to say to help Louie at the puppet show. For younger students, it's best to conduct this activity as a large group so you can deliver the statements for students to determine whether each statement is kind or unkind. You could direct older students to individually or in small groups write alternative statements they consider to be unkind.

Extend the Story: Louie and the Puppet Play

Read the story several times. Encourage students to read the story individually during independent reading time. Give students small paper bags and direct them to design puppets with them. Encourage students to be as creative as they wish. Tell students they will act out the story, *Louie*, as a puppet play. Assign students roles for the characters in the story, which include a narrator, Louie, Roberto, Susie, an unnamed student, and Louie's mother.

Kind Words for Louie	
Check the box if the statement is kind to Louie. If the statement is unkind, write an alternative statement.	
❏ "Hey, sit down!"	
❏ "C'mon, sit down, will ya?"	
❏ "Hi, Louie, nice to see you."	
❏ "The mouse and I have to get on with the show. Will you please sit down?"	
❏ "We can't see through you, Louie!"	
❏ "Hello, Louie. Go outside and follow the long green string."	

Figure 3.2: Kind words for Louie.

Visit *go.SolutionTree.com/diversityandequity* for a free reproducible version of this figure.

In this enactment, do not let students practice using harsh words. Assign several students to use kind words to get Louie to sit down, although he doesn't sit down until Gussie the puppet speaks to him. Repeat the puppet play several times so all students get to prompt Louie with kind words. Organize older students into small groups where they develop and present their own puppet show, demonstrating how to use kind words to help Louie.

Additional Readings

Extend the discussion on disabilities and differences through more children's books such as the following. This list contains books that focus on using kind words or fostering positive interactions with those with disabilities.

All Are Welcome by Alexandra Penfold and Suzanne Kaufman (2019; Primary)

This picture book depicts numerous examples of a welcoming classroom, neighborhood, and world. The pictures show diversity, representing cultures from around the world. The pictures also include children in wheelchairs, indicative of individuals with special needs. Engage students in discussions of each picture, noting the represented differences and how they could be instrumental in welcoming others.

The Invisible Boy by Trudy Ludwig (2013; Elementary)

Although this book is written and illustrated for primary students, it has a universal theme and could serve as an easy-to-read-and-discuss book for all elementary-aged groups. Brian feels "invisible" in his class, where his peers consistently overlook him for various school and play activities. A new student's unexpected observations and invitation help reveal some of Brian's talents and create a more wholesome school environment for Brian and his classmates.

The Woman Who Outshone the Sun: The Legend of Lucia Zenteno by Alejandro Cruz Martinez (1991; Elementary)

This story is about children who learn to speak kindly to a woman who is doing good things in their village. The story is written in both English and Spanish, which will give children the opportunity to practice Spanish words and more practice on delivering words in a kind manner.

Out of My Mind by Sharon Mills Draper (2012; Upper Elementary)

This fascinating chapter book tells the story of a ten-year-old girl, Melody, with cerebral palsy. With the aid of a brilliant and persistent homeschool teacher, Melody, who is nonverbal, learns to communicate through a computer device. The story tells of Melody's integration into public school and how she wins the admiration and hearts of her classmates. This is a very good story about students with disabilities. It has powerful messages about how students can empower others as well as assert themselves.

Wonder by R. J. Palacio (2012; Upper Elementary)

This story is about a ten-year-old boy with special needs. August has special medical issues with facial abnormalities. He has been homeschooled all his life, but he decides he wants to go to public school for fifth grade. Although August is an extremely bright boy with a terrific sense of humor, this is a challenging undertaking. This story expertly details the changes that occur with August and his classmates, a valuable learning experience for all. Discussions could center on what actions students had to take to make this beneficial for themselves and others.

Action Project: Peer Buddies

If your classroom includes students with disabilities, structure class learning and social activities so students with disabilities have the opportunity for meaningful and positive interactions with all their peers regardless of differences. These interactions could consist of simple indoor or outdoor games or small-group learning projects for the entire class. Monitor students to ensure they all use the skills taught in this activity, and treat students with disabilities with kindness and as equal peers.

If students with special needs are not integrated into your classroom, another option might be for students to become *peer buddies* for a class with students who have developmental disabilities. Children with developmental disabilities benefit greatly from social interactions with all their peers, regardless of differences. Depending on administrative and, if needed, parental permissions, your students could spend ten to fifteen minutes once or twice weekly coaching students with disabilities in social activities. This would take place during recess under teacher supervision.

Affirming Others From Different Religious or Cultural Groups

Religion is an important feature of most countries around the world. The United States and many other countries support freedom of religion. The U.S. Constitution guarantees people the right to practice any religion they wish as long as their religious behavior is consistent with the laws of the country (Constitution of the United States, n.d.). That means everyone must respect other religions and cultures that differ from their own. As with other differences, ignorance about religious groups may lead to unnecessary friction or hostilities toward, between, or among groups. Learning about different groups can be a means for creating acceptance and harmony. We use the terminology *religion or culture* because many individuals may be associated with a particular group but do not participate in the group's religious practices. There are many people, for example, who grew up in Christian households and celebrate holidays, such as Christmas and Easter, but are not practicing Christians.

Some of the key points for this book and related activities are (1) people are privileged to live in countries that accept people with different religious beliefs; and (2) people live very similar lives even if they have a different religious or cultural practice. For the first point, engage students in a discussion of religious groups. For primary students, limit the discussion to identifying the major religious groups (in the United States, for example, Christians, Muslims, and Jews), unless there are students in the class who practice other beliefs, such as one of the Eastern groups (for example, Buddhism). If students in your class represent other belief systems, enthusiastically include them in the discussion. Otherwise, students can discuss these other groups later in the activity or in upper elementary grades. Also, note that many people do not identify with any formal religious group or system. Avoid any discussion of the relative merits of one belief system over the other; rather, limit the discussion to symbols associated with each group. For example, Christians might wear the Christian cross, Jews might wear the Star of David, and Muslim women might wear a *hijab*, a head covering worn in the presence of any male outside of their immediate family. Point out to students in the United States and many other countries, people have the freedom to wear these symbols in public. These symbols are not intended to offend others who do not believe in the same way.

Second, it is important to emphasize for the most part, regardless of the religious symbols people display, they live their lives in very similar ways. People in all groups work hard to take care of their families, study to learn about the world, participate in entertainment and recreational activities, and do good things for their communities and others.

The purpose of this activity is to increase student awareness and possibly greater acceptance. Although there is no endorsement of any religious or cultural group and every effort should be made to present these activities in informative, nonjudgmental ways, we suggest you share the content of these activities with school administrators in advance to ascertain desired boundaries and avoid any community misunderstandings.

Literature on Affirming Others From Different Religious or Cultural Groups

This section focuses mainly on two groups: Muslims and Jews. There is a brief reference to Christianity, but the assumption is that most children in North America (and Western Europe) are familiar with Christian traditions. According to a 2017 Gallup Poll, about three-quarters of Americans identified as Christians, 2 percent Jewish, 1 percent Muslim, and 3 percent other groups such as Buddhist and Hindu, and 21 percent indicated no religious affiliation (as cited in Newport, 2017). If, however, your class has a majority of Muslim, Jewish, or other non-Christian students, expand the curriculum to include readings on Christians. Further, for older or more advanced students, you might expand to include additional religious or cultural groups from around the world. Structure these activities so they are informational, not judgmental. As is the case with all these activities, the intent is to affirm the others.

Book: *Under My Hijab* by Hena Khan (2019)

As noted previously, the steps for introducing each book to the class include present the story, clarify story concepts through discussion, clarify the features of the desired behaviors through enactments, practice the desired behaviors through real-life applications, respond appropriately to issues of diversity, and provide extension activities to maintain the desired behaviors.

Present the Story

Read the story to and with the class. If students have a hard copy of the book or if they can access the story online, they can follow along as you read aloud. If not, students can simply listen as you read.

Story Synopsis

The author of this book presents a variety of women in a wide array of hijabs. The effect is to remove some of the mystique and misperceptions associated with people who wear hijabs. In addition to the variety of hijabs and their special significance in public, the author shows the women in their private lives without wearing hijabs. The women include a grandmother who wears a hijab while working in a bakery but arranges her hair in a bun when she works in her kitchen at home. The narrator's mother wears a more brightly colored hijab while working as a dentist but reveals her long, attractive hair while working in the garden at home.

The author continues describing the different types of hijabs and different roles the women have in society, wearing hijabs when they work, play, or socialize in public but uncovering their hair when in private or just with other women. Essentially, women who wear hijabs live very much like all women in society. The women who wear hijabs belong to a particular culture and share religious beliefs, but not all people who subscribe to this culture or belief wear hijabs. At the end of the book, the author explains why some women wear hijabs.

Discussion

For each of the characters depicted in this book, ask students the following questions.

1. "Who has a grandma (or mother) who bakes cookies? Do you ever bake cookies with her? What is special about your grandma's cookies?"
2. "Who has a mother who is a dentist (doctor or some other professional)? What did your mother have to do to become a dentist (or other professional)? Tell us about your mother's work. What do you like about your mother's work?"
3. "Who has an aunt (or mother or another female) who is an artist? What kind of pictures does your aunt (or other adult female) draw? What does she do with her art? Do you watch her draw?"
4. "Who has a mother (or knows another female) who is a scout leader? What does this scout leader do? How does this scout leader help the scouts? Is it hard to be a scout leader?"
5. "Who has a sister (or knows another female) who is an athlete? What sport does your sister (or other female) play? What does she have to do every day to be a good athlete? Do you like having a sister who is an athlete?"

Point out that women fill these same roles in every other religious group. To further emphasize this point, have students identify the occupations or activities of family members or close friends, such as the following.

- Farmer
- Store clerk
- Teacher

- Religious leader
- Engineer
- Physician or veterinarian

Next, have students identify the religions of the people they identify, if possible. If your students are from different backgrounds, they should recognize that people of different belief systems are doing very similar jobs in their community. If the class is fairly homogeneous (for example, most identify as Christian), encourage them to identify someone in their community who wears a hijab who does the same work as a family member or close friend.

As part of this discussion, it is important to stress the commonalities among members of different religious and cultural groups. Encourage students to help you identify some of these commonalities for religious groups, such as the following.

- They have special buildings for worship, such as mosques, synagogues, and churches. If possible, display pictures of each building and help students specify ways they are similar and different.
- They have special holidays and celebrations such as Ramadan, Hanukkah, and Christmas.
- During these holidays and celebrations, they have special meals and invite friends and family to help them celebrate.
- They encourage members to share and help others who are poor, lonely, sick, or need special help.

Tell students now you are going to read a story to them about a religious group and then discuss one of its holiday celebrations.

Book: *Mrs. Greenberg's Messy Hanukkah* by *Linda Glaser* (2004)

As noted previously, the steps for introducing each book to the class include present the story, clarify story concepts through discussion, clarify the features of the desired behaviors through enactments, practice the desired behaviors through real-life applications, respond appropriately to issues of diversity, and provide extension activities to maintain the desired behaviors.

Present the Story

Read the story to and with the class. If students have a hard copy of the book or if they can access the story online, they can follow along as you read aloud. If not, students can simply listen as you read.

Story Synopsis

It is the first night of Hanukkah, and Rachel wants to make *latkes* (potato pancakes). Rachel's parents want to wait to make the latkes until later in the week when they have company coming to celebrate. Rachel's parents are busy with the holiday preparations, so Rachel asks to go next door to visit with her elderly neighbor, Mrs. Greenberg. Because she lives alone, Rachel thinks it would be a good idea to keep Mrs. Greenberg company on the first night of Hanukkah. Rachel bursts into Mrs. Greenberg's tidy house and tells Mrs. Greenberg they will be making latkes together. Rachel makes a huge mess in Mrs. Greenberg's house and when her parents come to pick her up, they scold her for making such a mess. Rachel begins to cry, but Mrs. Greenberg says this is the first time her house has felt lived in for years. After cleaning up the house, they all sit down and enjoy the latkes together.

Tell students that Rachel belongs to a religious or cultural group called Judaism, and one of the special holidays Jewish people celebrate is Hanukkah. Hanukkah celebrates a time when the Jews successfully defeated their enemies. Because Hanukkah is a holiday, this is a time to be with friends and family, and sometimes families give small gifts to one another. Rachel wanted to make sure Mrs. Greenberg was not lonely during Hanukkah, and she wanted to give Mrs. Greenberg a gift by helping her make latkes. Latkes are a favorite dish during Hanukkah. Help students understand Rachel practiced her religion and culture by befriending and helping others.

Discussion

Review the story to emphasize the following understandings.

- Hanukkah is a special holiday to celebrate with family and friends.
- Mrs. Greenberg lives alone and would not have friends and family visit for Hanukkah.
- Rachel is very thoughtful and kind because she does not want Mrs. Greenberg to be alone and wants her to celebrate Hanukkah.
- Rachel knows older people often need help doing things because their bodies are not as strong as the bodies of younger people.
- Rachel feels bad about making a mess.
- Rachel's parents and Mrs. Greenberg know Rachel means to be kind and helpful.
- Rachel's parents join with Rachel to help Mrs. Greenberg celebrate the first night of Hanukkah.

Remind students like other religious groups, Rachel's religious or cultural group (Judaism) has special holidays, which are celebrated with friends and family, and they encourage everyone to share with and help others.

Enactments

Discuss with students various situations in which they had the opportunity to learn about someone else's religion or had a positive interaction with someone from another religion. Some examples include the following.

- "Haleema is a new student in our class. Haleema wears a hijab. I welcomed Haleema to our class by saying . . ."
- "My friend Judah is Jewish. He lives on my street. My mom said I could invite Judah to my home for Christmas dinner. I invited Judah by saying . . ."
- "Ms. Jones lives alone and has no family in town. She is very lonely. My family is celebrating Hanukkah. What can I suggest to my family we do for Ms. Jones?"
- "My friend Jamal is Muslim. His family is celebrating Ramadan, and they invited me to a Ramadan meal with his family. What should I say?"

Real-Life Applications

Help students expand their knowledge and understanding of different religions and related cultures by applying them to real-life situations. Participation in some of the following activities depends on students' ability levels as well as their personal backgrounds.

- Encourage students to share about something they did in their religious group that helped others in need, such as serving in a soup kitchen for the poor.
- Ask students to share about a time they went to visit a different religious group's place of worship (for example, mosque or synagogue) with family or friends.
- Have students share about a time when they were invited to a holiday celebration in the home of someone of a different religion.
- Ask students to share about a time when their family invited someone of a different religion to their home to help them celebrate one of their holidays.
- Encourage students to share their favorite holiday traditions.
- Have students share about a time when they did something for someone who had special needs during one of their holidays.

Diversity Issues in These Stories

This activity focuses primarily on Judaism and Islam because some form of Christianity is dominant in Western cultures and its traditions and precepts are fairly well known. However, if the students in your class are from predominantly Muslim or Jewish backgrounds, you might allocate some time to discussing the origins and basic features of Christianity in broad terms, emphasizing the commonalities with other major religions of celebrating holiday traditions and altruism. Judaism, Islam, and Christianity all have their origins in the Middle East and are rooted in Jewish scriptures. Show students a map of the modern-day Israel and Palestine area. Each group uses an important book as a guide for daily living. These books include the Torah for Jews, the Quran for Muslims, and the Bible for Christians. Although these religions have their beginnings in the Middle East, they have spread all around the world and among every ethnic and racial group.

A major holiday and celebration for Muslims is Ramadan, which occurs in in the ninth month of the Islamic calendar and is remembered as the time when their messenger received the Quran. Ramadan lasts for either twenty-nine or thirty days; during this time, healthy adults fast during the day and break the fast at sundown with a special meal. The meals are often extensive and a time for inviting friends and family to feast.

Jews also celebrate special days and events, such as Hanukkah. According to the Jewish tradition, Hanukkah is a celebration of the occasion when thousands of years ago, the Jews defeated enemies who would not let them worship the way they wanted. They use a special candelabra, called a *menorah*, to light one candle for each of the eight days of the holiday. During Hanukkah, Jews like to eat certain foods, such as latkes, and like the other two religious groups, celebrate the holiday with family and friends.

Extended Literature Activities

Use these literature activities to further ascertain students' understanding of the story and desired social-emotional learning skills. Students use their own words to retell the story and specify appropriate ways to respond. You also could use the annotated book list in the section Books on Affirming Others (page 67) to assign more relevant readings to individuals or groups. For each book, we suggest general elementary reading levels.

Retell the Story

Encourage students to retell the stories in their own words. Have them explain their own positive reactions to how learning about the hijabs made them feel about the women wearing them. Also, direct students to identify Rachel's good intentions in trying to help Mrs. Greenberg.

Extend the Story: Welcome to My Ramadan, Hanukkah, or Christmas Celebration

On separate days, invite a parent or member of the community to class who is a member of one of these groups: Muslim, Jew, or Christian. You might consider including the Christmas celebration only if you have students in the class from other religious or cultural groups. Ask the parent or community member to talk to students about how his or her group celebrates Ramadan, Hanukkah, or Christmas. Restrict the presentation and student questions to the holiday activities, and avoid sensitive details of specific religious beliefs, religious comparisons, or evaluations of other religions. Encourage students to ask questions about the holiday celebrations.

To continue the activity, bring in an experienced cook (for example, one of the parents) representing each culture, or you might obtain some traditional recipes for traditional holiday dishes and try to prepare the food yourself. Recommended foods include latkes for Hanukkah, samosas for Ramadan, or cookies for Christmas. The book *Mrs. Greenberg's Messy Hanukkah*, for example, includes a recipe for latkes (Glaser, 2004). When you prepare the food, students invite their peers from another class to join them. Students can share food with peers and explain how a particular religious or cultural group celebrates the holiday.

Additional Readings

The following books contain more information about two main religious groups presented in this section: Islam and Judaism. The Curious George books are mainly for younger students, but upper elementary students will undoubtedly appreciate the greater detail of the customs of these two groups in some of the other books.

Divide the class into three groups, and assign each group one of the Curious George books to read. The students in each group will use their book to describe the holiday to the rest of the class.

Happy Hanukkah, Curious George by H. A. Rey and Margret Rey (2012; Primary)

Curious George and friends get to participate in key Hanukkah activities such as lighting the menorah, spinning the dreidel, and making latkes. A latke recipe is provided. George also gets to learn the importance of mitzvah.

It's Ramadan, Curious George by H. A. Rey, Margret Rey, and Hena Khan (2016; Primary)

Curious George helps his friend, Kareem, fast during the day and then joins Kareem in the evening for a special meal. George also helps Kareem make gifts for the needy and watch for the man on the crescent moon.

Merry Christmas, Curious George by H. A. Rey, Margret Rey, and Cathy Hapka (2017; Primary)

Curious George tries to help his friend select a Christmas tree; and in the excitement, he winds up at a hospital decorating the tree for children. George also gets to meet a jolly man in a red suit.

Chik Chak Shabbat by Mara Rockliff (2016; Primary)

This story tells about Goldie Simcha, a Jewish woman who enjoys making her special cholent recipe for her neighbors to enjoy on Shabbat. One Shabbat, Goldie is ill and cannot make her special recipe, so all her neighbors come together to make their own special dishes to share with her on this special day. This book teaches about important Jewish customs while also highlighting the beauty of a diverse community and friendship.

Yaffa and Fatima: Shalom, Salaam by Fawzia Gilani-Williams (2017; Primary)

This story talks about the friendship between two neighbors who are Jewish and Muslim. Both neighbors work together to help each other through hard times and share an appreciation for each other's differences. This book highlights that even though people may have different customs, they can find commonalities with those around them.

Mommy's Khimar by Jamilah Thompkins-Bigelow (2019; Primary)

In this story, a young Muslim girl plays dress-up with her mother's head scarves. As she tries on each scarf, she is reminded of her mother's love and beauty. This book showcases the beauty of diversity.

Crescent Moons and Pointed Minarets: A Muslim Book of Shapes by Hena Khan (2021; Elementary)

This is a beautifully illustrated book of the various shapes of Islam and the culture of the Muslim people. This picture book is intended for primary students, but it's also informative for all elementary-aged students, especially those unfamiliar with this religion or culture.

Hershel and the Hanukkah Goblins by Eric A. Kimmel (1989; Elementary)

This is a classic and favorite Jewish or Yiddish tale. It is a humorous trickster story about Hershel, who manages to outwit goblins during the eight nights of Hanukkah. Students would find this tale entertaining and gain more understanding about the culture people celebrate during Hanukkah.

The Kids Book of World Religions by Jennifer Glossop (2013; Elementary)

As students read these and other books, they may express an interest in reading about celebrations and traditions of other religious groups such as Buddhism, Hinduism, and so on. This book is useful for this purpose.

Amina's Voice by Hena Khan (2018; Upper Elementary)

This story highlights the life of Amina, a Pakistani-American who is struggling to maintain her identity while trying to fit in at school. This book highlights the challenges Amina faces as she tries to show her diverse community how to love and support one another.

Action Project: Celebrate Us

For each picture or symbol in figure 3.3, have students identify the appropriate religious or cultural group and share something about the holiday each group celebrates.

Crescent Moon and Star

Name a holiday for this group. What is one thing the group does on this holiday?

___

Star of David

Name a holiday for this group. What is one thing the group does on this holiday?

___

Cross

Name a holiday for this group. What is one thing the group does on this holiday?

Figure 3.3: Religious symbols.

*Visit **go.SolutionTree.com/diversityandequity** for a free reproducible version of this figure.*

When students discuss the religious or cultural groups in any of these exercises, make sure they note how the groups are alike; they all have special holidays and celebrate with lots of food, family, and friends; and they emphasize being kind and helpful to others.

Books on Affirming Others

Figure 3.4 offers a list of books featured in this chapter as well as additional culturally diverse literature that includes aspects of affirming others. Read these books as a class, and discuss some of the themes we note in the preceding activities and books. When appropriate, encourage students to read the books independently and allow them to share the books with the rest of the class, noting how story characters affirm others.

Title	Author	Story Summary
Primary		
Chik Chak Shabbat	Mara Rockliff (2016)	A Jewish woman makes a special recipe on Shabbat for all her neighbors.
Drawn Together	Minh Lê (2018)	A young boy learns to communicate with love and value his grandfather, even though they speak different languages.
Happy Hanukkah, Curious George	H. A. Rey and Margret Rey (2012)	Curious George and friends celebrate Hanukkah.
It's Ramadan, Curious George	H. A. Rey, Margret Rey, and Hena Khan (2016)	Curious George and friends celebrate Ramadan.
Last Stop on Market Street	Matt de la Peña (2015)	Through his grandmother, a youngster learns about examples of humanity and beauty among the impoverished.
Merry Christmas, Curious George	H. A. Rey, Margret Rey, and Cathy Hapka (2017)	Curious George and friends celebrate Christmas.
Mommy's Khimar	Jamilah Thompkins-Bigelow (2019)	A young Muslim girl dresses up in her mother's head scarves.
Yaffa and Fatima: Shalom, Salaam	Fawzia Gilani-Williams (2017)	This inspirational story highlights the friendship and kindness between Jewish and Muslim neighbors.
Elementary		
All Are Welcome	Alexandra Penfold and Suzanne Kaufman (2019)	This story depicts settings and ways of welcoming all people, despite their differences.
Crescent Moons and Pointed Minarets: A Muslim Book of Shapes	Hena Khan (2021)	This picture book features geometric images of the Muslim culture.
Dreamers	Yuyi Morales (2018)	This story tells of integrating in a new land.
Hershel and the Hanukkah Goblins	Eric A. Kimmel (1989)	This is a classic tale of how Hershel helps people celebrate Hanukkah.

Figure 3.4: Books on affirming others.

continued →

Title	Author	Story Summary
Home at Last	Susan Middleton Elya (2006)	A young girl narrates how her mother learns English and overcomes a retailer's aggression.
La Frontera: El Viaje Con Papá (My Journey With Papa)	Deborah Mills and Alfredo Alva (2018)	A young Mexican boy and his father make the journey to immigrate from Mexico to Texas.
Listening With My Heart: A Story of Kindness and Self-Compassion	Gabi Garcia (2017)	Children learn to be kind and affirm themselves.
Over the Green Hills	Rachel Isadora (1995)	A young Black South African boy goes on a journey in his homeland. The author describes the beautiful countryside and the kind, gentle lifestyles of people in this land.
The Day You Begin	Jacqueline Woodson (2018)	This story tells about learning to assert and affirm oneself, despite differences from others.
The Invisible Boy	Trudy Ludwig (2013)	A simple kind act changed the classroom dynamics for an "invisible" boy and his classmates.
The Kids Book of World Religions	Jennifer Glossop (2013)	This book presents the cultures and beliefs of people around the world.
The Woman Who Outshone the Sun: The Legend of Lucia Zenteno	Alejandro Cruz Martinez (1991)	Villagers taunt a kind woman. The woman leaves because of the taunting, and then the villagers greatly miss her and work to get her back.
Those Shoes	Maribeth Boelts (2007)	A young African American boy experiences the joy of sharing, even at his own expense.
Upper Elementary		
Amina's Voice	Hena Khan (2018)	A girl from Pakistan struggles to maintain her identity in the United States.
Fly Away Home	Eve Bunting (1991)	A widowed father and son who are homeless discover the way to freedom.
Out of My Mind	Sharon Mills Draper (2012)	Classmates of a young girl with cerebral palsy learn to value and embrace the main character.
The Hundred Dresses	Eleanor Estes (2004)	Classmates who ridicule a young girl daily realize the damaging results of their behavior and manage to make amends.
The Lunch Thief	Anne C. Bromley (2010)	A young boy who is homeless steals school lunches. Another student gains understanding and shares his lunch.
The Streets Are Free	Kurusa (1995)	Children in a poverty-stricken area work together to develop a community park.
Wonder	R. J. Palacio (2012)	A fifth grader with facial abnormalities learns and teaches valuable lessons on accepting others, despite pronounced differences.

Visit **go.SolutionTree.com/diversityandequity** *for a free reproducible version of this figure.*

Conclusion

Affirming others, especially across differences, is important to students' social-emotional learning. Affirmations involve the expressions of kind, caring behaviors, so to make these expressions more than rote superficial actions, one needs to have some knowledge of the other person's background, and, if possible, some personal interactions. Without background information, it is easy to misunderstand and victimize those who we see as different.

The differences in this chapter are poverty, disabilities, and religion. There are many other differences that we encounter, but this chapter offers a model with examples for using children's literature to affirm across differences. Children's literature can humanely present each of these groups to provide a means for discussing their characteristics and identify ways for real-life interactions. We suggest specific responses, and provide prompts so students can identify ways to affirm others within and beyond the classroom. We encourage students to expand their thinking so that, for example, they might identify some special talents or attractions of a classmate who cannot afford fancy shoes, or think of some fun things they can do with their friend who is in a wheelchair. Recommended books can help reinforce these and other social-emotional learning ideas.

Chapter Reflections

Individually or with a collaborative group, review and discuss the following questions to reflect on your learning in this chapter.

1. How important is it for your students to be kind to each other?

2. How important is it for your students to want to be kind to each other?

3. What is the likelihood that emphasizing affirmations among your students will help them learn to be kinder to others, regardless of differences?

4. Is there any teaching advantage for you (or learning advantage for your students) to increase students' kindness to each other?

5. Are these strategies working? Why or why not?

chapter four

Affirming Self

Self-affirmation pertains to valuing oneself to achieve some desired effect such as attaining the self-confidence to perform a specific task or reach a particular goal (Pauketat, Moons, Chen, Mackie, & Sherman, 2016). Everyone needs affirmation, but there are times when those affirmations are not forthcoming, and self-doubt may ensue if people are unable to affirm themselves. Further, people need to develop confidence within themselves, so they are not dependent on the appraisal of others. Adults providing affirmations for young children can set the tone for this internal dialogue, which subsequently can enhance children's self-confidence (Steele, 2010).

Claude M. Steele (2010), a social psychologist and emeritus professor at Stanford University who developed *self-affirmation theory*, describes self-affirmation as a "basic human motive to perceive oneself as good and competent . . . as 'morally and adaptively adequate'" (p. 172). According to Steele (2010), various experiences, such as being part of a devalued minority group, can seriously threaten people's perception of competence and thus undermine their performance. Steele (2010) uses the term *identity threat* to describe students from stereotyped groups (poor academic performers, for example) who are likely to be threatened and underperform when presented with challenging academic tasks. Steele (2010) and other researchers (Armitage & Rowe, 2011; Spitzer & Aronson, 2015) present a series of studies showing self-affirmations, such as creating a self-affirming narrative, which are effective in minimizing identity threat and improving overall performance across gender and racial groups.

We hope young students will develop the self-confidence to pursue novel experiences and challenges, even if their actions aren't guaranteed to be successful or enjoyable. Self-affirmations are especially important for students from minority groups, because there are often explicit or implicit communications that their differences alone will rule out certain aspirations. For example, girls should feel they have the right and ability to be mathematicians, scientists, or politicians, if they wish. Likewise, boys should be confident in all types of artistic expression, even those some frequently consider to be in the female domain. Educators should encourage all students, regardless of race, religion, socioeconomic status, or gender, to believe they have the right to aspire to any goal and be the best they can be.

Self-confidence or self-affirmation contributes not only to personal accomplishment but also to one's ability to support and affirm others (Craig, Brown, Upright, & DeRosier, 2016). Confident students are more likely to be socially competent as well as good achievers. These are the students who will contribute to the well-being of others in their environment simply by welcoming them and not doubting their ability to be friends. Self-confident students are particularly helpful to those students who might need the assistance and prompting of well-intended peers to fit in and adjust. The youngster from a culturally or linguistically different background who learns to affirm him- or herself will be an asset to self and others (Craig et al., 2016).

In this chapter, we focus on fictional and real-life stories of individuals who demonstrate the ability to affirm themselves in two areas—race and gender—and act accordingly. In some cases, they need to solicit help from others, but that is part of the process in learning how to affirm oneself. We use the book *Amazing Grace* (Hoffman, 2007) as a model for both themes, but we also provide other book suggestions as either supplements or substitutes for the model book. We encourage you to direct your students to develop and employ their own self-affirmations and corresponding self-affirming actions.

Affirming Self With Regard to Race

In this activity, educators help students understand that in many countries around the world, such as the United States and the United Kingdom: (1) people vary a great deal in physical appearance; (2) people come from many different countries; (3) even though people look different, they are very similar and like to do many of the same activities; and (4) most important, students should pursue activities according to interest and ability and not be restricted because of the color of their skin or their family's country of origin.

Sometimes, in the United States, we talk about people's differences according to their skin color, such as Black, White, or Brown. Other times, we might describe people according to place of origin such as Hispanic, Caribbean, Asian, European, and so on. Descriptions according to place of origin are very common elsewhere in the world. In the story *Amazing Grace* (Hoffman, 2007), Grace lives in the United Kingdom, where many people are White or European. However, the UK also is a culturally diverse country. Many people of color live there, like Grace, who are referred to as Black (from the Caribbean or Africa) or Brown (from China, India, Mexico, and Middle Eastern countries like Syria; PBS News Hour, 2020). Grace is from a Caribbean country named *Trinidad*.

Show the students pictures of children representing different groups from African, European, Asian, Middle Eastern, and Hispanic or Latin countries or geographic areas. Point out that people from any or all of these different groups might live in the same country, state, city, or community.

In previous chapters, we focus on students learning to affirm or value others despite background or special situations. In this chapter, we encourage students, especially those from minority groups, to learn how to affirm themselves even if they want to pursue activities that are at odds with common norms. An important understanding is they should pursue goals because of their interests and abilities and never be denied because of race or gender.

Literature on Affirming Self With Regard to Race

We use *Amazing Grace* (Hoffman, 2007) to address two somewhat distinct issues: (1) affirming oneself with regard to race and (2) affirming oneself with regard to gender. Although it is not possible to totally separate these two issues within the story, the first activity focuses mainly on race and the subsequent activity focuses primarily on gender.

Book: *Amazing Grace* by Mary Hoffman (2007)

As noted previously, the steps for introducing each book to the class include present the story, clarify story concepts through discussion, clarify the features of the desired behaviors through enactments, practice the desired behaviors through real-life applications, respond appropriately to issues of diversity, and provide extension activities to maintain the desired behaviors.

Present the Story

Read the story to and with the class. If students have a hard copy of the book or if they can access the story online, they can follow along as you read aloud. If not, students can simply listen as you read.

Story Synopsis

This is a story about a young Black girl named Grace who lives in the United Kingdom. Grace lives with her mother and grandmother, who originally came from the Caribbean country Trinidad. Grace loves stories, especially adventure stories she not only listens to but also subsequently likes to act out. Grace likes to act out a range of stories from pirate adventures on the sea to fairy tales such as *Aladdin and the Magic Lamp* by Ellen M. Dolan (1987). When Grace's class decides it will put on the play *Peter Pan* by James M. Barrie (1904), Grace volunteers to play the main character of Peter Pan. The class tells Grace she can't play that part because Peter Pan was neither a girl nor Black. Grace is sad and shares the students' comments with her mother and grandmother. That weekend, Grace's grandmother takes Grace to see a ballet in which a Black ballerina plays the main role of Juliet in William Shakespeare's (2011) *Romeo and Juliet*. What she sees encourages Grace. She practices the role of Peter Pan all weekend. At the class auditions the following week, Grace outperforms all her classmates in the role, and they choose her to be Peter Pan. Grace truly feels she can be anything she wants to be.

Discussion

Use questions such as the following to help students get a deeper understanding of this story and how others helped Grace affirm herself. Briefly review with students the story of Peter Pan. Peter Pan is a fictional character who could fly and who lived in Neverland where he never had to grow up. This is a fairy tale, and neither Peter Pan nor Neverland is based in reality. Help children understand the importance of race in this activity by asking questions such as the following.

1. "What is the skin color of Peter Pan in pictures of this story?" (White)
2. "Is Peter Pan a real person or is he made up?" (Made up)
3. "Because Peter Pan is not real, do you think he has to be White?" (No, Peter Pan can be any color or from any cultural group.)
4. "Why do you think the author who wrote the story made Peter Pan White?" (It's probably because the author is White.)
5. "Even if Peter Pan was a real person, do you think the person who plays him has to be White?" (No, because character, not race, is the focus of this play.)
6. "What is most important about the person who plays Peter Pan?" (The person does a good job acting as Peter Pan.)
7. "If someone with a different skin color did a good job of playing Peter Pan, could you enjoy the show?" (Yes)

Continue the discussion along these lines until students demonstrate an understanding that the person's performance, not skin color, is what is important. Help each student understand he or she has the right to affirm him- or herself, even if others want to discourage the student because they feel he or she does not "look" the part (that is, he or she does not have the right skin color, body, hair, or something else). Ask the following questions to help guide this discussion.

- "How did Grace feel when her classmates told her that she couldn't have the part because she was Black?" (Very sad and disappointed)

- "What do you think Grace might have said to herself?" ("I will never be able to star in a play because all the lead roles will be for White students.")
- "What helped Grace think she could play Peter Pan in spite of her skin color?" (Her grandmother took her to a ballet in which a Black dancer starred in a role traditionally a White ballerina performs.)
- "What do you think Grace said to herself after she went to see the ballerina from Trinidad?" ("The ballerina got her part because she practiced and became very good. I can practice and become very good too.")
- "What did Grace do that helped her get the role of Peter Pan?" (She practiced and learned her lines before the tryouts.)
- "What did Grace say to herself after she got the role of Peter Pan?" ("I did it! I can be whatever I want to be!")

Enactments

Tell students it is important that they learn to affirm themselves. This means not listening to people who tell them they cannot do something because of their race or skin color. If there is something they want to do and can do it, they need to: (1) tell themselves they have the right to do it if they want to, (2) find out what they need to learn to be good at doing the skill or activity, (3) study and practice the skill or activity until they can do it well, and (4) compliment themselves if and when they do it well. To affirm herself, Grace told herself she could have the lead role in the play if she was good at it, and then she practiced the role until she was very good.

Give students scenarios such as those in figure 4.1 (page 76), which are based on the lives of real African American women. For each of the women (left-hand column), there is speculation of what she might have said to herself (middle column), and then what she did to achieve her goal (right-hand column). Discuss each scenario with students. Note in each case, the woman was afraid she might not reach her goal simply because of her race. Also point out that often these women had help and encouragement, said positive things to themselves, and studied or practiced to accomplish their goals. These scenarios are from the book *Little Leaders: Bold Women in Black History* by Vashti Harrison (2017), which we note later in this activity.

Continue this activity by having students interject themselves into the scenarios. Prompt them in how to respond for the second and third columns. For example, for the third scenario, students might tell themselves they are very good dancers. They know how to dance a special part in *The Nutcracker* (Wiley, 1985). What do they do? They tell the director they would like to

Person	What Might She Have Said?	What Did She Do?
Mae Jemison was a Black doctor who wanted to be an astronaut. There were no Black female astronauts, and she was afraid the National Aeronautics and Space Administration (NASA) would reject her because of her race.	"I know how to do this. I can do this even though I am a Black woman."	She applied and became the first Black female astronaut.
Oprah Winfrey was a journalist who wanted to own and produce television shows.	"I know how to do this. Being Black should not stop me from doing my own productions."	She studied the business and started her own production company, Harpo Productions.
Misty Copeland was thirteen years old when she decided she wanted to be a ballerina. She was told she was too old to start dancing, and "Black girls are not ballerinas."	"I am a good dancer, and this is what I want to do, no matter what."	Misty affirmed herself and continued dancing. She became the first Black female in the American Ballet Theatre and is an internationally recognized prima ballerina.
Bessie Coleman wanted to fly airplanes, but none of the U.S. schools would teach a Black girl how to fly.	"I know I can do this even though no schools will admit me to flying school. I will learn to fly in France, another country, where they will let me go to flying school."	Bessie learned how to fly in France. Bessie became the first Black woman to get a pilot's license in the United States and become a famous pilot.
Rosa Parks disliked segregation in her hometown of Montgomery, Alabama. She wanted to remain in her seat while riding the bus home. The bus driver wanted her to stand to give her seat to a White woman.	"I paid my fare, and I have every right to be in this seat. I do not have to give up my seat just because I am Black. I will remain in my seat."	Rosa was arrested, but later she earned the right for everyone to be treated fairly on the buses. Everyone has the right to ride the buses and sit wherever they want.

Source: Adapted from Harrison, 2017.

Figure 4.1: Famous affirming Black women.

audition for the part. They practice very hard and know their part perfectly before the audition. Use figure 4.2 to complete this activity with students.

Primary students may not have had personal experiences in which others rejected them because of race, but they can understand stories about historical figures who were kept from pursuing some career or activity because of race. You could briefly discuss historical figures such as Marian Anderson, who the Daughters of the American Revolution would not permit to sing at Constitution Hall in 1939 because of her race. She later sang at many major venues throughout the United States. She sang for U.S. presidents and received some of the highest honors in the country. Also consider discussing individuals who became the first of their race to pursue a career or goal some others would not expect. One example is Dominique Dawes, who became the first African American woman to join the U.S. Women's National

Your Character	What Do You Say?	What Do You Do?
You are a Latino girl and a very good ballet dancer. You want to dance the part of Clara in *The Nutcracker* ballet, but some of your classmates tell you that only White girls should have that part.		
You are a Black boy. You like to swim and study sea animals. You want to be a deep-sea diver, but your friends tell you that Black boys cannot be deep-sea divers.		
You are a White girl. You like to play musical instruments. You want to play jazz on the trumpet like Louis Armstrong or Wynton Marsalis. Your friends tell you that White girls do not play jazz on the trumpet.		
You are a Latino American boy. You want to become the president of the United States. Your friends tell you that no Latino American has ever been the president of the United States.		

Figure 4.2: Self-affirmations.

*Visit **go.SolutionTree.com/diversityandequity** for a free reproducible version of this figure.*

Gymnastics Team. Discuss her successes, such as winning five gold medals in one competition, and how intimidating it must have been to do this with the whole world watching.

For older students, you might use books such as *Little Leaders: Bold Women in Black History* (Harrison, 2017) or *Little Legends: Exceptional Men in Black History* (Harrison, 2019) or *Be Bold! Be Brave! 11 Latinas Who Made U.S. History* by Naibe Reynoso (2020). Assign each student in the class one of the characters (for example, Marian Anderson, Ida B. Wells, Arthur Ashe, Sonia Sotomayor, and so on). Assign students across race and gender so they assume characters that do not match their own race or gender. Students can read from these and other books to get information about their character and then share out with the rest of the class. Their presentations should include (1) who the person was, (2) the person's dream or goal, (3) what the person did to achieve that dream or goal, and (4) what that person did to become famous.

Real-Life Applications

Encourage students to talk about people in their family or community who might have been the first to pursue a career or goal different from their group. For example, an Asian girl became a hip-hop artist or a Latina became an astronaut. If possible, invite people from the community who can share personal stories of barriers to their careers or goals due to racial differences. For example, Gwen Cartledge had such an experience during elementary school. She was the only non-White student in her class. When Gwen told her White teacher she wanted to be a teacher, her teacher said it was a good idea, and Gwen could become a teacher in the southern part of the United States, where "they could use good teachers like her." The teacher's message was clear: people of Gwen's race could not teach in the western Pennsylvania community where she lived because all the teachers are White. Self-determination, as well as support from family and her community, helped Gwen to more than exceed her stated goals. For this activity, try to include individuals of different racial and ethnic groups, both men and women.

Help children understand the importance of not excluding others simply due to race. Refer to Grace's classmates and how they all voted for her when they saw her wonderful performance. Ask questions such as the following.

- "Was the play better or worse with Grace in the role of Peter Pan? Why?" (Better)
- "Did Grace's race hurt the play? Why or why not?" (No)
- "Were the students happy with Grace? Why?" (Yes)
- "Should you judge people by race or performance? Why?" (Performance)
- "Were the students wise to vote for Grace? Why?" (Yes)

Encourage students to engage in higher-level thinking. Avoid rejecting any students' responses, but help them think through their rationales. For example, if a student answers the play was worse because Peter should be White, discuss when or if cross-cultural or cross-racial entertainment is OK. For example, should American ballet companies perform *The Nutcracker* (Wiley, 1985) because it originated in Russia, or should White Americans perform or sing songs originally produced by Black musicians and composers (for example, jazz)? Follow each student's answer with the question, "Why?" or "Why not?"

By the end of the discussion, help students realize the class's good judgment to select Grace even though she didn't look like what they originally thought Peter Pan should look like. What would have happened if they insisted on physical characteristics (rather than acting skill) for the role of Peter Pan?

Ask students to think about people from different racial backgrounds they interact with in positive ways. Tell students to note the following people from different racial groups who they:

- Invite to their play groups
- Read about in their story books
- Watch in their movies
- Greatly admire
- Listen to their music

Diversity Issues in This Story

The United States and other Western countries are growing in diversity, and people of different racial and ethnic backgrounds are commonplace (NCES, 2019). This increased diversity results in the need to make changes in people's expectations and ways of doing things. Even the term *race* is not easy to define. In the 1780s, various groups attempted to organize humans into racial categories such as Negroid, Caucasoid, and Mongoloid, but these terms are now considered obsolete and offensive (AAPA, 2019). Although the AAPA and other scientists (for example, Templeton, 2016) contend that race is not an accurate representation of humans, the U.S. Census Bureau uses the term *race* and organizes U.S. citizens into groups according to skin color and place of origin within a minimum of five groups—White, Black, Indian, Asian, and Pacific Islander—and permits people to self-identify in more categories as well as designate place of origin (Pew Research Center, 2020). Physical traits, language, and place of origin are not necessarily definitive. There are many people who do not look like the group they identify with. Many people who look White, for example, come from and identify with the Black or African American community.

Review the previous discussion with students about the racial features of Grace compared with the mythical features of Peter Pan. Emphasize again which was more important, her physical attributes or her performance? Point out because the United States, in particular, is so diverse that race or the way people look cannot be the basis for what they can do. Emphasize this point by showing students all the different skin tones and looks of people in the United States. The internet has a variety of sites for this purpose such as, "Images for the Range of Skin Tones in the U.S." (shorturl.at/etEO5). Other sites might show the range of skin colors of persons around the world or in one family.

Review again with students what Grace did when others discouraged her because of her race. She shared her disappointment with people who cared about her (her mother and grandmother). She learned about someone who looked like her and attained her goal against the odds. Grace practiced hard and achieved her goal anyway. Remind students that overcoming these kinds of obstacles is a way to affirm themselves if someone tells them they cannot do something simply because of their race.

Extended Literature Activities

Use these literature activities to further ascertain students' understanding of the story and desired social-emotional learning skills. Students use their own words to retell the story and specify appropriate ways to respond. You also could use the annotated book list in the section Books on Affirming Self (page 93) to assign more relevant readings to individuals or groups. For each book, we suggest general elementary reading levels.

Retell the Story

Have students work in small groups to retell the story using their own words. Ensure each student gets an opportunity to participate in the retelling. During these retellings, help students understand why it was unfair to tell Grace she couldn't play Peter Pan, what her family did to help her get the part, what Grace did to help herself get the part, and why students in the class were fair to select Grace for the role of Peter Pan. Also ensure students understand that by seeking help and practicing hard, Grace was affirming herself. Also point out the students were being fair when they voted for Grace following the audition because they were selecting her for her performance, not rejecting her because of her race.

Extend the Story: Affirming Myself

This is a rather sensitive activity because educators are encouraging children to affirm themselves in regard to race. We recommend you conduct this exercise in a large group and prompt students to give appropriate responses. In this exercise, students tell others how they might affirm themselves or others according to race or ethnicity (see figure 4.3). Initially, only present the scenario in the first column, and then gradually coach students to offer some appropriate actions, such as those in columns two and three of figure 4.3. If possible and appropriate, have students generate scenes and possible resolutions from their own lives.

Additional Readings

Extend the discussion of race with books such as the following.

I Am Enough by Grace Byers (2018; Primary)

This simply written, beautifully illustrated, and poignant book is intended to affirm young girls (grades 3–5), particularly girls of color. It is written in first person, so the girls in the story are self-affirming. Especially noteworthy are statements that underscore these girls are here to be everything they can be, and their worth is not based on looking or being like others.

What Happened	What He or She Said or Did	What Others Did
José is a new student in class. The boys would not let him play kickball because he came from El Salvador.	José asked Harold to play kickball with him. He showed Harold what a good kicker he is. They had lots of fun. José told Harold about the great kickball players in El Salvador.	The other boys watched Harold and José playing. They realized what a good player José was. They decided to play kickball with José and Harold.
Some of the girls in Jenny's class called her ugly because they thought her skin was too dark.	Jenny told the girls her father tells her every day that she is beautiful. He reads her stories of beautiful Black women such as Gwendolyn Brooks, Oprah Winfrey, and Serena Williams, who have skin like hers.	The girls read stories with Jenny about these famous Black women. They like to share these women's stories and make up plays about them.
The neighborhood children were planning a Christmas party. They were not going to invite Adaobi because she was a different race and from Nigeria in Africa.	Adaobi told the children she wanted to come to their party to learn about Christmas in the United States. She promised to tell them how her family celebrated Christmas in Nigeria.	The children thought it was a great idea. They decided to have an international holiday party and also invite children of different races and religions.
During recess, the children liked to dance to their hip-hop and rhythm songs. Kyong, who just came from Korea, did not know the dances, but he knew he liked to dance.	Kyong asked Josh to show him how to do some of the hip-hop dances and began to show Josh some of his steps from Korea. They had a great time.	Kyong began to join the others at recess, and they all had fun teaching him the dances and making up new steps based on Kyong's Korean-inspired dancing.

Figure 4.3: Affirming self and others.

Dream Big, Little One by Vashti Harrison (2018; Primary)

This book is similar to the previous one but for much younger students (grades K–3). It is a board book with far fewer pages, personalities, and words. This attractively illustrated picture book is one that primary students will enjoy reading. You might display the pictures while orally giving fuller depictions of the characters' lives.

A Girl Named Misty: The True Story of Misty Copeland by Kelly Starling Lyons (2018; Elementary)

This story is about how Misty Copeland came from a modest background to become one of the first Black leading ballerinas in the American Ballet Theatre. It tells how she overcame discouragement, poverty, shyness, and many other difficulties to achieve her dream of becoming a prima ballerina.

I Am Perfectly Designed by Karamo Brown and Jason Brown (2019; Elementary)

Self-affirmation is the theme of this unique and well-written book by a Black father-and-son team. The book tells of how the father's constant assurances of his son's "perfect design" contribute to his son's self-confidence and ability to self-affirm.

Little Leaders: Bold Women in Black History by Vashti Harrison (2017; Upper Elementary)

This is another lovely book useful in addressing racial differences that could lead to self-affirmation. It provides brief histories of forty Black women who distinguished themselves in the United States in literature, science, performing arts, visual arts, social activism, and athletics. Students can read the brief biographies, or you might summarize these women's stories for emerging readers.

Little Legends: Exceptional Men in Black History by Vashti Harrison (2019; Upper Elementary)

This is the male version of the book about women by Harrison (2017). It provides detailed stories about at least thirty-five major personalities, including historical figures such as Frederick Douglass, writers like Langston Hughes, and social activists. As with the book on women, Harrison (2017) gives suggestions for reading and learning about many other famous and important personalities.

Action Project: Getting to Know You

Create opportunities for students to interact positively with racially diverse classmates. For example, if you teach a racially diverse class or have considerable diversity in your school, form small, cooperative diverse groups in which students spend short periods solving a puzzle or playing simple games. Another option is to take students on field trips that provide experiences in racial diversity. For example, go to museums that focus on one particular racial or ethnic group, such as the local African American museum or Native American museum. You also can take students to the community museum and visit ethnic rooms such as the Chinese room or Egyptian room. Prepare students beforehand about the particular group and something special they should look for. In the African American museum, for example, students might look at the work of two or three of their favorite people in Black history, such as Bessie Coleman (the pilot) or Mae Jemison (the astronaut).

Affirming Self With Regard to Gender Differences

As educators recognize the continuum of identities across the gender spectrum, considerations of these issues may become more salient in the classroom. In some social-emotional learning inquiries, researchers note differences, suggesting females may be more caring and polite, have greater preferences for intimacy, and tend to be less physically aggressive than males (Choi, Johnson, & Johnson, 2011; Zentall, Kuester, & Craig, 2011). On the other hand, relational aggression, mostly associated with females, is characterized by social distancing, ostracizing, and other actions more likely to cause psychological rather than physical harm (Powell & Ladd, 2010). Of course, these traits and social proclivities emerge among all identities, and approximately 5 percent of the U.S. population identify in nontraditional gender categories beyond the binary male or female classification (UCLA Williams Institute, 2011). These nonbinary groups have become highly visible and are recognized in the law and literature, and thus, school-age populations may recognize these groups more as well.

Literature on Affirming Self With Regard to Gender Differences

Affirming oneself with regard to gender is not just limited to females. Discussions also include male affirmations and comfort with one's gender identity.

Book: *Amazing Grace* by Mary Hoffman (2007)

As noted previously, the steps for introducing each book to the class include present the story, clarify story concepts through discussion, clarify the features of the desired behaviors through enactments, practice the desired behaviors through real-life applications, respond appropriately to issues of diversity, and provide extension activities to maintain the desired behaviors.

Present the Story

Read the story to and with the class. If students have a hard copy of the book or if they can access the story online, they can follow along as you read aloud. If not, students can simply listen as you read.

Read the story *Amazing Grace* (Hoffman, 2007) again. Depending on students' ages and skill levels, encourage students as a class to retell the story, noting the key points: Grace enjoys acting out stories, she wants to play Peter Pan in the play, and classmates discourage her because she is neither male nor White. However, after learning that a non-White ballerina was chosen to play Juliet in Shakespeare's (2011) *Romeo and Juliet*, Grace was encouraged to pursue the role of Peter Pan. Remind students in the last activity, they focused on race or skin color. The class in the story decided it did not matter if Grace's skin is darker than Peter's in the original story or that she is a girl rather than a boy. In this activity, ask students to focus on gender or the things that girls and boys can do if they have the skills and enjoy doing them.

Share with students a bit of the history of the play, *Peter Pan* (Barrie, 1904). Point out that the play was first produced in England in 1904, and the first Peter was a woman named Nina Boucicault. The producers decided Peter should be a woman because if they used a young boy, the other children in the play would have to be much smaller and younger. At that time, there were laws against using children under fourteen in plays. A woman would be the right size for the other children, who would be at least fourteen years old. Other women played the part of Peter Pan in England, and Mary Martin played the part of Peter in the first musical in the United States. Very few males played the part of Peter in the play, *Peter Pan* (Rice, 2014). A male or female could play the part of Peter; she or he just needs to be a very good entertainer.

Discussion

Continue the discussion using figure 4.4. For each occupation listed in the left-hand column, have students indicate whether both men and women could perform the job. If students respond *no* to any of the occupations, have them explain in the last column why they believe both genders could *not* do the job.

Occupation	Yes		No		Why Not?
	Girl	Boy	Girl	Boy	
Dressmaker					
Nurse					
Doctor					
Teacher					
Dancer					
Baseball player					
Member of the armed forces					
Astronaut					
Farmer					
Plumber					
Chef					
Minister, priest, rabbi, or imam					
United States president or other country leader					
Housekeeper					

Figure 4.4: Occupations and gender activity.

*Visit **go.SolutionTree.com/diversityandequity** for a free reproducible version of this figure.*

Encourage students to generate roles or occupations they would like to discuss. Some of those listed in figure 4.4 might be a bit controversial (for example, priest, U.S. president, or member of the armed forces) because they have not yet been open to women, or their respective organizations permit few women in these careers. But for the most part, women have been successful in traditional male roles or occupations and vice versa. Discuss Grace's feelings in the book *Amazing Grace* (Hoffman, 2007). Ask students questions such as the following.

1. "How do you think Grace felt when her classmates said Peter Pan was a boy, and she could not play a boy?" (She probably thought it was unfair because she likes adventure stories, and most of the adventure stories give the best parts to boys.)

2. "How do you think Grace would have felt if her teacher had told her that women have usually played the role of Peter in the play *Peter Pan*?" (She probably would have been encouraged rather than feeling sad.)

3. "What matters most in selecting someone to play Peter Pan?" (Whether or not the person is a good entertainer.)

4. "What does a good Peter Pan have to do?" (He or she has to know the lines, and be a good actor, acrobatic, and a good singer.)

5. "What helped Grace self-affirm and make sure she had a right to want to play the part of Peter Pan?" (She learned her skills are more important than her race.)

Students should understand when they want to pursue an activity or role, they should focus not on gender but on whether it is something they want to do and are willing to work hard to do it.

Enactments

Review with students points from previous activities on the importance of affirming themselves and the steps for making these affirmations. If you want to do something that you enjoy, you should try it even if you are a girl and boys usually do it. The reverse is also true; that is, boys should not hesitate to choose an activity simply because girls traditionally do it. As noted previously, if there is something students want to do, they need to: (1) tell themselves they have the right to do it if they want to, (2) find out what they need to learn to be good at doing the skill or activity, (3) study and practice the skill or activity until they can do it well, and (4) compliment themselves if and when they do it well. Point out that Grace had to affirm herself regarding gender (being a girl) as well as regarding race. Take students through one of the previous activities, but this time focus on gender rather than race. Figure 4.5 (page 86) shows an example.

Person	What Might She Have Said?	What Did She Do?
Sally Ride studied science and physics in college and was an outstanding student. She worked for the National Aeronautics and Space Administration (NASA) and wanted to be an astronaut. She helped many girls learn mathematics, science, and engineering.	"I like to study science. I am good at science. I can be a scientist if I want to. Studying science and being an astronaut are not just for boys."	Sally spent her life working in science and became an astronaut. She helped many girls become mathematicians, scientists, and engineers.
Mae Jemison was a Black doctor who wanted to be an astronaut. There were no Black female astronauts, and she was afraid NASA would reject her because she was a woman and Black.	"I know how to do this. I can do this even though I am a Black woman."	Mae applied and became the first Black female astronaut.
Blanche Stuart Scott (born in 1885) loved riding her bicycle, driving, and exploring. At age twenty-five, she was the second woman to drive across the country, but she also wanted to learn how to fly an airplane. Glenn Curtiss, an aviator, agreed to teach her but thought it a waste of money to teach a woman to fly.	"I know Glenn doesn't want to teach me, but I will show him that I can learn to be a good pilot. He will learn that women can be good pilots just like men."	Blanche became the first female American aviator in 1910. Blanche learned to become a very good pilot and continues to be remembered as the second woman to drive across the United States, the first woman to fly an airplane, and the first woman to ride in a jet.
Bessie Coleman wanted to fly airplanes, but none of the U.S. schools would teach a Black woman how to fly.	"I know I can do this even though flight school administrators will not admit me to flight school. I will learn to fly in France, another country, where flight school administrators will let me go to flight school. Boys are not the only ones who can learn to fly airplanes."	Bessie learned how to fly in France. She became the first Black woman to get a pilot's license and become a famous pilot.
Marcelite Harris decided to join the U.S. Air Force and study courses in aircraft maintenance and business management. Marcelite was very good at her job.	"Even though the U.S. Air Force mostly recruits men, I can do this job. I can study and learn how to maintain U.S. aircraft. I can study and work hard."	Marcelite became the highest-ranking woman in the U.S. Air Force. She received many awards, created many opportunities for women in the air force, and was promoted to major general.

Figure 4.5: Famous women and what they said and did.

Similar to the previous activity, continue by having students interject themselves into the scenarios. You can use scenarios such as those in figure 4.6 for this purpose. As before, show students how to respond in the second and third columns. For example, in the first scenario, the student can respond by saying there are no laws stating that only men can be president of the United States. The student continues studying about the presidents and U.S. laws and policies as she goes through school, college, and her beginning careers.

Person	What Would You Say?	What Would You Do?
You are a young girl. You enjoy reading and listening to stories about the presidents of the United States. You also talk with your parents about the presidents. You tell your friends you want to become president when you grow up. They tell you that it's not possible because no female has ever been president.		
You are a young girl. You like to play sports such as baseball and basketball. You like to go with your parents to professional baseball games. You like to call the plays for your favorite team. You are good at calling the plays. You tell your friends you want to be the manager for a baseball team when you grow up. They tell you that it's not possible because only males can be baseball team managers.		
You are a young boy. You like to watch television programs about helping people who have been hurt or are sick in the hospital. Your parents bought you a medicine kit for your birthday. You tell your friends that you want to be a nurse when you grow up. Your friends tell you it's silly because only girls become nurses.		
You are a young girl. You like to play softball. You are the best pitcher in the neighborhood, and you want to play on the boys' team. The manager of the boys' team tells you that you can only play on the girls' team. This makes you very sad.		
You are a young boy. You volunteer with some of the other fourth-grade students to tutor the kindergarten children in your school during recess. You like teaching the kindergarteners. You tell your friends you want to be a kindergarten teacher when you grow up. They tell you that only girls become kindergarten teachers.		
You are a young boy. Your mom has a lot of work to do. You tell your friends you cannot play soccer after school because you have to help your mom with the housework and cooking. You like baking in particular and want to open a cookie shop when you grow up. They tell you that baking cookies is a girls' job.		

Figure 4.6: Affirming my gender.

*Visit **go.SolutionTree.com/diversityandequity** for a free reproducible version of this figure.*

Real-Life Applications

Encourage students to think about situations in their own lives when they wanted to do something or have something, and close friends or family, based on societal norms, discouraged them from pursuing it because of gender. For example, a girl wants to buy a blue bicycle, but her sister tells her to buy the pink one because "blue is for boys and pink is for girls." Similarly, a friend tells a boy not to buy a pink item "because it is not a boy's color." Discuss with students how others should not steer them toward certain items or colors simply because their choice is consistent with what others generally view as for their gender. It is perfectly fine if girls want to select pink and boys want blue, or vice versa. The point is others should not prohibit them from choosing items or activities simply because they are atypical for their gender. Encourage students to share personal experiences in this area.

Make sure students do not get the impression that the purpose of the activity is simply to identify the most unusual activities or occupations; rather, they should select things they are genuinely interested in doing, whether or not those choices are common for their gender. If it is common for their gender, such as when a young girl says she wants to become a nurse, compliment her for it. Ask her if she knows of any male nurses and if so, what does she think about that person? Ask students if it is OK for a male to be a nurse in their hospital or school. The major issue is for gender equity and individual freedom of choice, regardless of gender. Encourage students to respect and support the choices of others. Remind them people shouldn't reject others simply due to gender. Address the five questions in the Real-Life Applications section from the previous activity (see page 78) with students.

If possible, bring in people from the community (for example, family members of students in the class) who can relate personal experiences of overcoming gender barriers. For example, read the following story from Amanda Yurick, one of the authors of this book, who had an experience as a child that challenged gender barriers.

> As a youngster, I loved sports and baseball most of all. I often played with the neighborhood children, mostly boys. When it came time to sign up for Little League in the neighborhood, I went to register. My mom and I were turned away because the league was only open to boys. Because all the boys in the neighborhood I typically played with were on the team, I wanted to play as well.
>
> My mother went several times to complain to the city that the league should not prevent girls from playing and eventually, the league gave permission for me to play. Still, being the first and only girl to play in the boys' Little League came with challenges. Other players were angry and thought the league shouldn't allow me to play. When I came up to bat, the other team's catcher would taunt and intimidate me because I was a girl playing with the boys.

> When some neighborhood boys heard of the treatment I received, they helped me by staying nearby during pregame activities and practices. The support from the neighborhood boys helped buffer me against the taunts of other players. Eventually, the other players saw that my friends from the neighborhood accepted me and came to accept me as well.

Diversity Issues in This Story

The gender issue in this story is not just whether the role of Peter Pan is for a boy or a girl, but whether others will support girls and boys to move beyond traditional images they have for males and females. Gender differences in things such as colors, occupations, and sports are becoming less pronounced than in the past. For example, for colors, present pictures of men wearing bold-colored clothing, especially items such as athletic shoes. Likewise, women are increasingly becoming political leaders and top officers in major companies. In sports, women are still likely to be separated into parallel teams (such as women's basketball, tennis, or gymnastics, and so on), but their sports are getting much more recognition and respect. Further, there have been at least fifteen full-time female coaches in the National Football League in the United States, including Katie Sowers of the San Francisco 49ers (Kepner & Wagner, 2020). And Major League Baseball appointed the first female manager, Kim Ng, to manage the Miami Marlins (Kepner & Wagner, 2020).

There are some recognized gender social differences, such as preferences for gender-type toys. These patterns tend to persist over age more for boys than girls, and the relative role of environment versus biology is not entirely clear (Todd et al., 2018). Nevertheless, these commonalities should not rule out exceptions and force all individuals to conform to social dictates. Girls and boys have the right to pursue equally their heart's passions, whether they are in the sciences, corporate offices, homemaking, sports, and so on.

Discuss with students the times when they might have unfairly rejected someone because of gender. Examples might include not letting boys play house with the girls, or boys not letting a girl play a game of kickball or some other sport. There are legitimate times when boys or girls want to be in separate groups, but the exclusions should be fair, not simply because, for example, they don't want a girl to be a leader even though the girl is quite capable (or even more capable) of being the leader.

Extended Literature Activities

Use these literature activities to further ascertain students' understanding of the story and desired social-emotional learning skills. Students use their own words to retell the story and specify appropriate ways to respond. You also could use the annotated book list in the section Books on Affirming Self (page 93) to assign more relevant readings to individuals or groups. For each book, we suggest general elementary reading levels.

Retell the Story

Because students retold the story in a previous activity (on race self-affirmation), consider changing it by having students pretend they are Grace and journal about how they felt when the students said she couldn't have the role of Peter Pan because she was the wrong race and gender. Then have "Grace" write what she did to get the role and how she felt when she was told that she had the role. You can adapt this activity for primary students by having them draw pictures rather than write how they felt. Some students might enjoy doing both. This exercise helps students understand the feelings of someone who is denied his or her dream for reasons he or she cannot control.

Extend the Story: Affirming Self

In this activity, students think about and provide ideas on how they will affirm themselves with regard to gender. Figure 4.7 shows an example of how students might approach this activity. Present the problem and coach students to responses such as those in columns two and three.

Additional Readings

Continue to read and discuss some of the books for the activity on race self-affirmation, as they also have special relevance with regard to gender.

I Need You to Know: The ABC's of Black Girl Magic by Lora McClain-Muhammad (2019a; Primary)

This is a special book that deals with race and gender. This unique coloring book makes a positive statement about young Black girls on each page. The book contains more than twenty pages with words from each letter of the alphabet, from *amazing* to *zany*. Ask each student to select the picture and word each feels best represents him or her. Or you could present the book as a typical picture book, and then have students draw a picture of themselves with their own "magic," using one of the words from the book (for example, *courageous*) and telling you and the class why they chose that word to represent themselves. You could extend the concept to include students from all racial or ethnic backgrounds. Make all students feel valued for their own special "magic."

It's Okay to Be Different by Todd Parr (2001; Primary)

In this delightful, easy-to-read book, the author tells children that even if they have a disability or are a different color or size, or make a mistake, they can take pride and appreciate just being who they are.

What Happened	What Did They Say?	What Did They Do?
Lucy and Joy like to make clothes for their dolls from construction and crepe paper. Miguel is very creative and loves to make doll clothes too. He makes great clothes, but Lucy tells Miguel he cannot make clothes with them because he is a boy. This makes Miguel sad.	That evening, Miguel makes an outstanding outfit for one of his dolls. When he shows the doll to Lucy and Joy, they are very excited and ask Miguel to join them in making paper dolls and doll clothes.	Lucy, Joy, and Miguel decide to let Luca join their doll-dressing group. They make beautiful clothes and put on a play for the neighborhood children to show off their doll clothes. Miguel is the best designer. They have fun together.
Loriana is a very good student. She knows how to conduct a meeting, and she knows all the rules. She wants to be class president, but the students in her class say the president should be a boy. Loriana is upset because she does not know why the class president has to be a boy. The students say the president should be Alex.	Loriana discusses this situation with her teacher, who responds that Loriana and Alex should conduct a class campaign, and students should vote for who they think has the best campaign. Loriana works hard and presents a good campaign.	Loriana gets the most votes and becomes class president. The students are happy, and Loriana turns out to be a very good president.
Anaya enjoys mathematics and wants to be a mathematician. Her teacher tells her she should study journalism because she is a good writer and journalism is a good career for girls. Anaya is disappointed because she loves mathematics the best.	Anaya continues to study mathematics. She gets her parents to enroll her in a Saturday mathematics program. Anaya gets the highest score on a national mathematics exam.	Anaya's teacher agrees that Anaya should continue to study mathematics. Anaya works with her teacher to help other students learn mathematics too.

Figure 4.7: Affirming self.

This Little Trailblazer: A Girl Power Primer by Joan Holub (2017; Primary)

Gender and female affirmation are the focus of this book, one of several books that present women from all ethnic groups who were trailblazers. This is a board book with pictures and brief descriptions of each woman, such as Florence Nightingale, Rosa Parks, Maria Tallchief, Sonia Sotomayor, and many more.

I Need You to Know: The ABC's of a Young King's Greatness by Lora McClain-Muhammad (2019b; Primary)

This is the male counterpart to the book *I Need You to Know: The ABC's of Black Girl Magic* (McClain-Muhammad, 2019a). It is also a coloring book with adjectives about male greatness from A to Z. Each page has provocative, encouraging words. We recommend using this book in a manner similar to what we suggest for the preceding book.

The Day You Begin by Jacqueline Woodson (2018; Elementary)

This is a beautifully written and illustrated picture book that addresses all kinds of differences across ethnicity and gender. The author encourages children to affirm themselves, regardless of socioeconomic, language, cultural, athletic, and ability differences. Your differences make you special and "no one is quite like you."

Pink Is for Boys by Robb Pearlman (2018; Elementary)

This book simply asserts that children should not be pigeon-holed by gender. In this case, the focus is on colors, stating that boys and girls have the right to enjoy all colors. By extension, they can similarly pursue activities, careers, and endeavors according to interest and ability, not gender. It is a beautifully written and enjoyable book for students to explore.

Introducing Teddy: A Gentle Story About Gender and Friendship by Jessica Walton (2016; Elementary)

This is a sensitive and gently written story about gender and friendship that focuses on accepting and befriending others with gender differences. It also has implications for gender-different individuals accepting themselves.

Julián Is a Mermaid by Jessica Love (2018; Elementary)

This book takes a position of gender fluidity and challenges some prevailing social norms and biases. It describes a little boy who travels through an urban setting with his grandmother and observes three women dressed as beautiful mermaids. Julián is so obsessed with this glamour that he decides to adorn himself accordingly. Instead of disapproving, his grandmother offers him more glitz and takes him to join the parade of the mermaids. The text is nicely sprinkled with Spanish words.

It Feels Good to Be Yourself: A Book About Gender Identity by Theresa Thorn (2019; Elementary)

This book also addresses gender fluidity, specifically targeting transgender and gender-identity issues. Using various examples, the text discusses how it is not easy to determine gender by physical appearance at birth. The author presents scenes demonstrating affirmed gender differences in the family, among peers, and within oneself.

Action Project: Celebrating Firsts

In December 2019, Charlotte Nebres played the leading role of Marie in the New York City Ballet's annual production of *The Nutcracker*. Nebres is a mixed-race (Black and Filipina) eleven-year-old girl, who was the first Black person to ever have that role (Kourlas, 2019). Use portions of *The New York Times* article to share Nebres's story and some of the discussion about non-White ballet dancers—both male and female—who now have the opportunity to have major roles in dance and other art productions, as well as any other endeavor in which their abilities would lead them (Kourlas, 2019). In discussing portions of this article, it's especially important to have students note Nebres's thoughts about getting the role and what she hopes it will mean for other young people. An interesting aspect of this story is that Misty Copeland, the first African American female principal dancer for the American Ballet Theatre, inspired Nebres. In conjunction with this article, you might want to read portions of Copeland's story in the book *A Girl Named Misty* (Lyons, 2018). This might help students understand how seeing the success of others who look like them can encourage students to pursue similar goals.

In addition to entertainers, take note of other people who might have been firsts in your community, such as the first female mayor or police chief. Other examples might include the first Black, Hispanic, Asian, or Native American sheriff, school principal, superintendent, coach of the high school football team, and so on. If possible, invite that person to your class and ask him or her to use pictures to give a brief sequence of his or her life experiences for this achievement.

Books on Affirming Self

Figure 4.8 (page 94) offers a list of books featured in this chapter as well as additional diverse books that include aspects of self-affirmation. Read these books as a class and discuss some of the themes we note in the preceding activities and books. When appropriate, encourage students to read the books independently and allow them to share the books with the rest of the class, noting how story characters affirm themselves.

Conclusion

The ability to affirm or encourage oneself is key to social-emotional learning. Self-affirmations help us remain goal oriented even in the absence of external approvals. There are many conditions under which we experience threats, not just race or gender. You can apply the models presented in this chapter to a variety of circumstances, as long as you recognize the need to analyze the situation clearly, seek support in overcoming the threat, and respond in ways to avoid harming yourself or others. Elementary students are not too young to begin to "think big." Even though these aspirations may change frequently over time as they grow, they should be encouraged to aspire according to their interests and abilities. Thoughts relative to immutable characteristics (for example, race, gender, or ethnicity) should not interfere with these aspirations. Stories about individuals who overcame such barriers should be inspiring. Real-life enactments could further aid these appropriate pursuits.

Title	Author	Story Summary
Primary		
Dream Big, Little One	Vashti Harrison (2018)	This attractive board book features brief histories of outstanding Black women.
I Am Enough	Grace Byers (2018)	This book is about affirming oneself and others.
I Need You to Know: The ABC's of Black Girl Magic	Lora McClain-Muhammad (2019a)	A young Black girl affirms herself using words beginning with letters of the alphabet.
I Need You to Know: The ABC's of a Young King's Greatness	Lora McClain-Muhammad (2019b)	This is a coloring book of affirmations for boys of color using words beginning with letters of the alphabet.
It's Okay to Be Different	Todd Parr (2001)	This book provides self-affirmations across a variety of differences.
This Little Trailblazer: A Girl Power Primer	Joan Holub (2017)	This book offers stories about women from diverse backgrounds who were trailblazers.
Elementary		
A Girl Named Misty: The True Story of Misty Copeland	Kelly Starling Lyons (2018)	This is the story of how Copeland became the first Black prima ballerina with the American Ballet Theatre.
All Are Welcome	Alexandra Penfold and Suzanne Kaufman (2019)	This is a book about embracing everyone, regardless of differences.
Be Bold! Be Brave! 11 Latinas Who Made U.S. History	Naibe Reynoso (2020)	This book features brief histories of Hispanic female leaders.
I Am Perfectly Designed	Karamo Brown and Jason Brown (2019)	An African American father teaches his son to value and affirm himself.
I Love My Hair	Natasha Anastasia Tarpley (2001)	A young Black girl notes the special joys of her hair.
Introducing Teddy: A Gentle Story About Gender and Friendship	Jessica Walton (2016)	This gentle story features gender differences and friendship.
It Feels Good to Be Yourself: A Book About Gender Identity	Theresa Thorn (2019)	This is a special story about gender identity.
Julián Is a Mermaid	Jessica Love (2018)	This tender story focuses on gender individuality.
Pink Is for Boys	Robb Pearlman (2018)	This story offers gender affirmations.
The Day You Begin	Jacqueline Woodson (2018)	This story is about learning to affirm yourself despite your differences from others.
Upper Elementary		
Little Leaders: Bold Women in Black History	Vashti Harrison (2017)	This book provides brief histories of African American female leaders.
Little Legends: Exceptional Men in Black History	Vashti Harrison (2019)	This book provides stories of Black male historical figures.

Figure 4.8: Books on affirming self.

*Visit **go.SolutionTree.com/diversityandequity** for a free reproducible version of this figure.*

Chapter Reflections

Individually or with a collaborative group, review and discuss the following questions to reflect on your learning in this chapter.

1. Why are many leadership or high-profile roles in society considered to be gender or race specific?

2. How should you help students think about positions that traditionally have been occupied by only one gender or race?

3. Do you think children's literature is a good first step in helping students think about alternatives to traditional gender and racial roles? Why?

4. How can you translate these ideas to other immutable traits that tend to serve as barriers, such as disabilities or childhood poverty?

5. What other strategies would you suggest for helping students to think big?

6. What other suggestions do you have for ways students can affirm themselves to pursue their goals?

chapter five

Asserting Self

Self-assertion is the act of putting forward one's opinions or of taking actions that express one's needs, rights, or wishes (APA, n.d.). For social-emotional learning, we want learners to develop the self-confidence to take steps to achieve socially appropriate goals and meet their needs. It also means they are respectful of others and can reduce conflict. Students can learn to be more socially assertive.

Scott W. Ross and Robert H. Horner (2013) trained teachers of upper elementary students to equip learners with a simple assertiveness strategy to prevent bullying and reduce the conflict in their environments. Upon observing an ensuing conflict, students were taught to use the following three-step strategy: (1) tell the bully to stop; (2) if step 1 is not effective, walk away and get others to walk away; (3) if still not effective, talk to an adult. According to Ross and Horner (2013), students became significantly more assertive (especially third and fourth graders) in reducing conflict, suggesting that such strategies may be more powerful if initiated in lower grades with younger students. Asserting self is the extension of affirming self.

For the purposes of this book, *assertion* essentially refers to the positive action an individual takes after affirming themselves. The books we use for the activities, as well as the books we list for additional readings, provide examples of culturally and linguistically diverse individuals who first feel a bit challenged by their differences but manage to self-affirm and then act on a newfound sense of self. This change might take a major action such as reading and writing books about one's differences, or it might be a small action such as summoning the courage to make friends with new classmates. Activities in this chapter emphasize students learning to perform the steps to self-affirm and then make the requisite positive behaviors to assert themselves. Additionally, this chapter focuses on two main issues: (1) asserting self while encountering ethnic and cultural differences and (2) overcoming major challenges of being a solo immigrant or migrant to a new land.

Asserting Self With Regard to Ethnic and Cultural Differences

Self-assertion is especially challenging in situations that include significant differences such as language, appearance, culture, and so on. Psychologist and researcher Abraham Maslow notes wanting to belong is a basic human need (as cited in Lussier, 2019), especially for young people searching for their personal identity and trying to fit in. Students who present substantial cultural differences from the larger group may struggle with conformity at the expense of their own cultural identity. The stories and activities in this chapter focus on ways the main characters, who present pronounced cultural differences, are able to first affirm themselves and then use various assertion strategies to successfully integrate themselves into U.S. society. Both of the model books we use in this chapter feature people who come from different countries and, initially, speak different languages. The main character in the first story is an elementary-aged student, while the second story centers on an adult. We recommend several books to reinforce the basic concepts we present in this chapter.

Literature on Asserting Self With Regard to Ethnic and Cultural Differences

The desire to fit in and be accepted is universal, but people also have the need to take pride in who they are, their personal identity. This activity and related readings have important understandings for appreciating everyone's uniqueness and the differences of others.

Book: *The Name Jar* by Yangsook Choi (2001)

As noted previously, the steps for introducing each book to the class include present the story, clarify story concepts through discussion, clarify the features of the desired behaviors through enactments, practice the desired behaviors through real-life applications, respond appropriately to issues of diversity, and provide extension activities to maintain the desired behaviors.

Present the Story

Read the story to and with the class. If students have a hard copy of the book or if they can access the story online, they can follow along as you read aloud. If not, students can simply listen as you read.

Story Synopsis

Unhei (pronounced Yoon-hey) is a new student who just moved to the United States from Korea. She is excited about this new land, but she is also nervous because she knows there will be differences. One important difference is names. The children at her school do not know how to pronounce her name, and some of them tease her about it. Unhei decides she needs to change her name to an American name, so it will be easy for the other students to pronounce, and they will not tease her. The class creates a name jar and puts in many different names familiar to them for Unhei to select one for herself. While thinking about these names, Unhei remembers that her parents and grandmother carefully selected her name, which means *grace*. After considering many American names, Unhei finally decides she likes her Korean name the best and introduces herself to the class using her Korean name, spelling it in both English and Korean. Unhei, along with the other students, also comes to realize it is OK to be different.

Discussion

Begin the discussion by making sure students can pronounce Unhei's name (Yoon-hey). Model the correct pronunciation and then direct students to say the name several times, both as a group and then individually. Then review the details of the story, using Unhei's name as often as possible. The more often children hear unfamiliar-sounding names, the more comfortable they will become using the name.

During the discussion, point out the following.

- Unhei was not only new to the school but also new to the United States.
- Unhei had many new things to learn.
- One of the most important things for Unhei to learn is a new language.
- Like all children, she wants to be liked and make friends.
- Unhei does not want to be teased because she does not have an American name.
- She wanted to change her name so she could be like the American students.
- Unhei realized her name has a special meaning.
- Unhei learned she does not have to change her name to make friends in her class.

Some key understandings from this story include the following.

- People value their names and the meaning behind them.
- You should respect everyone's name and not make fun of other people's names.
- It is very hurtful when people are teased about anything, especially their name.
- You should be proud of your name and defend your name if others tease you.
- People's names often have special meanings; for example, Unhei's name means *grace*.
- People want to show the good meanings of their name.

Among other things, students should learn to assert themselves by respecting and defending their own culture. Help students understand what Unhei did to assert herself.

- She learned how she got her name.
- She learned her name means *grace*.
- She learned other people (grandmother, mother, grocer) think Unhei is a beautiful name.
- She learned to like her name, so she kept it.
- Unhei affirmed herself.
- Unhei asserted herself by respectfully and proudly sharing her Korean name with the other students and asserting that her Korean name is what she prefers to use.

Enactments

Direct students to go through the following simple enactments. Although the primary focus of this activity is on self-assertion, particularly relative to cultural issues, it also is important to emphasize the importance of respecting the cultures of others. Provide students a list of international names, such as those in figure 5.1, and assign each student an international name. Tell students the country or continent of the name's origin, how to pronounce the name, and its meaning. Have students stand in two rows, facing each other. The two students facing each other are partners. When you give the signal, students in row A say to their partner with the international name, "You're new to our class. What is your name?" The students in row B say their name, tell how to pronounce it, and say what it means. The first student pronounces the new name and says, "Welcome to our class, (international student's name). We are glad to have you." Continue this way until every student has the opportunity to welcome a student with an international or unusual name to the class.

Country or Continent of Origin	Name	Meaning of Name
Korea	Areum (F)	Beautiful
Korea	Haneul (M or F)	Heavenly
Africa	Ayo (M or F)	Full of joy
Africa	Amare (M or F)	Immortal
Hispanic countries	Alma (F)	Caring
Hispanic countries	Arsenio (M)	Strong
Hispanic countries	Valentia (F)	Brave
Hispanic countries	Fernanda (F)	Adventurous
Hispanic countries	Javier (M)	Full of light
Hispanic countries	Norma (F)	One who can rule
Poland	Zofia (F)	Has wisdom
Japan	Kenta (M)	Healthy and strong
Philippines	Marical (F)	Great or noble
India	Ulhas (M)	Full of happiness
India	Aarau (M)	Peaceful
India	Navita (F)	Fearless
Vietnam	Hao (F)	Good, perfect
Vietnam	Hieu (M)	Respectful
Vietnam	Hoc (M)	Studious
Vietnam	Duc (M)	Moral, good
China	Ah Lam (F)	Peace
China	Ai (F)	Lovable

Figure 5.1: International names and meanings.

When all the students in row B have followed the three steps, have partners switch roles, so students in row A now follow the three steps. If students cannot do this in large groups (due to lack of space to line up), have all students sit down and watch as each pair performs these steps under your supervision.

Real-Life Applications

This activity helps students become knowledgeable about their own names and, thereby, assert themselves to take pride in their names and culture. Note again that students will need time to investigate the meanings of their names, as most will not know that information ahead of time. Have students ask their parents or family members the origin of their names or why their parents gave them their specific names. This is a voluntary activity, so educators should not penalize them if students fail to get this information. Some students will share that they are named after relatives, such as grandparents, aunts, parents, and so on. Some students will indicate they received part of each parent's name, such as a girl named Lennette because her father is named Leonard and her mother is named Antoinette. Some students will discover they were named after famous personalities or from someone in the family's ethnic group.

Ask students, "Do you know what your name means?" If they don't, use a website, such as *Belly Ballot* (https://babynames.net), to search the name and meaning. Create a chart of their names and related meanings for the entire class (see figure 5.2). If students are sufficiently skilled, create a roster with all the names and require students to write in the meaning beside their own name. Make sure all the meanings are positive, with characteristics in which students can take pride.

Student's Name	Meaning of Name
Addy	Graceful and noble
Nicole	Triumphant
Josephine	Will grow or increase
Estelle	Star
Agueda	Good-hearted
Carlos	Free man
Bonita	Creative or beautiful

Figure 5.2: My name and its meaning.

Some native-born U.S. students have uncommon names for their country. Stress that students should respect everyone's name. In situations where a website does not yield a specific name and meaning, tell students to make up a meaning for their name. These should have positive meanings such as *courageous, thoughtful, kind, generous, helpful, good student, good reader, creative, good artist,* and so on. Tell students they should live up to the meanings of their names. If their name means *good-hearted* (or they selected that meaning for their name), students can tell you the things they do and can do to demonstrate their name's meaning.

Again, organize students into two facing rows. When you give the signal, students in row A ask their partners in row B, "What is your name?" Each student in row B responds by saying (1) "My name is (gives name)," (2) "I like my name because it means (gives name meaning)," and (3) "I try to live up to my name because I (something he or she does or did)." If some of these meanings do not reflect positive character traits, such as hard worker or kind, help children select an additional meaning that requires them to demonstrate positive social attributes such as *cares for others*. When all the students in row B have followed the steps, have partners switch roles, so students in row A then follow the steps. If students cannot do this in large groups (due to lack of space to line up), have all students sit down and watch as each pair performs the steps under your supervision.

If there are students with international names in your class, give these students an opportunity to share their names and culture with the class. The latter part should be voluntary, but you may choose to have students follow these steps.

1. Tell the class your name. ("My name is Ravindra.")
2. Tell the class how to pronounce your name. ("You pronounce my name so the *v* almost sounds like an *f*: *Raf-vin-drah*.")
3. Tell the class the origin of your name. ("My name is a Hindi name from India.")
4. Explain the meaning of your name. ("The main meaning of my name is *lord of the sun*, but it also has other meanings such as *someone who wants to help others*.")
5. Tell a little bit about the culture of your name. ("India is a very big country with many people. It is near China. Only China has more people than India.")

As time permits and is appropriate, encourage students to share interesting and important facts about their respective cultures of name origin. It is important for them to share and for others to receive this information with respect, recognizing these traditions are not only different but also not superior or inferior to other cultures.

Diversity Issues in This Story

U.S. classrooms are increasingly diverse with individuals from all parts of the world (NCES, 2019). Unlike in the past when many new immigrants anglicized their names, today's immigrants are likely to keep first and last names reflecting their birth countries (Roberts, 2010). These international and unusual names often present challenges for English speakers, but they are not insurmountable and can be exciting. As a matter of fact, you could view these different names as special opportunities to see how quickly you can learn to pronounce a unique name and learn something about another area of the world.

Laughing at or demeaning someone's name can be a personal affront. That is, the individual who is the object of ridicule could associate the negative perceptions of his or her name with him- or herself (for example, "I have an inferior name; therefore, I am inferior"). Likewise, students may conclude they should reject those with different names, languages, or cultures. From the time children begin to socially interact with peers, they must learn that *different* does not mean *bad*. That is, it is OK to have a name or background that is different from others in the group. That difference does not make you a bad or undesirable person. There are many different ways of doing things (for example, cooking, dressing, dancing, traveling, and so on) that are worthwhile, good, pleasurable, and beneficial.

Although you might be most comfortable with the things you are used to, no one culture is inherently better or worse than any other. Present other cultures positively, and help students enjoy learning about others. Along the same lines and consistent with the focus of this activity, help students from different cultures present themselves and their native ways of doing things with pride. Native-born and internationally born students should relish learning about one another.

Extended Literature Activities

Use these literature activities to further ascertain students' understanding of the story and desired social-emotional learning skills. Students use their own words to retell the story and specify appropriate ways to respond. You also could use the annotated book list in the section Books on Asserting Self (page 115) to assign more relevant readings to individuals or groups. For each book, we suggest general elementary reading levels.

Retell the Story

If students have mastered working effectively in small groups, conduct this activity in small groups. If not, conduct it in a large, teacher-directed group, allowing students to respond chorally as well as individually, as time permits. Direct students to retell the story. During the retelling, ask students to include these facts: (1) Unhei is from a different country (Korea), and she has a different name from the other students in the class; (2) at first, the students tease Unhei about her name; (3) Unhei feels bad and wants to change her name; (4) the other students want to help her change her name; (5) Unhei realizes she had a good Korean name and does not have to change it; and (6) Unhei is happy to keep her birth name.

Extend the Story: I Am Unhei

Conduct this exercise as a large group. Help students understand how Unhei felt when others teased her, when she tried to change her name, and when she decided to keep her own name. Point out to students that they should not feel obligated to make other people happy by doing what they want them to do; rather, they should do what they know is right and best for themselves. Tell students they are going to pretend to be Unhei, and this is what Unhei should say to assert herself (see figure 5.3).

Student Taking the Role of Unhei	Student Taking the Role of a Welcoming Classmate
"My name is Unhei."	"My name is _____."
"This is the way to say my name: Yoon-hey."	"Yoon-hey."
"Unhei is a Korean name. It means *grace* in English."	"That is a good name. Welcome to this class."
"Thank you. I know I will like this class."	"That's good!"

Figure 5.3: I Am Unhei example.

As time permits, give each student the opportunity to take the role of Unhei and also the role of the welcoming student.

Additional Readings

Extend the discussion on cultural self-assertion through reading some of the following books.

Alma, and How She Got Her Name by Juana Martinez-Neal (2018; Primary)

This attractive, award-winning book continues the topic of naming and shows how it is done in another culture. Young Alma thinks her name is too long and wants to shorten it, but her father tells her about the origin of all her names. Alma has five names, but she learns that she is named after some pretty exciting family members. Alma then decides she likes her names and the stories behind each. This story provides a nice segue into the pattern of Hispanic naming and the action project we suggest in the next section.

Your Name Is a Song by Jamilah Thompkins-Bigelow (2020; Primary)

This story tells of a young African American and Muslim student who decides she is not returning to school because teachers and classmates continue to mispronounce her name. Her mother teaches her about the beauty and musicality of her name, as well as the names of children from other cultures. Her mother's stories encourage her, and the young girl readily returns to school empowered and prepared to assert herself.

Bee-Bim Bop! by Linda Sue Park (2008; Elementary)

This delightful book helps students understand Korean culture by telling the story of a young girl who helps her mother make a favorite Korean dish called *bee-bim bop*. The dish is a rice bowl that contains various egg, meat, and vegetable combinations. These rice bowls, originally from Asian countries, have gained much popularity in North America, and you can use this story as an example of cultural differences being neither good nor bad, simply different.

Dumpling Soup by Jama Kim Rattigan (1993; Elementary)

Dumpling Soup is another book about Asian or Pacific Island culture. Although the story is set in the U.S. state of Hawaii, many of the Hawaiian people are originally from Asian countries such as Korea, Japan, and China. This story is about making dumpling soup, which is a traditional Korean soup eaten first thing on New Year's Day. In the story, young Marisa learns to affirm and assert herself in her first successful effort to make dumpling soup with her grandmother. This story provides interesting cultural information on how these families celebrate New Year's Day.

Knock, Knock: My Dad's Dream for Me by Daniel Beaty (2013; Elementary)

This book tells of a young African American boy who draws from his father's former image and loving actions to assert himself. This boy is deeply hurt by the permanent loss of a previously loving and engaged father. Over time, he learns to internalize his father's words to assert himself and become the kind of person his father wanted him to be.

Action Project: What's in a Name

If conditions are amenable in your school, arrange for your class to celebrate names and cultures. This activity helps cultural-minority students affirm and assert themselves. At different times of the year, select a specific international group, one particularly well-represented in your area. One example might be Somali names and culture. In a small assembly, designate students with a Somali background to present their names, the meaning of their names, and some aspects of their culture. A parent or official in the Somali community might come to your school to share information about Somali names and their culture. The female name Aamiina, for example, is also Aminah, which is fairly common in the United States. It means *feel safe* and is believed to be the name of the mother of the Prophet Mohammed. Somali names have three parts. The first is a given name, the second is the father's name, and the third is the child's paternal grandfather's name. The names often narrate the story of their ancestral or social background (Marohn, 2016).

Students may be intrigued to learn how parents from other countries systematically determine their children's names. Some cultures have special rules for naming children. To keep from stigmatizing or alienating a particular group of students, you might alter this activity with something such as a *naming celebration*, in which two or three students from three or four different groups (for example, Somali, Honduran, Indian, and U.S.-born White students with a Western European background) would get the opportunity to talk about the origin and meanings of their names.

Over a period of weeks, make sure all groups are represented, permitting as many students to participate as who wish to do so. Make sure students know everyone respects all names, and no names are better or worse than other names.

Asserting Self Across Immigrant and Migrant Groups

Immigration and migration are unique features of U.S. history. Except for Native Americans, who make up only approximately 1 percent of the U.S. population (Wells, Fox, & Cordova-Cobo, 2016), the source or origin for the remaining 99 percent of U.S. society is from some other country. Immigration continues and remains an important feature of life in the United States. It is an especially prominent factor in the education and socialization that occurs in U.S. schools. This activity highlights ways immigrants can assert themselves.

Literature on Asserting Self Across Immigrant and Migrant Groups

These readings give special insight into the difficulties and exceptional effort needed when moving to a different country. Being assertive under these circumstances inevitably means a combination of abilities such as ingenuity, creativity, and industry.

Book: *Dreamers* by Yuyi Morales (2018)

As noted previously, the steps for introducing each book to the class include present the story, clarify story concepts through discussion, clarify the features of the desired behaviors through enactments, practice the desired behaviors through real-life applications, respond appropriately to issues of diversity, and provide extension activities to maintain the desired behaviors.

Present the Story

Read the story to and with the class. If students have a hard copy of the book or if they can access the story online, they can follow along as you read aloud. If not, students can simply listen as you read.

Story Synopsis

This story is autobiographical. The author tells of coming to the United States from Mexico. She travels here with her infant son. She does not know the language or many things about this new country, but she and her son travel around to see many things. A very important discovery is the library, where she and her son spend many hours looking at and eventually learning to read numerous books. They think of libraries as magical places. They learn to speak English, read English books, and eventually, write many good books for children. This is one of those books. An important message is everyone can be dreamers—to learn, to hope, and to love. Another important lesson is people must be brave when they move to different countries or places.

This beautiful picture book is attractive to young children and adults alike. It's useful for learning about self-assertion because it talks about having the courage to explore and pursue a novel environment to become linguistically competent and comfortable in a new land. This self-assertion leads the author and her son to not only become comfortable in the United States but also make valuable contributions to others who are willing to become dreamers about the promises of lands throughout the world.

Discussion

In this story, the central character is a mother who tells of her adventures with her very young child. During the discussion, help students grasp the following ten key points.

1. The child is a newborn.
2. The mother loves the child very much.
3. The mother and child travel to a new land where everything is different.
4. The mother and child are not allowed to return to their previous land.
5. In this new land they are called *immigrants*.
6. They must learn many new things, such as a new language and how to travel around a new city.
7. They discover libraries where they spend lots of time reading books.
8. These books help them learn the language and about their new country. This helps them gain the confidence to assert themselves.
9. They learn to read and write books.
10. They learn to dream about all the wonderful things they could do and become.

During the discussion for each of these key points, allow students to look at the pictures in the book and speculate how the mother and her child must have felt. For example, the mother was probably afraid to travel around a big city where most people did not speak her language. She would have to be very brave and *assert* herself. Help students see she asserts herself by asking people for help until she finds someone who speaks her language and can help her. She does this over and over until she learns her way. Make sure students realize the story takes place over a period of a couple of years, from the time right after the child's birth to about the time the child is two or three years old. Students can speculate about how the child probably develops even beyond the time span of the story. Do students think the little boy continues going to the library? What do students think are some of his favorite books? What are some other things he might enjoy doing?

Enactments

Remind students the mother in this story asserts herself and helps her son understand how to be assertive by learning how to do important things in a different land. For example, they figure out how to go different places, even though they are in a new city. In this exercise, students practice how to obtain various things, even though they are different or new to them. Figure 5.4 (page 110) presents specific scenarios and a suggestion for how the student should respond. For the final six scenarios, the response column is blank so students can generate their own responses. This works best as a teacher-directed, large-group exercise.

Real-Life Applications

This activity could be a variation of the preceding activity except the scenarios and responses should reflect real-life events. That is, students either share a situation when they demonstrated how they asserted themselves or present a scenario of how they would like to assert themselves. For example, Jordan tells of the time when Abioye, a new immigrant boy, moved into his neighborhood, and he invited him to play softball. Then Abioye taught Jordan how to play soccer and some other games he used to play in his native country. Give students prompts of things they might have done to assert themselves. Encourage them to give details about the event, demonstrating how they asserted themselves. Possible examples include the following.

- I am a new immigrant to the United States. Last week, I went to the neighborhood store to buy some groceries for my family.
- I am a new immigrant to the United States. I escorted my younger sister to school.
- I am a new immigrant student in this school. Last week, I went to the library by myself.
- I am a new immigrant to the United States. I invited Alaina, my neighbor, to my birthday party.
- I am a new immigrant student in this school. Last week, I went to the principal's office to deliver the class roster.

Scenario	Assertive Response
You and your family just immigrated to the United States, and you are at a new school. On the playground, you see some students playing kickball. You want to play kickball too. What do you do?	If you do not know English, ask the school translator to ask the students if you can play with them. Also ask the translator to tell you how to say, "May I play?" in English.
You are at a big shopping mall with your father. You get separated from him and are a little afraid. You have not learned English. What do you do?	You look for a security guard or a salesperson in the mall. Show them your name and telephone number. Wait with them until your father comes.
You just immigrated to the United States, and you do not speak much English. You like to study about dinosaurs. You want to get dinosaur books so you can learn more about dinosaurs as well as practice English. What do you do?	Ask your teacher to help you get books from the school library on dinosaurs. Return the books to the library so you can take out more books on dinosaurs.
You are a new immigrant in the United States. You want to be a musician. You want to play the violin in the school orchestra. You do not have a violin. What do you do?	Tell the school music teacher you want to play the violin. Ask the teacher what you can do to get a violin. If you are able to get a violin, practice every day.
You are a new immigrant. Harold asks you to play American football, but you do not know how to play. What do you do?	Tell Harold you would like to play the game. Ask for the rules. Watch the others play, and then join the game.
Your best friend has moved away. You miss your friend. What do you do?	
Your name is Carlos. You are a new immigrant to the United States. You and your family just moved into your neighborhood. You want to play ball with children on your street. What do you do?	
You are a new immigrant to the United States. In your new class, the students ask your name. You know your name sounds different, and you are afraid they will tease you. What do you do?	
You are a new immigrant student in the United States. It is your birthday. You want to invite the class to your birthday party. You do not know how to invite them, but your new friend Olivia does. What do you do to get help?	
You are a new immigrant student in your class. You want to take the bus to buy some school supplies. You don't know how to do this, but your classmate does. What do you think you could do?	
You are a new immigrant student in your class. You need someone to help you with your spelling words because no one in your family speaks English. Alex, a friendly student in your class, is a good speller. What do you think you could do?	

Figure 5.4: Responding assertively.

*Visit **go.SolutionTree.com/diversityandequity** for a free reproducible version of this figure.*

I Am an Immigrant

This is a voluntary activity you should base on students' maturity and skill levels. Give students the assignment to interview their parents to identify at least one parent, grandparent, great-grandparent, and so on who was born in another country and then came to the United States. The student should tell the country the relative came from, the language he or she spoke, and something special or unique about that culture, such as a special soup this relative used to make for the family. If there are Native American students in the class, these students could talk about their particular group and something special about their culture. Native-born African American students are not likely to have identified a specific country in Africa of their ancestors' origin. Under these circumstances, they can simply select one of the countries in Africa (for example, Nigeria) and tell something about the Nigerian culture. Or students may have information about their immediate and extended family roots within the United States and can share their families' journey across the United States or stories of deep roots within their own communities.

Habla Español

This is an exercise where both immigrant and native U.S. students can practice assertiveness. If you have immigrant students with a different language background, switch this exercise to the language of those students. Native English-speaking students will teach immigrant students key English words, and immigrant students will, in turn, teach native English speakers words from their language. Point out to students there are real advantages to learning a second language. It can help them communicate with people with different languages; it can make visiting other countries more fun; and it can help them understand other cultures better. As an educator, knowing another language can help you assert yourself and be helpful when students speaking different languages enter your class. Take students through the exercise in figure 5.5 (page 112), pretending you just got a new Spanish-speaking student in your class. You can use the blank rows for additional phrases. You also may substitute Spanish phrases for whatever immigrant language is most represented in your class.

Diversity Issues in This Story

In this activity, the focus is on the immigrant population in the United States. According to the Pew Research Center (2020), the United States has more immigrants (approximately forty million) than any other country in the world, making up about 13.6 percent of the total population. About three-fourths of these are legal immigrants, and the remaining one-fourth are undocumented. Immigrants come to the United States from all over the world.

English Phrase	Spanish Translation
Hello	Hola
Welcome to our class.	Bienvenida a nuestra clase.
What is your name?	¿Cómo te llamas?
My name is Michael.	Mi nombre es Michael.
Come play our game with us.	Ven a jugar nuestro juego con nosotros.
Come have lunch with us.	Ven a almorzar con nosotras.

Figure 5.5: Habla Español.

*Visit **go.SolutionTree.com/diversityandequity** for a free reproducible version of this figure.*

Most new arrivals to this country are from Asia, with India being the top country of origin. During this discussion, you might distinguish between voluntary immigrants and refugees. *Refugees* are individuals who usually come from countries where there is a lot of warfare, such as the Democratic Republic of the Congo, Syria, or Burma, and the people are fleeing for their lives. They also could be coming from a country with a major natural disaster, such as the 2021 earthquake in Haiti. A world map could help students understand the general areas where immigrants come from, such as Hispanic, Asian, African, and European countries. Most Americans believe immigrants make major contributions to their country (Budiman, 2020). Engage students in a discussion of some things people identify with recent immigrants. Some examples might include sports (soccer), food (chili sushi, rice bowls), and dance and music (salsa, cha-cha, calypso).

Most immigrants (a little more than half) who come to the United States know how to speak English, but many others still have to learn the language (Budiman, 2020). Although language differences can present communication barriers, they also offer the opportunity for both immigrants and English-speaking Americans to learn a new language. Learning new languages facilitates social interactions and aids in gaining information about other cultures. Most U.S. public schools require students to take a world language, often starting as early as kindergarten (DeGerolamo, 2020).

Elementary-aged students learn new languages more easily than adults. Encourage them to exchange words and phrases with their language-different classmates. Allow some time in class for students to share newly acquired words from their classmates and how they are informally aiding English-learning students in English.

Extended Literature Activities

Use these literature activities to further ascertain students' understanding of the story and desired social-emotional learning skills. Students use their own words to retell the story and specify appropriate ways to respond. You also could use the annotated book list in the section Books on Asserting Self (page 115) to assign more relevant readings to individuals or groups. For each book, we suggest general elementary reading levels.

Retell the Story

In small or large groups, direct students to retell the story of *Dreamers* (Morales, 2018), being certain to make the following points: (1) the mother dreams of a new life; (2) this dream takes her to a new country; (3) in this country, everything is different; (4) she has to learn a new language; (5) she has to learn to travel to different places; (6) often she is afraid but learns how to get help; (7) she is very happy in the library, learning new things from books; and (8) she learns to read and write English.

Read several of the books in the Additional Readings section. For each story, have students identify one aspect about the new location that makes the main character frightened or unhappy and how that person asserts him- or herself to solve the problem. For example, in the story *Home at Last* (Elya, 2006), the mother began to learn English so she could assert herself with the grocer who was being unfair to her.

Additional Readings

The focus in this activity is on asserting oneself when moving from one location to another, whether as an immigrant, refugee, or migrant. There are always major adjustments that call on substantial inner and external resources.

Home at Last by Susan Middleton Elya (2006; Elementary)

This is a heartwarming story about a family immigrating from Mexico and trying to maintain all the important features of family life while adjusting to a different culture and learning a new language. The mother of the family is especially stressed about carrying out her family duties until she begins to use her newly acquired English to assert herself with vendors and others outside her home.

I Have Heard of a Land by Joyce Carol Thomas (2000; Elementary)

This is another encouraging story and somewhat related to the previous story. This award-winning book is about a migrant (not immigrant) Black family moving from the southern part of the United States to Oklahoma, where they could get free land for their homes and get some relief from the suffering many of the ex-enslaved people were experiencing. Especially noteworthy are the strength and courage the grandmother displays to help build her own home, grow all her own food, and care for herself and her family.

Mango, Abuela, and Me by Meg Medina (2015; Elementary)

Learning a new language and new ways of doing things not only challenges immigrants in their interactions with native members of their new country but also presents certain barriers for these immigrant children with their own family members. This book gives a vivid example of this dilemma in which a young girl learns to communicate with a loving grandmother who speaks Spanish, not English.

Drawn Together by Minh Lê (2018; Elementary)

Similar to the previous story, a young Asian American boy learns to assert himself to communicate with love and to value his grandfather, even though they speak different languages.

Listening With My Heart: A Story of Kindness and Self-Compassion by Gabi Garcia (2017; Elementary)

This bilingual book offers a separate edition in Spanish. It provides good examples of a young girl affirming herself and others. Give special attention to the way Esperanza asserts herself (for example, extending friendship) to help Bao, a new student from Vietnam, to feel like he belongs in his new school.

The Other Side by Jacqueline Woodson (2001; Elementary)

This is a beautiful and poignant book about a somewhat different, but powerful example of assertive behavior. Two young girls—one White and one Black—in a racially segregated town, gradually decide to assert themselves to defy the admonitions of their parents and the mores of their community to go to the other side of the fence to play with each other. Someday someone will come along to knock the fence down.

Ben's Trumpet by Rachel Isadora (1991; Elementary)

This is an award-winning book about a young boy who loves jazz music and dreams about playing the trumpet. Ben dares to assert his dream just by constantly "playing" his imaginary trumpet. Others ignore, reject, and ridicule his obsession with trumpet playing except for a master trumpeter who begins to mentor Ben in playing a real trumpet.

Action Project: Special Centers for Immigrants or Refugees

This action project focuses on refugees who come to the United States because they are escaping war or persecution in their birth countries. Most cities have international rescue centers or committees that help refugees adjust in their new country. In addition to helping the new families get shelter, clothing, food, and jobs, these centers often pair the new families with mentors who help them with issues of everyday living. One center in Boise, Idaho, tells the story of the Balubwila family from the Democratic Republic of the Congo matched with a Boise family (Kyle, 2016). The children in these two families tell how they befriended one another. The American children taught the African children things, such as how to participate in a snow fight and how to attend an American football game. The African children taught their American friends words in Swahili. See if there is a comparable center in your community. In some towns, churches serve in this capacity. Invite a representative from one of these facilities to share with your class some of the things they do to help refugees. Ask the representative to tell students some of the major things young refugee children must learn, including how to assert themselves to be successful.

If there are no refugee services available in your community, perhaps someone in the community has been a refugee and is willing to come to your class to speak to students. A church for an ethnic group (for example, Hispanic or African), a synagogue, a mosque, and so on might aid in identifying people who could possibly come to your class for this purpose. A family with children the same ages as your students would be ideal. Of particular importance is learning how young children adapt to their new country and school, and how they learn to affirm and assert themselves.

Books on Asserting Self

Figure 5.6 (page 116) offers a list of books featured in this chapter as well as additional diverse books that include aspects of asserting self. Read these books as a class and discuss some of the themes noted in the preceding activities. Where appropriate, encourage students to read the books independently and have them share the books with the rest of the class, noting how story characters assert themselves.

Conclusion

Learning to assert oneself, acting in the interest of oneself and the common good, is an essential feature of social-emotional learning. Children need to know not only how to value self and others but also how to act on those values. They should learn to act independently and decisively and honor themselves and others. Assertive behaviors from students might consist of very simple and elementary acts, such as claiming they like their name, or much more threatening situations, such as standing up for a classmate who is being bullied or trying to make friends in a strange land with a strange language.

Title	Author	Story Summary
Primary		
Alma and How She Got Her Name	Juana Martinez-Neal (2018)	A young Hispanic girl learns to appreciate her unusually long name.
Your Name Is a Song	Jamilah Thompkins-Bigelow (2020)	A Muslim mother teaches her daughter the beauty of her name and how to be assertive and proud of it.
Elementary		
Bee-Bim Bop!	Linda Sue Park (2008)	This book celebrates a very popular Korean dish.
Ben's Trumpet	Rachel Isadora (1991)	Ben, a young African American boy, realizes his fantasies about playing the trumpet.
Drawn Together	Minh Lê (2018)	A young Asian boy learns to love and value his grandfather, who speaks a different language.
Dumpling Soup	Jama Kim Rattigan (1993)	A young Asian girl learns to master a special holiday dish.
Home at Last	Susan Middleton Elya (2006)	A young Hispanic girl narrates how her mother learns English and overcomes a retailer's aggression.
I Have Heard of a Land	Joyce Carol Thomas (2000)	A Black family encounters the special pleasures and challenges of moving west to Oklahoma territory.
Knock, Knock: My Dad's Dream for Me	Daniel Beaty (2013)	A young African American boy draws on his father's former image and loving actions to assert himself.
Listening With My Heart: A Story of Kindness and Self-Compassion	Gabi Garcia (2017)	Children from all different ethnic backgrounds learn to be kind and affirm themselves.
Mango, Abuela, and Me	Meg Medina (2015)	A young Hispanic girl learns to communicate with a loving grandmother who speaks a different language.
The Empty Pot	Demi (1996)	A young Chinese boy learns the rewards of honesty and integrity.
The Other Side	Jacqueline Woodson (2001)	Black and White girls assert themselves to play together despite admonitions of segregation.

Figure 5.6: Books on asserting self.

Visit go.SolutionTree.com/diversityandequity for a free reproducible version of this figure.

The classroom activities in this chapter can give students guidance and practice in being assertive. When students not only think but act on affirming statements, that is being assertive. As teachers, we need to identify the assertive behaviors students need most and then provide explicit instruction for those behaviors. Adult prompting, classroom practice, and readings from children's literature can be useful for this social-emotional learning.

Chapter Reflections

Individually or with a collaborative group, review and discuss the following questions to reflect on your learning in this chapter.

1. How much attention do you think school personnel should give to the social-emotional adjustment of immigrant or migrant students at your school?

2. How much attention and preparation should school personnel give to domestic students who are about to receive immigrant or migrant students into their classrooms?

3. What kind of assertive skills do domestic students need who transfer from one school within the district, across districts, or across the country?

4. What are the most critical assertive skills needed by the students in your class?

5. Have you provided explicit instruction on being assertive for the students in your class? If so, how successful were you? If not, what kind of instruction might you provide to help students learn to be more assertive?

6. What additional understandings regarding childhood assertion would you add to this discussion?

Part III

Dealing With Aggression and Conflict Through Diverse and Culturally Relevant Children's Literature

Interpersonal conflict, to varying degrees, is a constant among students in schools. Teachers must manage conflict in order to teach, and children must learn to manage conflict for school and adult success. Conflict can be especially troubling when one or more individuals oppose or dislike others primarily due to misinformation relative to in-group threats and out-group negative stereotypes. The pluralistic U.S. society is made up of many different cultural and racial groups. Throughout the United States, practices such as racial housing patterns, racialized school zoning, magnet schools, charter schools, White flight, and so on have resulted in some areas with highly segregated schools (Chang, 2018; Hannah-Jones, 2019). Segregated schools limit the opportunities for interaction or understanding across diverse groups. Further, many of the smaller groups get relatively little authentic curriculum exposure about themselves, increasing the possibilities for false and negative perceptions (Adam, Barratt-Pugh, & Haig, 2017; Fleming et al., 2016). Negative perceptions based on ignorance or misinformation can easily escalate into hostility, creating conditions for conflict and possibly aggression.

We present the following three conflict-management strategies in part III. The featured stories involve culturally diverse populations managing strife among, between, or within groups. These strategies are key to growth in interpersonal problem solving.

1. **Responding to aggression:** The way people respond to aggression is a major factor in whether the aggression persists, becomes worse, or goes away. The goal in conflict management is to make it go away and, if possible, establish more positive interpersonal relationships.

2. **Playing and working cooperatively with others:** Play and work are important social arenas for children and adults. It is under these conditions people learn and grow socially. This literature helps students think about ways to avoid conflict through cooperation. It also emphasizes the importance of cooperation with others of different backgrounds.

3. **Questioning unfair practices:** A pervasive refrain for many young people, particularly those from culturally and racially diverse backgrounds, is that some rule or consequence is unfair. These complaints are not always without justification, but people often do not know how to address them to bring about the best outcomes. This literature of culturally and racially diverse characters uses some examples of blatantly unjust laws, as well as a contemporary story of subtler questionable practices, to point out productive actions under these circumstances.

chapter six

Responding to Aggression

Conflict that escalates may lead to *aggression*—when individuals intend to harm one another physically or psychologically. For example, name-calling or teasing, triggered by differences, is a common form of school conflict. Diversity is associated with peer victimization, but equitable diversity under positive school and classroom conditions is important for more favorable interracial attitudes and student interactions (Donoghue & Raia-Hawrylak, 2016; Hoglund & Hosan, 2013; Juvonen, Kogachi, & Graham, 2018). Students enter a classroom or school with distinct differences in physical features, language, dress, physical or intellectual abilities, and places of origin and backgrounds. Because these differences are novel, and educators typically do not prepare students on how to treat a new student with noticeable differences, taunting is likely. When discussing aggression and conflict, consider using the story *Angel Child, Dragon Child* (Surat, 1989), which deals with students taunting a child from a different country who looks and speaks differently from her classmates at school. The abuse escalates until the harm becomes physical.

In this story, a wise principal helps the students use their words to resolve this conflict. Although peer conflict often can resolve itself naturally, reconciliation is more likely to occur with adult intervention. Further, psychological pain (for example, name calling) can be just as harmful and more long lasting than physical aggression. Thus, student conflict should concern school personnel and other adults. There are many good reasons for adults to teach students how to manage conflict appropriately. Research on student aggression and bullying provides the following three understandings (Powell & Ladd, 2010; Ross & Horner, 2013).

1. Young people are often unaware of how damaging their unkind words and deeds are to taunted classmates. Bullies often state their actions are meant for fun or discount the severity of their acts; but if the fun is not reciprocal, it is most likely abuse.

2. Taunted students often do not know how to stop the bullying without doing more harm. They are prone to use physical strategies that may hurt others or themselves. Or they may simply blame themselves, which can be emotionally self-destructive.

3. Young students tend not to be skilled in using assertive strategies, such as planful ignoring or seeking help, to resolve conflict.

School personnel and other adults must be aware that children typically need adult intervention to solve problem situations. Likewise, adults need to be aware of conditions of ongoing peer conflict and the strategies useful in preventing or reducing it. Additionally, researchers Melissa D. Powell and Linda D. Ladd (2010) state the following.

- Most young people will not report when they are being bullied.

- Males are more likely to use physical aggression such as fighting.

- Females use more psychological or relational aggression. They will emphasize exclusion or alienation tactics to exclude students from friendship or play groups.

- Strategies to address student conflict should include the entire class or school.

- In addition to the bully and the victim, there are at least two other constituencies involved: (1) student enablers, who behind the scenes support the bully's behavior; and (2) silent students, who ignore or avoid the situation. Both of these groups help perpetuate the conflict. Complicity for the first group is obvious. The second group must learn that even their silence may inadvertently appear to endorse or encourage the bully's negative behavior.

In this chapter, we focus on books that feature two types of aggression: (1) physical and (2) verbal. Although we might think of physical aggression as being more dangerous or damaging, verbal aggression also inflicts harm. Harm resulting from verbal aggression may not be immediately obvious, but it can be even more long lasting.

Responding to Physical Aggression

There is no one way to respond to physical aggression because of situational specificity, but generally, social learning researchers advise children and others to try one or a combination of the following four strategies: (1) ignore or avoid the aggressor, (2) get away from the aggressor, (3) go for help, or (4) give an assertive response such as telling the person to leave you alone (Cartledge & Kleefeld, 2009, 2010; Sokol, Bussey, & Rapee, 2016). When dealing with aggressive or bullying behaviors, authorities recognize it is not enough to simply focus on the bully and victim. Equally, if not more, important is the peer group who reinforces the behavior by attending to it, laughing at the victim, or simply avoiding condemning it (Ross & Horner, 2013). We cannot overstate the importance of the peer group or larger audience in efforts to reduce peer aggression in schools or society (Palmer, Rutland, & Cameron, 2015).

Ross and Horner (2013) taught elementary students to employ a simple peer-confrontation strategy to address bullying in their schools. Some of the implications from this study are the importance of adult involvement and early intervention. Educators could engage older elementary students (grades 4–5) and adolescents (grades 6–12) in developing peer-intervention strategies. In the story *Angel Child, Dragon Child* (Surat, 1989), the principal is able to stop the immediate physical aggression, but wisely recognizes the importance of full school involvement to relieve the larger problem of peer aggression. In addition to teaching students very specific skills (such as walking away), peer group involvement is critical, especially in situations in which certain students or groups are the targets for abuse.

Literature on Responding to Physical Aggression

When educators permit microaggressions to fester and persist, escalation into more serious aggression is inevitable. The following readings illustrate this eventuality and offer constructive alternatives.

Book: *Angel Child, Dragon Child* by Michele Maria Surat (1989)

As noted previously, the steps for introducing each book to the class include present the story, clarify story concepts through discussion, clarify the features of the desired behaviors through enactments, practice the desired behaviors through real-life applications, respond appropriately to issues of diversity, and provide extension activities to maintain the desired behaviors.

Present the Story

Read the story to and with the class. If students have a hard copy of the book or if they can access the story online, they can follow along as you read aloud. If not, students can simply listen as you read.

Story Synopsis

This story is about an elementary school child who immigrates to the United States with her Vietnamese refugee family. The main character and narrator is named Hoa (pronounced *Hwa*). Hoa is her true name, but she prefers the name Ut because in Vietnamese culture, it is the loving name of the youngest daughter or son. Hoa's family name is Nguyen, but in her culture the family name comes first, unlike in many other countries, such as the United States, in which the family name comes last.

Hoa is a new student in a U.S. school along with her two older sisters. Dressed in their native garb, Hoa is shy and afraid as she approaches the new school, but her sisters remind her they must follow their parents' directions to go to this school. The children have come to the United States with their father; their mother, who Hoa misses greatly, is still in Vietnam. Hoa remembers her mother's instructions; she should be an *angel child* (good and happy), and a *dragon* (brave and noble). Hoa tries to be good and brave, even though the U.S. children at school laugh and tease her about her clothes and speech.

One day, Hoa's main antagonist, Raymond, throws a "snow rock" (an icy snowball) that hurts her sister. Hoa angrily throws a snow rock at Raymond, who then attacks Hoa, and the two begin to fight. The school principal stops the fighting and puts the two in the same room with the directions that Hoa will dictate her Vietnam story to Raymond, who will write the story as Hoa dictates it. After a brief period of sulking, the children begin talking, and Hoa reveals her mother is still in Vietnam, and they need money so she can travel to the United States to join her family. After learning of Hoa's story, the school children, including Raymond, decide to help Hoa and her family.

Discussion

Review the events of the story with students, making sure they not only can relate to the events of the story but also gain an understanding of the underlying feelings relevant to the story characters. Have students describe Hoa, pointing out the following.

- She is a new student in the school.
- She is new to the United States.
- She is just learning English.
- She wants to be a good student but doesn't understand everything the teacher says.
- She doesn't have the same kind of clothes as the other students.
- She misses her mother.
- She is very afraid.

- She does not know what to expect in her new school and country.

Ask students to think of times when they were in a new place (for example, school, class, city), and they were not sure what to do or how to feel. Ask them to discuss how they felt and how they wanted others to treat them. How did others help them?

Help students describe the native-born American students in Hoa's school. Tell them these students are very much like them, which means that these students probably have the following in common.

- They are familiar with the school.
- They know the language.
- They understand the teacher's directions.
- They have made friends in the school.
- They dress in typical U.S. clothes.
- They enjoy going to their school.
- They can speak regularly with their mother and father.
- They have not had students in their school who look or talk like Hoa and her sisters.
- They are unprepared to welcome students who look, dress, and talk in a different way than they do.

Discuss some of the unkind things Hoa's classmates did to Hoa.

- They made fun of her clothes.
- They made fun of her being quiet and her poor English.
- They did not try to make friends or play with her.
- Raymond threw a snow rock at her sister and fought with her.

Discuss with students how sometimes people are unkind to others who are different because they don't know them and have not had the opportunity to play, talk, or do things with them. Help students understand it is important to avoid conflict and fights with others. Discuss why students should avoid getting into fights with other students, including the following key points.

- When you fight, you cause others to feel bad.
- When you don't fight, you can avoid being punished.
- When you don't fight, you can do more fun things in and out of school.
- When you don't fight, you will have more friends to do fun things with.

- You can do the following to avoid fights with other students.
  - Say positive things to other students.
  - Offer help to students who need it.
  - Help new students learn the classwork or speak English.
  - Avoid laughing at or teasing new and different students.

Explain to students that there is something they could have done to keep Hoa and Raymond from fighting. Even students who were not directly involved in the conflict could help. Discuss each student or set of students as follows.

- **Raymond:** He likes to tease or bully Hoa. He needs to learn how to welcome Hoa into the school and say positive things to her.
- **Hoa:** When Raymond teases Hoa, she is first intimidated and hides behind her desk. But when Raymond hurts her sister, Hoa lashes out with aggression. Hoa needs to learn to be assertive and use her words to tell Raymond she doesn't like what he is doing, or tell a helpful adult if Raymond doesn't stop.
- **Students who laugh when Raymond teases Hoa:** Students should understand they are being unkind to Hoa and are encouraging Raymond to be unkind.
- **Students who ignore or do nothing when Raymond teases Hoa:** Students must know when they say or do nothing, bullies often keep bullying. Instead, students should try to discourage bullies by being kind to Hoa, helping her in the class, and playing with her during recess. Students could also tell Raymond it is unkind to tease Hoa or throw snow rocks at her sister.

Finally, discuss with students how everyone in the school feels when they decide to help Hoa and her family bring Hoa's mother to the United States. Point out that Hoa and her family finally bring their mother to live with them. Also, the students in the school learn about Vietnam and are very happy to help someone. Helping others often makes people happy.

Enactments

Engage the class in role-playing positive behaviors for each of the story characters (Raymond, Hoa, students who laugh, and students who do nothing).

Raymond, the taunting and bullying child: Teach Raymond to make positive statements to Hoa, and welcome her to the school and to participate in school activities. Following are some examples of positive statements and actions.

- "Hello, Hoa. Welcome to our school."
- "My name is Raymond. What is your name?"
- "I can help you speak English."
- "I can help you understand the teacher's directions."
- "Hoa, the teacher wants you to stand up and say your name."
- "Hoa, how do you say *teacher* in your language?"
- "Hoa, do you want to play ball with us when we go outside?" (Show students how to use body language with words for someone who doesn't speak English.)

Encourage students to identify other positive statements they could make to a new refugee or immigrant student in their class and school. For example, they could explain the school schedule, give a tour of the school, describe the class lessons and play activities, and so on. As the refugee student's English improves, he or she could teach classmates about his or her native country, activities, food, and language.

Hoa, the taunted child: Help students understand although it is hurtful when others tease or bully someone, there are several things they can do to possibly stop the teasing and bullying. These actions include the following.

- **Planful ignoring:** This means you do not look at the bully, you do not say anything to the bully, and you do not let the bully know you are aware of him or her or the behavior bothers you. In the story, although Hoa initially did not say anything back to her classmates, she hid her angry face (passive) and later she fought back (aggressive). Show students how to planfully ignore someone. That is when someone throws a barb or insult, and you say aloud you will not look at the person or say anything to the person. Then just walk away. Give students the opportunity to practice this behavior. For class enactments, make sure you or some other adult suggests a mild barb; downplay the barb and emphasize the student's constructive response.

- **Assertive statements:** Help children identify things they could say to a bully, such as the following.
    - "Please stop calling me *pajamas*; my name is Hoa."
    - "I don't like it when you laugh at me. Please stop it."
    - "Stop that. You are not nice when you call me names."

Encourage students to use their own words to tell someone they do not like what the person is doing and to stop it, and then say what the bully should do instead.

- **Tell someone and get help:** Tell students that finding a helpful authority figure is often the best option when dealing with a bully who will not stop after you've tried other things. In this story, the school principal is very helpful in stopping the bullying and fighting. Identify good authority figures such as the following.

    – School principal

    – Teacher

    – Guidance counselor

    – School nurse

    – Parent or guardian

    – Custodian

    – Classroom aide

    – School psychologist

Practice with students how they might relate to the problem (for example, "Raymond and the other children are laughing at me about my [clothes, speech, and so on], and it hurts my feelings. Could you help me?"). Note that instead of punishment, the principal in the story helps the students get to know each other, which eventually leads to friendship. Direct students to identify some things the bullies and bullied students might do to foster positive relationships. You or another adult might facilitate actions such as the following.

– Tutor a refugee student in English.

– Tutor a refugee student in academic content.

– Eat lunch with a refugee student and discuss food differences.

– Include a refugee student in play activities at recess.

– Share stories with a refugee student about respective families.

– Study the country of the refugee student (for example, Vietnam).

– Assign a bullying student to help present to the class content on a refugee student's country.

- Learn some words from a refugee student's language.
- Teach a refugee student some U.S. songs, games, dances, and so on.

Students who laugh and encourage taunting: Help students understand when they laugh at or encourage bullying, they are just as guilty as the bully and help the bullying to persist. Students must realize that although they did not initiate the bullying, they can be part of the solution. Help students identify positive actions to counter or mitigate unkind or bullying behavior, such as the following.

- Greet the taunted or refugee student with a smile and welcome him or her to the school.
- Introduce yourself and ask the student his or her name.
- Review the positive behaviors similar to those suggested for Raymond, the bully.

Students who ignore or do nothing when bullying occurs: This group of students is just as important as, if not more important than, the previous group. Undesired behaviors are more likely to persist when "good" people or students remain silent. Encourage all students to find a way to speak out in the interest of the group and the bullied student to do good. Help students identify some ways that they can speak out and help Hoa and her sisters, including the following.

- Tell Raymond what he said to Hoa was unkind.
- Tell Hoa to ignore Raymond.
- Invite Hoa to join you in lessons or play.
- If the bullying doesn't stop, encourage Hoa to tell a teacher or the principal she is being bullied.
- If Hoa is likely to be injured, report the problem to a responsible adult like a teacher or principal.
- Consider positive behaviors similar to those suggested for Raymond, the bully.

Real-Life Applications

Talk to the class about any new refugee or immigrant students in the school and how these new students might feel the way that Hoa felt. Prompt students to do the following.

- Speak kindly and introduce yourself to any new students.
- Welcome all students to the class or school.
- If appropriate, offer to help the new students.

- If others are teasing or taunting the new student, do not join in with the bullies.
- If others are teasing or taunting the new student, discuss this with the teacher.

If there are no refugee or immigrant children in the school, identify refugee or immigrant children in the community, city, state, or country. These might include young people from Somalia, Syria, Ecuador, Sudan, Russia, and so on. Select one group located closest to where you live. Help students find out something about that group, such as why they are refugees in the United States, their native language, their native clothes, and what their native schools are like.

Diversity Issues in This Story

Some Vietnamese believe the legend that they are the products of an Angelic Fairy and a Dragon King; thus, their society expects each person to possess the attributes of a good angel and a noble dragon, which explains the title of this book (Surat, 1989). Discuss with students the country of Vietnam, some aspects of its culture, and the differences from U.S. culture. Present a map of the world and locate Vietnam, positioned in the East, just south of China. Point out that for nearly one thousand years, the northern part of Vietnam was part of China and much of its traditional culture and ways of doing things in Vietnam are similar to those of the Chinese, such as aspects of religion (Buddhism), food, dress, and language.

In many Asian countries such as Vietnam, people consider children's behaviors to reflect on their family, and there is considerable emphasis on not bringing shame on the family. Within traditional families, parents teach children not to question adults and authority figures. Therefore, many children from Asian backgrounds may appear shy or anxious, not willing to express opinions or feelings in public.

The United States fought with Vietnam in that country's last war. When the war ended, many Vietnamese fled to the United States out of fear that the new government would harm them. These people were called *refugees*. Discuss with students how they think they would feel if they had to leave their home with one of their parents to come to a new country where nearly everything is different. Discuss with students a couple of obvious examples, such as food and school.

A popular food in Vietnam is *pho* (pronounced /fuh/), which is a soup consisting of broth, rice noodles, a few herbs, and meat, primarily either beef or chicken. Pho is a popular street food in Vietnam and in restaurants around the world. Obtain a picture of pho. Discuss with students the popular U.S. soups made with noodles, such as chicken noodle soup. If possible, obtain samples of pho (chicken or beef) for tasting, and have children describe similarities and differences.

Another example is the differences in schooling. In Vietnam, children go to school six days a week, Monday through Saturday, but only for half days. The school year is from September through May. As we noted in the story, children usually sit in small groups and respond in unison. Discuss with students how these practices differ from those in their U.S. school.

Extended Literature Activities

Use these literature activities to further ascertain students' understanding of the story and desired social-emotional learning skills. Students use their own words to retell the story and specify appropriate ways to respond. You also could use the annotated book list in the section Books on Responding to Aggression (page 145) to assign more relevant readings to individuals or groups. For each book, we suggest general elementary reading levels.

Retell the Story

Arrange students in small groups to recap the story together. Ensure everyone has a chance to participate in the retelling, or summarizing, of the story. After each group has retold the important points of the story in its own words, assign a follow-up task to the groups. This task could include drawing a strip of four or five pictures to depict the story, or students could generate an additional ending to the story (for example, the class invites Hoa's mother to visit, along with a translator so she can share about her trip to the United States). Students might also perform a simple drama for the class in which they demonstrate how they welcome Hoa to their class, show her about their class and school, and learn about Hoa's culture.

Extend the Story: More About Hoa

Assign students to small groups of five or six students. Try to make the groups diverse in terms of gender, race, ability, and so on. Give each group a large sheet of paper such as newsprint, butcher paper, or art paper. Direct groups to extend the story by telling something the class and Hoa did after the fair. For example, one group might decide Hoa brought a thank-you card to the class with a beautiful picture of her former country. Then the class drew pictures of things they liked best about the fair and put their pictures on the class bulletin or white board with Hoa's card as a centerpiece to the pictures. Allow each group to use large sheets of paper to illustrate its extended story. Encourage students to be creative in their stories, but also make sure they continue kind, thoughtful interactions with Hoa.

Additional Readings

The way students treat one another, particularly new students from diverse backgrounds, is an important theme in this story and is particularly pertinent in dealing with aggression. None of the following stories deal with physical aggression, but they lend themselves to discussions on how the story characters avoid hostility and aggression through acts of kindness and inclusion.

The Invisible Boy by Trudy Ludwig (2013; Primary)

This story continues the aggression theme with a few twists. It deals with relational aggression; all the students in the class systematically ignore and reject one student. Brian, the maligned student, is not from a diverse background; the other students just don't like him. A new student from Korea joins the class and other students briefly ridicule him. Brian, however, befriends the Korean student, and this simple act of kindness provides an entree for Brian and the new student's class acceptance. This story provides for a good discussion of how others, who failed to show kindness, treated the boys unfairly. You can also use this story during discussions on verbal or social aggression.

The Day the Crayons Quit by Drew Daywalt (2013; Primary)

This is a somewhat unusual book for the topic of aggression. However, the author describes Duncan, who wants to use his crayons to color, but each crayon gives a reason for quitting the crayon box because of feeling Duncan has unused or misused it. Duncan solves the problem with a beautiful picture including all the colors. You could use this as an analogy, assigning a different color to everyone in the class and noting how much more beautiful or fun it is when all are valued and included.

Those Shoes by Maribeth Boelts (2007; Elementary)

Unkind teasing and peer ridicule over his shoes spurs Jeremy to commit an extraordinary act of kindness for one of his classmates. A discussion of Jeremy's empathic, rather than angry and aggressive, actions is relevant to this theme.

The Name Jar by Yangsook Choi (2001; Elementary)

This book gives another look at students responding more compassionately toward an ethnic-minority new student. We feature *The Name Jar* in another section of this book (see page 98), but you could revisit it here. Emphasize how far, although a bit misguided, the students are willing to go to help their new classmate from a different country. Discuss further with students the things they could do to help classmates, regardless of diverse backgrounds.

All Are Welcome by Alexandra Penfold and Suzanne Kaufman (2019; Elementary)

This is a simply written and inviting book you can use as follow-up reading for this theme. It depicts children from all backgrounds and conditions as being welcomed into the community.

Action Project: Our Special Guest

Identify a recent refugee or immigrant from your community who is willing to come to your class to talk about the country he or she left, and why he or she came to the United States. Prepare students with a set of questions they might ask the guest (for example, "What are some of your favorite things about your former country?" "What are some of the things you like about the United States?" "How are schools the same or different?" and so on). Review the questions with students beforehand and how they will welcome and accommodate their guest.

Responding to Verbal Aggression

Like physical aggression, verbal aggression is intended to inflict harm. The injury may not be immediately obvious but can be quite damaging. In this section, we group several related terms of aggression (Donoghue & Rai-Hawrylak, 2016). *Verbal aggression* can include teasing, name calling, or insulting others. It also can include threats to harm someone such as, "I'm going to fight you after school." *Social* or *relational aggression* (Risser, 2013) occurs when someone tries to cause harm to a relationship. Often the effort is to get someone or a group of people to not like another person or group. Another related type of aggression is *cyber aggression*, in which an individual uses technology (such as the internet or a cell phone) to post negative, embarrassing, or threatening things about someone or a group of people (Powell & Ladd, 2010). *Nonverbal* or *psychological aggression* also includes situations in which an individual intentionally refuses to speak to or respond to another person to offend them.

Intentionality and frequency are important factors for determining aggressive behavior. An occasional teasing episode or threat is common among children. Parents, teachers, and school clinicians (for example, psychologists, social workers, and counselors) might consider it developmental or typical of most school children. Psychologists who study teasing and aggression in students observe these behaviors varying within this population according to age, often peaking in mid-adolescence (thirteen to fifteen years old), and according to the intensity of the peer relationship (Heyes, 2020). Repeated taunting, however, with the obvious intent of social or psychological harm, is aggressive behavior. Racially and ethnically diverse children also are at risk of others subjecting them through social isolation or abuse, and their risk is higher if their peer group sees them as outsiders rather than group members (Palmer et al., 2015).

The interventions to counter verbal and related aggression are similar to those for physical aggression. Because these latter forms are subtler, you and other adults must exercise greater vigilance and concern for abused students. We endorse a whole-school or classroom approach through alternatives to aggressive behaviors (Donoghue & Raia-Hawrylak, 2016), especially within a culturally diverse context.

Literature on Responding to Verbal Aggression

Words do hurt and can cause lasting damage. Contrition and wise, prompt actions are powerful antidotes. The following readings highlight these points.

Book: *The First Strawberries: A Cherokee Story* Retold by Joseph Bruchac (1993)

As noted previously, the steps for introducing each book to the class include present the story, clarify story concepts through discussion, clarify the features of the desired behaviors through enactments, practice the desired behaviors through real-life applications, respond appropriately to issues of diversity, and provide extension activities to maintain the desired behaviors.

Present the Story

Read the story to and with the class. If students have a hard copy of the book or if they can access the story online, they can follow along as you read aloud. If not, students can simply listen, as you read.

Story Synopsis

This Native American (Cherokee) legend started long ago as a means to explain how strawberries came to be. In this story, the first man and woman on earth are married. When the man speaks harshly to the woman, she becomes angry and decides to leave. The husband is sorry about his unkind words and does not want to lose his wife, so he follows her. During her walk, the wife discovers wonderful strawberries the sun has sent. The wife shares the strawberries with her repentant husband, and they reunite as a couple. The strawberries are a symbol of friendship and respect.

Discussion

Although this is a short, easy-to-read story, the main concepts are appropriate for discussion among all ages, accordingly. Begin by pointing out this story is one of many old myths Native Americans and others use to explain the world. Embedded in many of these stories are suggestions of how people might behave to live better lives. Although simply told, this is a beautiful, universal creation story. The husband and wife live in an idyllic garden setting where they help and enjoy each other. Review the chronology of the story from the perspective of each character. You might choose to illustrate this with a timeline of the following events.

1. The husband comes home from hunting, looking for a prepared meal.
    a. How might a day of hunting make the husband feel physically? (He feels tired and hungry.)
    b. As the husband walks home, what might he be thinking about that would make him happy? (He wants a good hot meal and a quiet evening with his wife.)
    c. How do you think he felt when he did not see the meal he was looking for? (He felt disappointed and angry.) What do you think he might have said to himself to lead him to feel this way? ("I've been working all day to feed us; at least she could work to prepare the food.")

2. The wife had not prepared the meal but picked flowers.
    a. What do you think made the wife want to pick flowers? (Probably the beauty of the area where they live; she probably wants to please the husband and may have lost track of the time.)
    b. How do you think she felt as she was picking the flowers? (Probably happy; she might have been thinking that these flowers would make the husband happy.)

3. The husband speaks to the wife in anger.
    a. Why do you think the husband uses harsh words? (He is hungry and annoyed that she hasn't prepared his meal.)
    b. Do you think he wants to make the wife angry? (No, he probably thinks he would get his food faster.)

4. The wife responds to the husband's words with anger and walks away.

a. Why does the wife walk away? (The husband uses unkind words. She is angry.)

b. What thoughts do you think cause the wife to become angry? (She may think the husband does not like her. He does not appreciate that she is trying to do something nice for him.)

5. The husband follows the wife but cannot catch her.

    a. How do you think the husband feels when he is following the wife? (He's probably afraid he might lose her.)

    b. How does the husband feel about the unkind words he uses with the wife? (Walking probably helps him quiet down. When he quiets down, he begins to feel sorry and sad.)

6. The sun agrees to help the husband get the wife back.

    a. Why does the sun agree to help the husband get the wife back? (The sun sees that the husband is genuinely sorry for being unkind to the wife. The sun does not want the husband and wife to be in conflict.)

7. The sun helps by using its rays to cause berries to grow.

    a. What are the berries that the sun helps produce for the wife? (It produces raspberries, blueberries, blackberries, and strawberries.)

    b. Why does the wife not stop until she sees the strawberries? (She is too angry to stop until the strawberries glow like fire before her.)

8. The wife stops to pick some of the berries.

    a. How does the wife react to the berries? (She loves the taste of the berries, and they made her happy.)

    b. What does she decide to do with the berries? (Share them with the husband)

9. The husband catches up with the wife.

    a. What does the husband say to the wife? (He apologizes for his harsh words.)

    b. What does the wife do? (She shares the strawberries.)

10. What do strawberries represent for the Cherokee people?

    a. We should be kind to each other.

  b. Friendship and respect are as sweet as ripe red strawberries.

How does this wife respond to the aggression? Review what the wife does when the husband uses harsh words with her.

1. She tells the husband that she does not like what he said. She tells him his words hurt her.

    a. Discuss why it is good to let someone know when something he or she does or says hurts your feelings or offends you.

    b. Help students think about what would have happened if the wife decided to say unkind things to make the husband feel bad. (An argument or bad feelings would escalate.)

2. She walks away.

    a. Discuss with students why sometimes it is good to walk away when someone says unkind things to you.

    - You might need to get away from a dangerous situation.
    - It gives you an opportunity to think about what you did and helps you cool down.
    - Walking is a good exercise when you are angry.

After discussing the events of the story and the wife's response to the aggression, finish the class discussion by talking about what others might do in this situation, even if they are not directly involved in the conflict. You might remind students what they learned through the discussion of the students who either laughed or did nothing to help Hoa in *Angel Child, Dragon Child*. In this story, the sun could represent the role of a good friend or observer who helps a friend (or friends) in conflict. The sun does not tell the husband he is right to be angry with the wife; instead, the sun tells him it will help him when he says he's sorry and wants the wife back. The sun does all the following to help mediate the conflict.

- Did not tell the husband he was right to use harsh words with the wife
- Encouraged the husband to apologize for being unkind
- Helped the wife to slow down so the husband could catch up to her and apologize

- Used the strawberries to remind the wife of how happy she had been with the husband, so she would accept the husband's apology
- Helped the wife realize it would be good to accept the husband's apology

Similarly, as good friends or helpful observers, students could be peacemakers by helping their classmates and friends avoid hurting others. As teachers and other supervising adults, do not encourage students to insert themselves into dangerous situations. On the other hand, educators should help students understand they are not being good friends if they encourage or let a friend hurt someone else. The sun is being a good friend to the husband and wife because it finds ways to help the couple apologize and be good to each other. Some of the things good friends would do include the following.

- Encourage your friend and the other person not to remain angry.
- Help your friend think of ways to apologize to the other person for some unkind word or deed.
- Help your friend realize that everyone is happier when they are friends than when they are enemies.
- Help your friend accept the apology and forgive the other person if both want to avoid hurting each other.

Enactments

Help students identify and act out appropriate responses to aggression, as in this story. Begin with the wife's responses. Point out that becoming angry when someone says or does something unkind is normal. However, students should learn to control or channel their anger so they can avoid increasing the aggression or conflict.

1. **The wife** makes a good (assertive) statement by telling the husband his words hurt her.

    a. Help students to identify ways to tell someone they do not like or are hurt by what the person said or did. For example:

    - "Please don't say that to me; it hurts my feelings."
    - "I don't like it when you call me that name."
    - "My name is _____. Please call me that name or don't call me at all."
    - "Please don't say that to me; it's rude."

- "Please stop."
- "Don't do that; I don't like it."
- "Stop it!"

2. **The wife** walks away from a hurtful situation.
   a. Discuss with students why there are times when it's good to walk away from a situation.
      - When someone is trying to hurt you with their words
      - When someone is trying to hurt you physically
      - To avoid saying mean or unkind things to the other person
      - To get help or advice from someone who can help solve the conflict

3. **The husband** feels sorry for his hurtful words and apologizes.
   a. Help students understand why the husband's apology is a good one. The husband follows these steps.
      - He genuinely feels bad about his unkind words.
      - He tells the wife he is wrong.
      - He asks her to forgive him for his angry words.
      - He does not make excuses for being unkind to her.
      - He does not tell her it was her fault he was angry or unkind.

4. **The sun** helps the husband and wife let go of their anger and be friends again. Discuss with students the steps they could take to help two quarreling people resolve their conflict. Some steps to take include the following.
   a. Tell the person it is better to be friends.
   b. Find out if the person is truly sorry for his or her unkind words or deeds.
   c. Tell the person to apologize.
   d. Tell the person not to make excuses for his or her wrongdoing (for example, "I was angry because I was hungry").
   e. Tell the person not to blame the other person for his or her angry words or deeds (for example, "I was angry because you were late").

To further illustrate possible actions under these circumstances, give students the following scenarios and discuss how they might respond. Older students can discuss these scenes in small groups and then present to the entire class. Prior to discussing these scenes, point out that fighting is not an option for what the person should do.

- **Scene 1:** Ravi is a Native American who is new to his class. He used to live on a reservation, but his family moved to the city where he attends a public school. Ravi is eight years old and in third grade. He is a handsome boy with very long hair, but the other students tease him about his hair. He is the only boy in the school with long hair. He wants to cut his hair, but his father tells him the men in his culture wear their hair long as a symbol of manhood and strength. Ravi tries to remember this and takes pride in his hair, but the next day at school, Brandon starts teasing him and calls him Ramona, which is a girl's name. The teasing hurts Ravi's feelings. He does not like to be called Ramona. What does Ravi do?

Help students identify some good (assertive) statements Ravi can make that might cause Brandon to stop teasing him. They also might consider some way to use humor in such a way that Ravi makes fun of himself and gives Brandon the impression that his taunting doesn't hurt him. For example, if Brandon teases Ravi about being a slow runner, Ravi can laugh and say "Yep, I've got slow feet. You want to race?" Another option is for Ravi to invite Brandon to share an activity in which Ravi excels, such as making paper sculptures or doing mathematics. There is no guarantee that these or other assertive actions would be successful, but students should consider trying some alternatives before seeking adult assistance. Counter aggression is not an option.

- **Scene 2:** Ravi has been unable to get Brandon to stop teasing him. The next day on the playground, Brandon and four other boys in the class gather around Ravi and start calling him Ramona. Brandon tells Ravi he thinks Ravi is a girl, and he should pull Ravi's hair to see if it feels like girl's hair. The other boys laugh and start telling Brandon he should pull Ravi's hair. The other boys start chanting, "Pull it, pull it!" Other students stop playing on the playground and gather around Ravi, Brandon, and the chanting students. What does Ravi do?

Help students understand this situation could possibly cause someone to get hurt. Ravi should walk away. He also should go to an authority figure (for example, a teacher, playground supervisor, or principal) for help. Discuss with students the kind of help the adult might give. Refer back to the *Angel Child, Dragon Child* story to think about ways the principal helped Hoa. Point out that simply punishing the taunting student is not enough. The desired goal is for genuine remorse and for students to develop wholesome relationships.

- **Scene 3:** In the previous scene in which Brandon and his other friends are taunting Ravi and threatening to pull his hair, several students gather around but are not chanting. They are just watching. One student, Rufus, has been a good friend of Brandon's. Rufus played often with Brandon and knew Brandon could be lots of fun. He did not want to see his friend get in trouble. Rufus does not know Ravi, but he knows Ravi is a new student in the class. He knows Ravi has some special talents and does not want to see him leave his school. What does Rufus do?

Suggest a few peacemaking options for Rufus, such as quietly asking Ravi if he wants to play kickball with him, or asking Brandon to come play kickball with him, and reminding Brandon that taunting Ravi will get him in trouble. He also could talk Brandon into inviting Ravi to play kickball with him and the other students on the playground, or ask Ravi to teach him and other interested classmates how to play lacrosse.

- **Scene 4:** Ravi's father is a highly recognized storyteller and college professor. The principal invites Ravi's father to tell the students some stories about his native culture, and he plays some instruments while telling his stories. Ravi's father has written several books for young people about his culture. He tells students about Ravi's name and shows them how Ravi can use paints to illustrate his stories as he tells them. The students in Ravi's class are fascinated with Ravi's father's stories, especially Brandon. Brandon is a good artist. He likes to draw and would love to illustrate one of Ravi's father's stories the way Ravi does. Brandon apologizes to Ravi and asks him if he could draw one of his father's stories with him. What does Ravi do?

Discuss with students the way Ravi should respond to Brandon's request. He should kindly agree to this request. Help students understand this is now a respectful friendship.

Real-Life Applications

Give each student a piece of paper, and ask them to title it *Responding to Aggression*. If possible, have a small picture of a Native American woman in an upper corner of the paper to remind the student of the story for this activity: *The First Strawberries: A Cherokee Story* (Bruchac, 1993). Tell students to think of a time in the last week when someone said something they felt was unkind or hurtful. On the paper, have students write answers to the following three questions.

1. "What did you say?"
2. "What did you do?"
3. "Did the person say, 'I'm sorry'?"

On the following day, give students a similar sheet of paper with the following questions. Ask students to think about a time when they said or did something unkind to someone, and the person told them they hurt his or her feelings. On the paper, ask students to answer the following three questions.

1. "How did you feel when the person said you hurt his or her feelings?"
2. "What did you say to that person?"
3. "Did the person accept your apology?"

Create a one-week *counting club*. As members of this club, ask students to observe themselves for one week and count the number of times they act appropriately when someone says or does something unkind to them, and the number of times they apologize to someone for something that they said or did that caused someone else to feel bad. Students do not have to report their numbers to the entire class; they can simply turn their numbers in to you. At the end of the week, you can report the numbers for the entire class and then congratulate students for their thoughtfulness in acting kindly toward others.

Diversity Issues in This Story

Although Native Americans make up approximately 1.3 percent of the population of the United States (U.S. Census Bureau, 2019), they are a powerful factor in the history and culture of U.S. storytelling. Storytelling is an important feature of Native American life, and many of these stories are renditions of myths or legends, such as the story for this activity. Many of these stories highlight the environment and emphasize the importance of harmony with others and nature. Other key features reflect generosity toward others and contributing to the common good of the group.

The rich resource of stories, books, and plays is an effective way for teachers and others to help students learn about and appreciate Native American culture. Native American culture, like every other culture, is made up of several different groups (for example, Cherokee, Hopi, Navajo, Cheyenne, Seminole, and so on), and each group has unique traditions. One highly recommended source is the book *Pushing Up the Sky: Seven Native American Plays for Children* by Joseph Bruchac (2019). This book contains seven different plays, each based on a different Native American tradition, for children to enact. Another entertaining book that gives the kaleidoscope of Native American life is *The Girl Who Helped Thunder and Other Native American Folktales* by James Bruchac and Joseph Bruchac (2008). In addition to retelling creation myths and animal stories, the book depicts the art and artifacts of various native peoples. For example, in addition to learning how the buffalo saved the Lakota people, the learner is enlightened about the specific patterns of native peoples' art and artifacts (for example, Navajo-style rugs).

Beyond myths, legends, and traditions, it is important students learn of the authentic history of Native Americans. These stories include the tragic *Trail of Tears* by Joseph Bruchac (1999), which tells about the Cherokee for primary students, or the more comprehensive version for older learners, *Trail of Tears: A Captivating Guide to the Forced Removals of Cherokee, Muscogee Creek, Seminole, Chickasaw, and Choctaw Nations* by Captivating History (2018), which details the painful forced removals of other Native American nations. Other nonfiction books that give an authentic picture of the historical Native American include *A Boy Called Slow: The True Story of Sitting Bull* by Joseph Bruchac (1994), an inspiring coming-of-age story communicating the importance of effort in bringing about success. The heroic deeds of the Navajo code talkers who helped save countless American lives during World War II are memorialized in the fictional account *Code Talker: A Novel About the Navajo Marines of World War Two* by Joseph Bruchac (2005), as well as a nonfiction work by J. Patrick Lewis (2016) called *The Navajo Code Talkers*.

Some exciting fiction, such as *Children of the Longhouse* by Joseph Bruchac (1998), gives an in-depth look at historical Native American life, but other stories, such as *The Warriors* by Joseph Bruchac (2003), give a relatively contemporary view of Native American culture as young people struggle with the stressors of navigating two cultures: traditional Native American and mainstream U.S. culture. Both of these stories feature lacrosse, a sport integral to Native American life, as well as the internal conflict the characters experience while trying to be true to peaceful, prosocial values of their culture.

Extended Literature Activities

Use these literature activities to further ascertain students' understanding of the story and desired social-emotional learning skills. Students use their own words to retell the story and specify appropriate ways to respond. You also could use the annotated book list in the section Books on Responding to Aggression (page 145) to assign more relevant readings to individuals or groups. For each book, we suggest general elementary reading levels.

Retell the Story

Help students retell the story using their own words. Allow students to draw pictures depicting the story, giving special attention to pictures of the berries. Have students identify their favorite berries and note the special importance of strawberries as symbols of friendship and respect.

Extend the Story: My Web Design

Assign student pairs who are diverse across gender, race, ability, and so on. Tell students each of them is a web designer who will design a website page for their partner. Of course, these are not real websites. Give each student a long sheet of paper (11" × 17", if available) or two sheets of 8.5" × 11" paper. Ask students to decorate the "websites" and provide information about their assigned partner. They should make this website as attractive and positive as possible. Students should spend brief periods (allow them ten to fifteen minutes per day over a period of a few days, as needed) interviewing each other to find out important things each student wants to put on the website about his or her partner. Such items might include name, age, favorite hobbies, movies, school subjects, sports, food, games, books, and so on.

Have partners collaborate on the websites. Encourage students to make them extremely positive and then present their partners to the rest of the class. You should review the websites beforehand to ensure they are indeed kind and positive. This activity gives students opportunities to practice written language and positive peer behaviors. Primary students with limited writing skills could simply draw positive pictures about their partners and describe them to the class.

Additional Readings

The following stories are selected mainly for their focus on Native American history and culture. You can note and discuss aspects of receiving and responding to verbal aggression in each of the readings.

How Chipmunk Got His Stripes by Joseph Bruchac and James Bruchac (2003; Elementary)

Brown Squirrel wins a bet with Black Bear and teases Black Bear to his peril. What happens when a brown squirrel teases a black bear? This is one of the creation myths so prevalent in the Native American culture.

The Rough-Face Girl by Rafe Martin (1992; Upper Elementary)

This is a story of a young girl whose face becomes scarred from sitting by the fireplace to cook and do all the household chores for her older, hard-hearted sisters. However, these scars do not keep her from seeing beauty in the world or others from seeing the beauty within her. Discuss with students how they could consider this a Native American *Cinderella* story. Discuss how the two tales are alike and different. Help students pick out the features of this book that are uniquely Native American, and identify aspects or main ideas of both stories that are the same. Help students note the similarities between cultures.

Soft Rain: A Story of the Cherokee Trail of Tears by Cornelia Cornelissen (1998; Upper Elementary)

This story depicts a bleak period in American history. It gives a personal account of a young girl's painful experience of enduring the hardship of the Trail of Tears. It is a story of courage and hope as the young girl reunites with her family. This is an important story in understanding and developing an appreciation for all groups in the United States.

For additional readings, note the suggestions we give in the previous section in the discussion of diversity issues.

Action Project: More About Tribal Nations

If possible, invite someone with a Native American background to class to share information about his or her particular Native American nation, traditional storytelling, and specific current interests or goals of this group. Have students prepare (teacher-preapproved and practiced) questions for the Native American guest in advance of the visit.

Books on Responding to Aggression

Figure 6.1 (page 146) offers a list of books featured in this chapter, as well as additional diverse books that include aspects of appropriate responses to aggression. Read these books as a class and discuss some of the themes. When appropriate, encourage students to read the books independently and then share the books with the rest of the class, noting how story characters respond to aggression.

Conclusion

As children grow, they must learn to manage conflict, which is common to the human experience. In this chapter, we discussed conflict in the form of aggression, noting its prevalent forms (physical and verbal). To illustrate these concepts, we used books highlighting Vietnamese and Native American cultures.

Racial and ethnic differences can be a major factor in triggering aggression toward others, especially if we have little or no information or if we are misinformed. A major aspect about the instruction to counter aggression under these conditions is to increase accurate information and stress similarities versus differences. Students need to learn that we all have a lot to gain from harmonious encounters with others, even if initially significant differences appear.

Title	Author	Story Summary
Primary		
The Day the Crayons Quit	Drew Daywalt (2013)	A child includes all the colors from a crayon box to make especially beautiful pictures.
The Invisible Boy	Trudy Ludwig (2013)	An ignored and rejected boy manages to make friends in his class.
Elementary		
All Are Welcome	Alexandra Penfold and Suzanne Kaufman (2019)	This book includes and embraces children with all backgrounds and abilities.
How Chipmunk Got His Stripes	Joseph Bruchac and James Bruchac (2003)	This creation myth is about how the chipmunk got its stripe.
Mufaro's Beautiful Daughters: An African Tale	John Steptoe (1987)	This African American Cinderella tale demonstrates the rewards of gentle words.
The Girl Who Helped Thunder and Other Native American Folktales	James Bruchac and Joseph Bruchac (2008)	This book features many Native American myths and aspects of the culture.
The Name Jar	Yangsook Choi (2001)	A young Korean girl decides her native name is enough.
The Woman Who Outshone the Sun: The Legend of Lucia Zenteno	Alejandro Cruz Martinez (1991)	Villagers taunt a kind woman. The woman leaves because of the taunting, and then the villagers greatly miss her and work to get her back.
Those Shoes	Maribeth Boelts (2007)	A young boy experiences the joy of sharing, even at his own expense.
Upper Elementary		
Children of the Longhouse	Joseph Bruchac (1996)	This book offers a historical portrait of Native American life.
Pushing Up the Sky: Seven Native American Plays for Children	Joseph Bruchac (2019)	This is a book of plays about different Native American traditions.
The Rough-Face Girl	Rafe Martin (1992)	This is a Native American Cinderella story.
A Boy Called Slow: The True Story of Sitting Bull	Joseph Bruchac (1994)	This is a Native American coming-of-age story.
The Warriors	Joseph Bruchac (2003)	This book offers a contemporary view of Native American life.
The Trail of Tears	Joseph Bruchac (1999)	This book features the relocation of Native Americans in the United States, with a focus on the Cherokee nation.

Figure 6.1: Books on responding to aggression.

Visit ***go.SolutionTree.com/diversityandequity*** *for a free reproducible version of this figure.*

Verbal aggression for students often presents itself as teasing but may become quite painful if it eventually emerges into bullying. Counter aggression is the least effective response for resolving this problem. We recommend a range of alternative actions that may ultimately culminate in the need to acquire adult intervention. Teachers and other school personnel need to be allies with students in addressing this problem and the students' social-emotional growth.

Chapter Reflections

Individually or with a collaborative group, review and discuss the following questions to reflect on your learning in this chapter.

1. Why do you think counter aggression is so popular when we face physically or verbally aggressive situations?

2. Are you more or less likely to be harmed if you aggress when threatened?

3. When you are angry or frustrated with students, what kind of model do you present? Why? How successful are you in achieving your goals?

4. How do you advise students to deal with aggression? Fight back? Ignore it? Stop tattling? Get tough? Something else?

5. What does it mean to use brains over brawn?

6. Do you think you can teach children to be thoughtful about conflict situations? Why should you? How should you?

chapter seven

Playing and Working Cooperatively With Others

Playing cooperatively with others is an important skill for all students to master. From the time children begin noticing peers in their environment, it is natural for them to want to engage. Often, babies and very young toddlers may encounter difficulty with peers because they have not yet developed the skills of sharing and playing cooperatively. For very young children (birth to three years), researchers use cooperative play behaviors, such as joint (shared) attention, turn taking, responding to overtures from others, conversation making, and so on, as markers of typical and atypical development (Hughett, Kohler, & Raschke, 2013).

Peers often isolate or reject younger children who lack desired cooperative behaviors, which can cause them to fail to develop key social communication skills (Hughett et al., 2013). Less cooperative older learners tend to be more negative and acquire fewer prosocial behaviors (Choi et al., 2011; Zentall et al., 2011). These children might be diagnosed with disabilities (Hughett et al., 2013; Yu, Ostrosky, & Fowler, 2014), as educational risks (Zentall et al., 2011), or as social bullies (Choi et al., 2011). Children who fail to master the requisite cooperative play and learning behaviors fall along a continuum from individuals with disabilities to those who are intellectually gifted, but nevertheless are at risk for unfavorable outcomes such as peer marginalization or antisocial outcomes.

Caregivers and preschool teachers intentionally seek to promote cooperative play because it is so vital to a child's success in many other settings. The ability to play cooperatively in early childhood has implications not only for social acceptance but also for successful group-oriented work skills, both in and out of school. There is, however, encouraging research showing that educators can teach preschool (Hughett et al., 2013) and elementary students (Choi et al., 2011) to develop more cooperative peer-interaction skills. For example, Hughett and colleagues (2013) taught preschool students with developmental delays to stay within a play group, to play with the other students in the group, and to talk with the students. Choi and colleagues (2011) find that elementary students who educators had taught to participate in cooperative learning classrooms display more cooperative prosocial behaviors than their peers in noncooperative learning classrooms. We recommend activities in this chapter consistent with these strategies on playing cooperatively.

Playing and Working Cooperatively Across Age Groups

Choi and colleagues (2011) suggest *cooperation* occurs when individuals "obtain resources through members' prosocial behaviors, and use the resources to promote the success of others and the common good" (p. 443). Under these conditions, the individual is not trying to exert influence over the group for his or her own personal gain. Group members recognize when everyone cooperates, everyone benefits. Whether the situation calls for cooperative play or cooperative work, the central tenets are the same (Cartledge & Kleefeld, 2009, 2010).

First, students must be familiar with the rules of the game or the directions for the task at hand. If students do not entirely understand what teachers expect of them, they may be unable to follow through in a successful manner. This may elicit a negative reaction from their peers. Often, if a student makes a mistake or doesn't understand the game, others may taunt the student or not choose him or her for future games. It's important for teachers to give students every opportunity to fully engage with the task.

Next, once students understand the rules and the task completely, they should put forth their best effort, follow the rules, and be fair. *Being fair* means not cheating or cutting corners, and it may be necessary for teachers to clarify this aspect to younger students. Sometimes it is tempting to cheat and put the odds in one's favor, but doing this eventually may lead to peer rejection. In addition to interacting fairly, students must learn the importance of putting forth one's best effort and maintaining a positive attitude regardless of group activity outcome. The desire to win or be successful is universal, but when people fall short, being gracious and using kind words are important for social-emotional development. Teach students to find ways to congratulate the winner and to accept congratulations graciously. This goes a long way to promote positive peer relationships that require group cooperation.

Children's cooperative play typically occurs within one's age group. If, however, same-age peers are unavailable, circumstances may require cross-age cooperative play. This play may be *lateral* (meaning children view themselves as equals, assuming similar roles) or the play may be *hierarchical* (where some players take on a mentoring or teaching role to aid the younger or less-skilled players).

A common example of the latter in the social-emotional learning research is to pair older or more-skilled students to teach cooperative play behaviors to the younger or less-skilled students (Hughett et al., 2013). Under these conditions, teach students how to promote, encourage, and reinforce other students in cooperative play skills. Peer trainers can help these students develop patience and gradually coach others into more cooperative play. Impatience is quite common among students toward their younger and less-skilled peers. Although the principal story in this activity (*When Jackie and Hank Met*) centers on two highly talented players, patience and understanding are key to making this a winning outcome for all (Fishman, 2012).

Literature on Playing and Working Cooperatively Across Age Groups

Cooperation in work or play often seems counterproductive to self-interest, but these stories help show that cooperation can benefit everyone. The readings in this chapter present cooperation as not only an alternative to conflict but also the preferred means to (1) winning and (2) school success.

Book: *When Jackie and Hank Met* by Cathy Goldberg Fishman (2012)

As noted previously, the steps for introducing each book to the class include present the story, clarify story concepts through discussion, clarify the features of the desired behaviors through enactments, practice the desired behaviors through real-life applications, respond appropriately to issues of diversity, and provide extension activities to maintain the desired behaviors.

Present the Story

Read the story to and with the class. If students have a hard copy of the book or if they can access the story online, they can follow along as you read aloud. If not, students can simply listen as you read.

Story Synopsis

This story recounts the common life experiences of two well-known figures in the history of American baseball: Jack Roosevelt Robinson and Henry

Benjamin Greenberg, also known as Jackie and Hank. The story begins by describing their respective childhoods, detailing that although their home lives, geographic locations, and family roots were different, they shared a love of baseball and also many similar experiences of racism, social isolation, and discrimination. The author follows the men from school age through young adulthood and describes each of their paths into both the military and the profession of baseball, accordingly. Each story is told separately but describes many common hardships due to lack of acceptance of Jewish people and people of color.

From childhood through adulthood, both young men were subjected to verbal taunts. According to the story as told by Fishman (2012), the two ball players literally collided on the field. They were separated no more. At the sight of the collision, the crowd urged Jackie and Hank to "Fight! Fight! Fight!" But they did not fight. They picked themselves up and kept playing the game. Later, Hank recalled having experienced similar hardships and obstacles to Jackie's. Because he was older, with more experience and time in the league, he supported the younger Jackie by encouraging him to, "Stick in there." That kinship and advice impressed and helped Jackie. He later told a reporter that, "Class tells. It sticks out all over Mr. Greenberg." The men were friends from then on. Each went on their life paths, with Hank later managing the Cleveland Indians and Jackie serving on the board of the National Association for the Advancement of Colored People (NAACP). Still, through their later experiences, the two men continued to work toward equality for all.

Discussion

The book, *When Jackie and Hank Met*, provides a rich story from which educators can derive many different topics of discussion, including the history of segregation in the United States, racial and religious discrimination, and perseverance in the face of hardship. We will address some of these themes in chapter 8 (page 169). However, this activity focuses more on the friendship between the two men and how their age and experience differences may have helped create a context for mentorship as well as friendship. That is, how can students help others, even those with different backgrounds, learn important things about getting along with others and be their friends?

To begin the discussion, ask the students to contribute examples from their own lives when someone older or with more experience helped, supported, guided, or mentored them in some way. Examples include things like an older sibling, relative, or friend who showed them how to do something interesting or fun, such as riding a bike, playing a new card game, or speaking another language. Let students generate their ideas on a form, like the example in figure 7.1. In the left-hand column, name the person, and in the right-hand column, write how having that support made the student feel.

Someone Who Helped Me	How It Makes Me Feel
My older sister showed me how to play a game on her phone.	I feel happy because I can play the game now.
My dad taught me to refill the air in my bike tires.	I feel I can take care of my bike better on my own and maybe help someone else who has a flat tire.
My cousin lives in a neighborhood with many Spanish-speaking people. She taught me to say friendly and helpful phrases so I could talk and play with the children who live there.	I feel proud of myself and less shy because I know I can talk with the neighborhood people.

Figure 7.1: Someone helped me example.

Everyone has been in situations when they have been a novice or rookie. Common feelings that accompany circumstances such as these may include anxiety, fear, shame, nervousness, or shyness. When you feel these emotions, it is more difficult to be successful in those settings. The support of someone who has "been there and done that" can be invaluable. Ask students to turn the tables and share examples, such as those in figure 7.2, of when they may have served as a mentor or coach to a younger person or someone with less experience than them, and how helping another person made them feel.

One Time, I Helped . . .	How It Makes Me Feel
My younger brother learn to play board games	I feel like a good big brother for teaching him how to play checkers.
A kindergarten student build a tower out of blocks	I feel I can work with a younger friend to build blocks.
A young girl on the playground because she was sad and no one asked her to play; she wanted to play kickball but didn't know how.	I can be a good friend because I taught her how to play kickball. Now the other kids invite her to play.

Figure 7.2: I helped someone play example.

Enactments

Continue the previous activity, directing students to describe how they helped or cooperated with a sibling or playmate. Make sure students explain these five things: (1) what they wanted to do with the other person, (2) how they approached the other person and what they said, (3) how long they played, (4) how the playmate felt, and (5) how they felt.

Real-Life Applications

Teaching and learning in a mentor-mentee relationship can be a very rewarding experience for students in grades K–5. The following activity allows students to engage in both sides of the relationship. First, divide the class in half. Each group will learn a previously untaught skill to later share with their mentee (a student from the other group). Decide on a novel skill to teach each group. This can be a crafting skill like constructing a paper star, a new type of writing such as cursive handwriting, or a communication skill such as the American Sign Language (ASL) associated with a well-known song like "Happy Birthday." Teach each group a different skill; students should be able to master the skills within a short time frame (for example, fifteen to twenty minutes). After teaching the groups their respective skills, pair a student from each group together to teach each other the new skills they just learned. The pairs should take turns in the mentor and mentee roles and learn the appropriate behaviors associated with being a good mentor and a good mentee. It is ideal to pair together students who are from different backgrounds or who do not appear to share a great deal in common. This activity may serve as an opportunity for students to get to know someone different from themselves. Emphasize the following points about each role.

To be a good mentor, do the following.

1. Break down the skill you will teach into manageable parts.
2. Practice each step until it is easy to show and explain.
3. Tell your mentee what he or she did right and what he or she needs to work on.

To be a good mentee, do the following.

1. Listen carefully to the instructions.
2. Try your best to do what your mentor shows you.
3. Thank your mentor for helping you.

When students are practicing their new skills in pairs, you might want to circulate around the room with these checklists of good mentor and mentee behaviors. When you observe students being good mentors or good mentees, provide a positive statement or a checkmark to indicate they are performing the activity correctly.

Diversity Issues in This Story

This story presents diversity issues related to the experiential commonalities between baseball players who are Black and Jewish. Black and Jewish Americans have a history of experiencing racial discrimination and prejudicial practices in the United States. The story spans the pre–civil rights era, through the civil rights movement, and beyond. Even though Jackie and Hank had different skin colors and ethnicities, they both experienced a lack of access to many resources afforded to non-Jewish Whites. Further, each had been on the receiving end of aggression and violence in speech and action.

Additionally, throughout U.S. history, many other groups, such as Native Americans, Asians, Latinx, as well as some ethnic Whites (such as Eastern and Southern Europeans), have encountered similar obstacles. The story of

Jackie and Hank shows that discrimination is not specific to one ethnic, racial, or religious group, but the threads of oppression are a shared experience of many or most types of people. This poor treatment harms everyone. Teach students to help others so everyone can lead better lives.

Extended Literature Activities

Use these literature activities to further ascertain students' understanding of the story and desired social-emotional learning skills. Students use their own words to retell the story and specify appropriate ways to respond. You also could use the annotated book list in the section Books on Playing and Working Cooperatively With Others (page 166) to assign more relevant readings to individuals or groups. For each book, we suggest general elementary reading levels.

Retell the Story

After reading the story as a group and engaging in discussion and real-life applications, organize students into small groups for retelling. Each student in the group should contribute to the retelling of the story. Encourage each group member to identify one main event for either Jackie or Hank. In turn, ask other group members to search the book for a similar or shared event for the other character. For example, if one student recalls that other players sometimes yelled at and taunted Jackie during games, another student can share that Hank shared a similar experience when as a child, children threw rocks at him. Students should work as a group to locate key details in the story that reflect Jackie and Hank's similar experiences.

Extend the Story: Personal Stories

After the retelling, it may be appropriate to open discussion for students to share their own experiences. Examples may include stories about being "the new kid on the block" or "a fish out of water." Other stories could detail ways in which a student was the first to do something, with or without help of a more experienced mentor. Carefully guide this share time to ensure all students feel safe and comfortable sharing personal details. Do not require students to share if they decline.

To open the discussion, it is helpful for you, as the teacher, to share a personal (and true) anecdote about yourself, preferably something that happened when you were close to your students' current age. This will help students feel a sense of connection and be more comfortable to share their own thoughts. For example, if you are teaching older learners, you might share a story about when you were transitioning to middle school and older classmates assisted you. Or, if you are teaching younger students, you may choose a story related to entering school for the first time and getting help from the teacher or an older sibling. The most important feature is that the story is authentic and relatable to the class.

Additional Readings

Jackie and Hank were from different sides of the United States, had different racial backgrounds, and were different ages (Jackie was eight years younger than Hank), but they fundamentally understood each other. To relate to someone different, it is not necessary to have the exact same experience at the same moment in time, but to have shared feelings and the ability to relate to similar events. This was the case with Jackie and Hank. The thread of common hardships, even if the details are contextually different, facilitated a friendship and bond that extended beyond age differences and beautifully illustrates how differences can become the ties that bind.

Stevie by John Steptoe (1969; Primary)

Robert's parents agree to let Stevie live with them during the week when Stevie's mother is at work. Robert, an only child, doesn't like this intrusion and refers to Stevie as a *crybaby* who he has to supervise and who limits his opportunity to play with others. Over time, however, Robert comes to realize how much he enjoys Stevie. This story provides for a good discussion on appreciating the special opportunities and talents of others.

Drawn Together by Minh Lê (2018; Elementary)

In this book, age and language differences impede a young boy's bonding experience with his grandfather. However, through a shared love of drawing, the two bridge the divide that language and age pose.

Virtues of a Great Warrior: An Adventure About Finding the Ancient Secret of Martial Arts and Also Something Greater by Ori Avnur (2014; Elementary)

This story follows a young warrior who learns fighting techniques and so much more from a great master. The cross-generational relationship illustrates you can pass on to younger people not only skills but also the philosophy of compassion and restraint.

Action Project: Cooperative Hands

Students may benefit from having the opportunity to extend the skills they learn and practice during this activity to other settings beyond school. Earlier in the activity, students served as mentors and mentees to one another in the classroom. It's important that students maintain these skills in other settings and with other people. When students generalize what they learn in the classroom, they can take more ownership of their learning, and their skill set has a chance to develop and become more fully integrated into their behavioral repertoire.

To begin this action project, show students the example of the cooperative hands action project in figure 7.3. Then provide them with a blank copy of the figure.

Things I Know How to Do	People I Could Share These Skills With
Bake bread	Neighborhood friends, my Aunt Tilly, my friend Sarah
Play the piano	The other students in music class, my grandma's community center club
Do card tricks	Family members, friends
Say "hello" in many different languages	Teachers, friends from other language backgrounds, online groups about learning languages
Do a cartwheel	People in gymnastics class, kids in my neighborhood, my siblings and other family members

Figure 7.3: Cooperative hands action project.

*Visit **go.SolutionTree.com/diversityandequity** for a free blank reproducible version of this figure.*

Ask students to identify a list of things they already know how to do and are comfortable doing, and record their ideas in the left-hand column. These can include playing a video game, tying shoes, writing letters, singing a song, making new friends, braiding hair, and so on. Once students generate ideas about skills they are comfortable doing, have them generate ideas for people or groups of people they could share these skills with, and record their ideas in the right-hand column. This list can include family members, church groups, youth clubs, swim teams, aftercare classmates, and so on.

Then guide the students to connect one skill from the first column with a person or group from the second column. Students may choose which activity and group they'd like to work with for their project. When students conduct their action project, remind them of the mentor steps they learned in the previous section of this activity.

1. Break down the skill you will teach into manageable parts.
2. Practice each step until it is easy to show and explain.
3. Tell your mentee what he or she did right and what he or she needs to work on.

When students return to school after completing the project, give them an opportunity to share which activity and the people or group they worked with and how the project turned out. Emphasize the ultimate goal of the project is to work together, regardless of whether or not others learned the skill. Teaching and learning in an informal way can be a great way to foster healthy relationships both in school and in other settings.

Playing and Working Cooperatively Across Racial and Ethnic Groups

Racial and ethnic issues are dominant in the previous story, *When Jackie and Hank Met* (Fishman, 2012). Hank's mentoring focused on helping Jackie tamp down the negative racial attitudes and behaviors interfering with cooperative, peaceful play. A harmonious atmosphere and a winning team are what most people want. A similar theme surfaces in the story *Angel Child, Dragon Child* (Surat, 1989). Here, race and ethnicity again emerge as dominant factors undermining cooperative and productive play and schooling. We emphasize race and ethnicity in this section of the chapter with the goal of helping students understand that hostility based on physical characteristics restricts people from achieving what they desire most: cooperative, enjoyable relationships.

Literature on Playing and Working Cooperatively Across Racial and Ethnic Groups

In the second presentation of this story, *Angel Child, Dragon Child*, we emphasize the benefits of classroom cooperation for everyone in the school as well as the key characters.

Book: *Angel Child, Dragon Child* by Michele Maria Surat (1989)

As noted previously, the steps for introducing each book to the class include present the story, clarify story concepts through discussion, clarify the features of the desired behaviors through enactments, practice the desired behaviors through real-life applications, respond appropriately to issues of diversity, and provide extension activities to maintain the desired behaviors.

Present the Story

Read the story to and with the class. If students have a hard copy of the book or if they can access the story online, they can follow along as you read aloud. If not, students can simply listen as you read.

Story Synopsis

Nguyen Hoa is a young girl from Vietnam. She prefers the name Ut, which is a tender name for *smallest daughter*, and members of her family use it. (We also discussed this story in chapter 6, page 123. The main character may be referred to as either Hoa or Ut.) Hoa and her sisters have recently immigrated from Vietnam to the United States and are attending a U.S. school for the first time. Hoa's introduction to the school proves difficult when she encounters a student, Raymond, who taunts her for her clothing, calling them *pajamas* and laughing loudly. Hoa goes on through her day somewhat uncertainly, as she is reluctant to speak English and is unfamiliar with the traditions of U.S. schooling, such as hand raising and individual answering.

When she gets frustrated, she hides her face and looks at a picture of her mother she keeps in her pocket. Hoa's mother had to remain in Vietnam when the family immigrated to the United States because the family could not yet afford her trip. Hoa misses her mother and remembers her mother's words encouraging her to be an angel child, not a dragon child, when things become difficult. Hoa tries her best to be an angel child; however, one day Raymond throws a "snow rock" that strikes her sister, Chi Hai, on the chin. Hoa could no longer be an angel child. In defense of her sister, she picks up a snow rock of her own and throws it back at Raymond. Raymond tackles Hoa, and they start fighting. The principal intervenes and places the two students in a room together, instructing them to work out their differences by having Hoa speak her story to Raymond using English words and, in turn, Raymond would write down Hoa's story on paper.

At first, the two cannot bridge their differences, but when Raymond starts to cry for his mother, Hoa sympathizes with him because she also knows what it feels like to miss her mother. She speaks to Raymond in English and offers him a piece of her cookie. Raymond is pleased to hear Hoa speak English, and the two begin to talk. As Raymond writes down Hoa's story of leaving Vietnam without her mother, he begins to understand her better and later suggests to the school principal that they hold a fair to raise money to help reunite Hoa's mother with her family in the United States.

The school community comes together and does just that. The Vietnamese fair features games, food, and decorations that represent Hoa's culture. At the end of the fair, the class has raised enough money for Hoa's mother's travels. The days and months pass, and at the end of the school year, when the *hoa-phuong* (flowers) are just beginning to blossom in Vietnam, Hoa comes home from school that day to find her mother at home, reunited with her family.

Discussion

In this activity, we use the story *Angel Child, Dragon Child* to illustrate the importance and value of cooperation. Cooperative play is something many students are already familiar with, especially if they engage in team sports or group-oriented games. However, interpersonal cooperation, outside of game playing, is also an important skill to develop. Pose the following questions to the class, and guide the discussion to develop a consensus on understanding and cooperation.

1. "What does the word *cooperation* mean?" (It means working together with others for a specific purpose.)
2. "Why is it important to cooperate with others?" (It's important in order to accomplish a shared goal in a peaceful fashion.)
3. "What are some things you might do if you are cooperating with others?" (Take turns, share items and resources, speak kindly and respectfully, try your best to problem solve, and be responsible for your part.)
4. "If you need to cooperate with someone you don't know very well or you don't have much in common with, how can you make sure your efforts are successful?" (You can be friendly and polite, share your things, and make sure to do your best work.)

Once students have a clear understanding of what cooperation means, steer the discussion toward the details of the story.

1. "When did Hoa need to be cooperative in the story?" (When the principal told her to work with Raymond to write her story together.)
2. "How did Hoa feel when she had to cooperate with Raymond?" (She felt it would be difficult, and he wouldn't understand her. She may have also felt angry and shy.)
3. "What happened that helped Hoa and Raymond begin to work together?" (Raymond began to cry for his mother. Hoa understood Raymond because she also missed her mother. Hoa comforted Raymond.)
4. "What did Raymond realize once Hoa began telling her story?" (Raymond understood Hoa's mother was far away and she missed her and wanted to bring her to the United States.)
5. "As a result of cooperating to write Hoa's story, did Raymond and Hoa begin to understand each other better?" (Yes. After they cooperated in writing the story, Raymond and Hoa got along better and became friends.)
6. "After writing Hoa's story, what did Raymond suggest to help Hoa's family?" (Raymond suggested to the principal the school have a Vietnamese fair to raise money to help Hoa's family bring her mother to the United States.)

7. "What happened when the school had the Vietnamese fair?" (Many people came to the fair and enjoyed games, food, and decorations. The community cooperated to help Hoa's family and also learned about Vietnamese culture.)

8. "How do you think Hoa felt once the school came together to help her family? How do you think Raymond felt?" (Hoa probably felt accepted and thankful for good friends. Raymond probably felt happy he could help Hoa.)

Help students understand that although initially Raymond and Hoa did not get along, they forged a friendship through the cooperative writing activity the principal assigned. In turn, that cooperative activity resulted in additional cooperative support in the school community when students held a Vietnamese fair to support Hoa's family. When people work together cooperatively, they can solve problems together and help one another in meaningful ways.

Enactments

Tell students it is important to learn to cooperate with others, even if they don't know them very well or get along at first. In many circumstances, people can solve problems or make the world better by working together with others. To cooperate with others, you must (1) understand what you are trying to achieve together, (2) identify ways you can help to achieve the goal, (3) be responsible for trying your best and getting your part done, and (4) be respectful and kind to everyone you work with.

Begin the following activity by drawing the chart on the board or putting up a large poster somewhere in the classroom. Place the students in small groups of three or four (consider grouping students with others they do not know very well or don't often work with). Assign each group one of the scenarios, such as those in figure 7.4 (page 162), and ask each group to complete each remaining step to demonstrate cooperation.

Use these scenarios or adjust them for situations that suit your students best. The scenario should state a relatable problem that will require more than one person to solve. Make sure each group member identifies explicit ways he or she will be responsible in helping to solve the problem. Remind students when they work together for a common goal, they usually can get more done in less time and possibly make friends in the process.

Scenario	Problem or Goal	How I Can Help Achieve the Goal	How I Can Show That I Am Trying My Best	Respectful and Kind Words I Can Say
Company is coming over in one hour, and the house is very messy.	The house needs to be cleaned.	We can divide up the rooms that need to be cleaned, and I can clean the room I am responsible for.	I can do my best work by being very careful and cleaning the room thoroughly. I can stay on task and try to get my work done quickly while still doing a good job.	I can tell the others I'm glad we worked together and thank them for doing their part.
While playing at the park, one friend's bike gets a flat tire.				
Your mom has a bad cold and needs to stay in bed. You and your siblings want to make dinner for your family.				
During indoor recess, many friends want to play checkers, but there's only one checkerboard.				
You have some classmates from Somalia who do not know how to use the lavatory.				

Figure 7.4: Cooperating to solve problems.

*Visit **go.SolutionTree.com/diversityandequity** for a free reproducible version of this figure.*

Real-Life Applications

Elementary school children will benefit from classroom activities that require them to work in cooperative groups. Following the enactments activity, discuss with students some problem or circumstances which they might work together to solve or achieve. Organize students into small groups of four or five. Give each group a blank version of the chart in figure 7.5 and an assignment, such as one of the following examples. You may post these assignments on the blackboard, a whiteboard, or chart paper.

1. Organize yourselves to walk quickly and orderly down the hall to the lunchroom.
2. Welcome a student to class who is new to the city or United States.
3. Correctly collect and store the classroom crayons.
4. Fairly select team members for a class kickball game.
5. Carefully care for the fish in the classroom fish tank.

My Group	Problem or Goal	How I Can Help Achieve the Goal	How I Can Show That I Am Trying My Best	Respectful and Kind Words I Can Say
Nevaeh, Olivia, and August	Care for the class pet.	Check the filter in the aquarium each day, and change it when it gets dirty.	Make sure that I do my job each morning before our classwork begins.	"I need help, please." "Thank you for taking very good care of our fish."
Zach, Gabriel, and Trae	Welcome a new student.	Volunteer to sit next to the new student during lunch, and include her in recess games.	Make conversation with the new student during lunch by asking her about her interests.	"I'm glad I have the chance to get to know you." "You seem like a cool and interesting person."
Elijah, Donte, and Caitlyn	Collect and store the classroom crayons.	Announce to the class that all students using crayons should put them in the upper-right corner of their desk for a classmate to collect.	Get everyone's attention (without yelling), and help organize the process by telling my classmates what we plan to do.	"Thank you for helping us organize the crayons." "Please listen to me so we can all help keep our materials neat."

Figure 7.5: My cooperation project.

Visit **go.SolutionTree.com/diversityandequity** *for a free blank reproducible version of this figure.*

Direct students to decide how they could cooperate as a group to complete or perform the chosen assignment. It would be wise to brainstorm about one or two of these examples before requiring students to work in small groups to complete their own assignments. Encourage and support students as they complete their assignments and give them several days for completion. Permit each group to present its plan to the entire class and get feedback on the plans. Decide with the class to adopt the plans, with appropriate modifications for the entire class. Display the plans on class bulletin boards.

Once the plans are complete, discuss the process with the class. What did they learn from working cooperatively in a group setting? How did it make them feel to be helpful to others? What problem did you help solve or what goal did they help achieve for the group?

Diversity Issues in This Story

This story describes the experience of a young Vietnamese girl beginning school in the United States. Hoa has brought with her the only experiences she knows, which are from Vietnam. The school and home cultures in Vietnam can be quite different, and these differences are threaded throughout the story. It may be helpful to review the story again with students, and at each point a cultural difference is evident, ask students to identify the difference and ways they express the same customs in the United States. Use the examples in figure 7.6.

Difference	Vietnamese Tradition	U.S. Tradition
Clothing (pp. 7, 26)	*Ao dai*, a long shirt, like a tunic over trousers	Jeans, T-shirts, pants, skirts, sneakers
School (p. 8)	Students sit together and chant as a group	Students sit separately and answer individually, usually by raising a hand
Greetings (pp. 9, 26)	"*Chao buoi sang*"	"Good morning" or "hello"
Decorations (p. 27)	Rainbow-colored dragon	Brightly-colored streamers and balloons
Food (p. 27)	Rice cakes, imperial rolls, sesame cookies	Pizza, chips, cookies, fruit, vegetables

Figure 7.6: Vietnamese and American traditions.

It is important to point out to students that although customs and traditions may appear different, all cultures have ways of expressing celebrations and common values. What is novel or different for some is very appropriate and common to others. Likewise, common traditions and customs in the United States seem very novel and different to people from other cultures. It is important to note this story includes names and words not common to English-speaking-only populations. Examples include Ut (*oot*), Little Quang (*Kwang*), Chi Hai (*chee hi*), Nguyen Hoa (*new-yen hwa*), chao buoi sang (*chow bwee sung*), hoa-phuong (*hwa fung*), and ao dai (*ow zi*). Include pronunciations at the bottom of each page these words appear. Practice the correct pronunciations of the words in context, so you can read aloud the passage accurately and fluently to the class. Mispronouncing or stumbling on these words may inadvertently communicate a lack of attention to and respect for cultural terminology.

Extended Literature Activities

Use these literature activities to further ascertain students' understanding of the story and desired social-emotional learning skills. Students use their own words to retell the story and specify appropriate ways to respond. You also could use the annotated book list in the section Books on Playing and Working Cooperatively With Others (page 166) to assign more relevant readings to individuals or groups. For each book, we suggest general elementary reading levels.

Retell the Story

Students benefit from becoming familiar with the story through readings and rereadings. After the class has read the story a few times and practiced the activities we describe in previous sections, encourage students to retell the details of the story to one another. In small groups, have students contribute details of the story in a round-robin fashion. You may consider structuring the retelling, so the speaker holds a baton or other item when contributing a detail about the story. Teach students to build on each detail in a sequence such as, "First, Hoa's family moved to the United States," and then pass the baton. "Hoa started school at a U.S. school," and then pass the baton. "A student named Raymond laughed at Hoa's clothing, calling them pajamas," and then pass the baton. Students should continue in this way until they tell all the details of the story.

Additional Readings

The following books provide various stories about being cooperative. They range from noting simple ways people can cooperate with others through exercises, such as yoga, to learning why it is so important for people to cooperate with others, even when there are times one would rather go alone.

Yoga Friends by Mariam Gates and Rolf Gates (2018; Primary)

This is a terrific book to extend the discussion on cooperation. This story describes how partners can work together to complete different yoga poses such as tree, lotus, octopus, and owl. It provides step-by-step instructions for each pose, along with colorful pictures of children completing the poses together. This book may also serve as an opportunity to learn practices commonly found in Indian culture.

Maybe Something Beautiful: How Art Transformed a Neighborhood by F. Isabel Campoy and Theresa Howell (2016; Primary)

This story is based on real-life artists Rafael and Candice López. A young girl named Mira, who lives in East Village near downtown San Diego, loves to paint and draw. She hands out her colorful pictures to families in the community and even tapes some to walls of buildings in her neighborhood. Mira feels this helps brighten her community, but not much. One day she meets a muralist who paints large, bright pictures on buildings. She tells him she is also an artist. They work together to bring color and life to otherwise drab-looking areas of their community. This book also is offered in a Spanish language edition.

Teamwork Isn't My Thing, and I Don't Like to Share! by Julia Cook (2012; Elementary)

This story describes the frustrations of a young boy, RJ, when his teacher asks him to work with other children in the class he does not particularly like. After school one day, RJ goes home to find one cookie left, and his mother asks him to share it with his sister, which frustrates him even more. Through the guidance of a football coach, RJ comes to understand the importance of cooperation and sharing at school, at home, and at play.

Action Project: Cooperation Coach

Many schools have a student council or peer-mediation program that encourages students to work for the good of the school community. If your school does not have a group of this sort, consider starting one or building a small-scale group in your classroom. Approach this group and ask if students can serve as *cooperation coaches* for other students or classes in the school. Cooperation coaches are available to assist other students having disputes; classroom teachers or school personnel who want student-to-student support with cooperative play and learning; or recess helpers.

Cooperation coaches are experts at the steps of cooperation in this activity. They know how to identify (1) what needs to be achieved, (2) how each person can help achieve the goal, (3) how each person can demonstrate he or she is trying his or her best, and (4) respectful and kind words to use. Have students work in teams to develop materials and resources that illustrate these steps in various forms. Designate groups that do some or all of the following: develop a visual display like a poster, act out role plays to show the steps, write a handbook for cooperation coaches to use and share with others, draw pictures that show students cooperating with one another, sing or write poems that relate to cooperative behavior, verbally describe the steps of cooperation and reasons to work together, and so on. Identify students' strengths and encourage students to apply those strengths to sharing this information with others. Students can be creative and helpful to the school community.

Books on Playing and Working Cooperatively With Others

Figure 7.7 offers a list of books featured in this chapter that include aspects of playing and working cooperatively with others. As time permits, read these books in class and discuss the themes we noted in the previous activities. Encourage students to read these books independently, when appropriate, and share their observations with you and the rest of the class.

Title	Author	Story Summary
Primary		
Maybe Something Beautiful: How Art Transformed a Neighborhood	F. Isabel Campoy and Theresa Howell (2016)	A young Latina girl cooperates with a muralist to improve their community through art.
Stevie	John Steptoe (1969)	A young boy learns to appreciate and enjoy a younger companion he initially resents.
Yoga Friends	Mariam Gates and Rolf Gates (2018)	This book describes how partners can work together to complete different yoga poses, featuring Indian culture.
Elementary		
Angel Child, Dragon Child	Michele Maria Surat (1989)	A young Vietnamese girl adjusts to beginning school in the United States.
Drawn Together	Minh Lê (2018)	Age and language differences impede a young Asian boy's bonding experience with his grandfather. A bond forms through a shared love of art and storytelling.
Teamwork Isn't My Thing, and I Don't Like to Share!	Julia Cook (2012)	Children learn the value of working together as a team and sharing with others.
Virtues of a Great Warrior: An Adventure About Finding the Ancient Secret of Martial Arts and Also Something Greater	Ori Avnur (2014)	A young Asian warrior forges a cross-generational relationship through martial arts.
When Jackie and Hank Met	Cathy Goldberg Fishman (2012)	This book features African American and Jewish baseball players Jackie Robinson and Hank Greenberg. It presents many common hardships of baseball players who are Black and Jewish, due to a lack of acceptance during the 1940s and 1950s.

Figure 7.7: Books on playing and working cooperatively with others.

Visit *go.SolutionTree.com/diversityandequity* for a free reproducible version of this figure.

Conclusion

From the time children become aware of others in their environment, caregivers often become intent to teach these young people how to share, work together, and play cooperatively. And this is with good reason! Our communal good depends upon these fundamental skills in important ways. Children who can share items and resources freely and fairly are more likely to achieve mutually desirable outcomes with peers. They are also more likely to be viewed favorably by others and to be recipients of others' generosity as well. Working and playing cooperatively not only gives a sense of mutual achievement, but also lends the benefit of a shared experience to draw on as relationships grow and mature. Through healthy cooperative engagement, children may learn important social-emotional skills that will allow them to build an increasingly sophisticated repertoire of positive, prosocial behaviors.

Chapter Reflections

Individually or with a collaborative group, review and discuss the following questions to reflect on your learning in this chapter.

1. What are the necessary social behaviors that are indicative of cooperation?

2. Why is it important to maintain a cooperative attitude with others?

3. How can you assist a person or a group that appears to be unskilled in cooperative behaviors and attitudes?

4. Is your own personal gain more or less important than the collective good of the group? Are these mutually exclusive objectives, or can they overlap?

5. Are there preconditions for working and playing cooperatively? If so, what are they? Is being cooperative always a good idea? Why?

chapter eight

Questioning Unfair Practices

"That's not fair!" How many times have parents and teachers heard this all-too-familiar refrain from their children and students? From the time children engage in peer play, they seem to have the innate capacity to identify something they view as unfair. In fact, literature suggests children can identify unfair practices and instances of inequality quite early on in childhood (Dunkerly-Bean, Bean, Sunday, & Summers, 2017). Yet, the types of inequalities or injustices children cite tend to change and become more complex across the developmental lifespan. Younger elementary students are more likely to identify lacking goods, items, or equal resource allocation as unfair (Hakovirta & Kallio, 2015). This concrete analysis eventually morphs into a more generalized, bigger-picture understanding of social inequities in older elementary students and adolescents (Elenbaas, Rizzo, & Killen, 2020).

The developmental nature of the understanding of fairness and justice is clearly conducive to curricular content and begs the opportunity for adoption into classroom instruction. Still, when students protest some rule or consequence as unfair, the typical response of parents and teachers is to dismissively tell students, "Well, life isn't fair sometimes." And while this may be true, it doesn't completely address a couple of important lessons. First, everyone should develop the discernment to correctly identify when a rule or consequence isn't fair. However, simply because one does not like or agree with something does not automatically guarantee it is unfair. Second, if people can correctly identify unfair or unjust practices, they should have developed an effective way of addressing that unfair practice and should follow through on those actions.

If people cannot correctly distinguish between something that is unfair and something that is simply disagreeable or not preferred, others are more likely to perceive them as chronic complainers or may not take them as seriously when they bring forward a valid concern. Third, if people lack the skills to take action against unfair practices, they allow injustices to persist and perpetuate harm to themselves and others. When students vocalize their perception that something is unfair, it is a teachable moment, and you and the class can explore what it means if something is unfair and what can be done about it.

School is a predominant environment for children and provides a valuable context to explore how they understand fair practices and also to teach and foster the development of a more critical analysis of what is just and unjust in greater society. A study by Robert Thornberg (2008), a professor of education and researcher, uses ethnographic fieldwork and group interviews to investigate students' thinking about the fairness of school rules and their perceptions of teacher behavior in relation to these rules. Thornberg (2008) discusses four rule categories for students: (1) *relational rules* (for example, being nice to others, not bullying others), (2) *protecting rules* (for example, no running in the hallways), (3) *structuring rules* (for example, raising hands to speak, respecting class property), and (4) *etiquette rules* (for example, no gum chewing, no wearing hats in the classroom).

Generally, students can identify fairness and value behind all rule categories except etiquette rules. The author notes students identify etiquette rules as arbitrary, without justification, and unnecessary for the effective and safe functioning of the school (Thornberg, 2008). In reference to the rule against wearing hats in school, one student notes teachers justify the rule by saying they need to see students' faces. In response, a fifth-grade student retorted, "Yes, maybe there's a small part of the forehead you can't see, but does that matter?" (p. 422). Implicit in this statement is questioning how much hats *matter* to student learning. This illustrates students relate fairness of rules with the rule's utility to school functions.

Further, students identify one of the structuring rules (the requirement they go outdoors for recess) as unfair because they observe the teachers not following the rule themselves. As one student put it, "They are the ones who made this rule, so they should have to follow it too" (Thornberg, 2008, p. 423). It appears students conceptualize fairness of school rules as requiring both applicability to the school's functioning and also more uniform compliance with the rules (for example, if students follow the rules, adults should do the same).

The author concludes the organization and establishment of these rules should be a "practice of deliberative democracy in school and an education in and a preparation for an active and competent citizenship in a democratic society beyond school" (Thornberg, 2008, p. 427). Indeed, Thornberg's (2008) position that rule construction within school, which is a student's analog environment to greater society, is an opportunity to teach important civic competencies is well noted, and educators should consider the rationale for teaching students how to question unfair practices.

The findings in Thornberg's (2008) study suggest students perceive rules as unfair or unjust when they are arbitrary and when not everyone in the environment uniformly follows them. A school environment that works in arbitrary and selective rule application is likely disempowering for students who experience those contexts. In contrast, other research notes when students attend schools that respect their rights and have a more just rule application, they are more likely to demonstrate increased engagement, feel more empowered, and perceive the school as a positive and welcoming place (Covell, Howe, & Polegato, 2011). This engagement is particularly important for students at risk of school failure (Covell, Howe, & McNeil, 2008).

As direct providers for students, teachers are well situated to begin the important work of shaping the common student refrain, "Hey, that's not fair!" to more thoughtful and productive actions of engagement with the concepts of just practices within the school framework. As researchers David Shriberg and Poonam Desai (2014) point out, this aspirational goal "involves viewing social justice as a verb, that is, a set of direct actions that researchers and practitioners can take" (p. 4).

Teaching students how to question unfair practices and take appropriate action to ameliorate aspects of injustice in their world is a worthy pursuit in the classroom, as it positively impacts students' immediate social sphere (the classroom) and also provides foundational skills to apply as they develop into engaged members of a just society. Explain to students that it is not enough to identify an unfair practice that only affects them; they should be aware of practices that affect others unfairly and speak up and take appropriate action. Appropriate action to take in response to an accurately identified unfair practice may vary depending on the situation. But regardless of whether that unfair practice is coming from a peer, sibling, parent, teacher, or someone in a position of authority or an even broader context, students first should address the individual directly.

Students can learn to advocate for themselves and others as a first means of action. The next step is to remove themselves or limit engagement as much as possible. If students identify an unfair practice, at the very least, they can refuse to continue to participate in it. Finally, instruct students to suggest solutions to appropriate audiences. If a student and her classmate are arguing about the rules of a game, she might first tell her classmate how the actions are unfair. Next, she may disengage from the game. And finally, she can suggest a solution to the argument and unfair practice to a teacher or other adult to help resolve the problem.

Teaching students these components (the ability to clearly define, advocate against, and resolve an unfair practice) will help them become skilled in self-advocacy and more effective problem solving, powerful tools as they grow into adulthood. The activities in this chapter use stories that illustrate unfair practices regarding two issues—race and poverty—and how the characters in the stories address the problems to arrive at a resolution.

Questioning Unfair Practices With Regard to Race

The United States is home to people of many different racial and ethnic identities. Along with such diversity comes a number of benefits as well as struggles to coalesce around people's differences. U.S. history tells a story of unified idealism against a backdrop of hard-fought conflicts for the actualization of equality. These conflicts range from overt and individualized expressions of racism to subtler and more covert institutional threads of racism woven into the fabric of daily life. These impacts are present not only in adulthood. San Diego State University assistant professor and early childhood educator Idara Essien (2019) observed microaggressions related to race in early childhood. Given that racialized issues affect everyone across the lifespan, it is worthy to address in developmentally appropriate ways. Indeed, institutional inequities related to race, such as structural racism, shape and have important implications for students in school and, as such, schools can be central to making change in their communities (Noguera & Alicea, 2020).

Teaching social issues through literature is an effective means for bringing these activities into the classroom. One teacher, Robin Cooley (2004), did just that. She used the book *Iggie's House* by Judy Blume (2014) to help her fifth-grade students distinguish the differences among acts of active racism, passive racism, and anti-racism. In the story, a Black family, the Garbers, moves into a predominantly White neighborhood. They are met with rejection from one of the neighbors in the form of a lawn sign and petition to remove the Garbers from the community (active racism). The primary character, Winnie, who is White, struggles with her own family's avoidance or lack of action against active racism (passive racism). Interestingly, the author stops short of narrating an ending with overtly anti-racist actions from the main characters. Instead, she opens the door for conversations about appropriate anti-racist actions that one could (and should) take when injustices occur. Cooley (2004) guides her students through analysis and classification of the different characters' actions (or lack of actions) throughout the story. In the author's words, it's important for students "to become more critically aware of the roles they can take when confronted with unjust situations" (Cooley, 2004).

The previous example illustrates how you can use literature to help elementary-aged students identify gradients of injustice related to race. It is clear through Cooley's (2004) work those young students have the ability to discern when actions are unjust. In another study and subsequent follow-up, Jill E. Flynn (2012, 2017), a University of Delaware professor, examines the impacts of a multicultural pedagogy on eighth-grade students' identification of structural racism and subsequent anti-racist work. In the initial study, eleven target students and two teachers engaged in the study of multicultural issues and race discussions throughout the school year. At the conclusion of the initial study, most students identified their understanding of racism developed through their work together as one of the most important ideas learned that year, and they were inspired to act and work toward becoming anti-racist leaders (Flynn, 2012). However, Flynn (2017) determines this promising foundation and intention immaterial. In the follow-up with some of the students four years later, Flynn (2017) observes a lack of action, and disillusionment is evident. As one student notes:

> They got us really pumped up to go out and *do* stuff to prevent racism, but then when we actually got out there, and . . . people don't really *care* . . . personally, all we can do is, like, when somebody's being racist say, "Hey, don't do that." And not be racist ourselves. (p. 211)

Although the students' framework for understanding the complexities of racial issues and even their verbalized intention of engaging in anti-racist work are encouraging, it is clear those outcomes are necessary but insufficient for tangible change. Flynn (2017) concludes teachers may advance the stages of understanding by locating activist groups that foster support for these emerging connections, as well as encouraging students to cultivate cross-race friendships, and providing students with *tools* to help sustain the benefits of multicultural work in and beyond the classroom. We posit the tool students need to move beyond the understanding and identification of unjust or unfair actions related to race is to teach them the skills to appropriately and effectively question these unfair practices once students identify them. Using literature to teach questioning unfair practices related to race is one approach to achieve those outcomes. In *Anti-Bias Education for Young Children and Ourselves*, coauthors Louise Derman-Sparks, Julie Olsen Edwards, and Catherine M. Goins (2020) offer effective anti-bias activities to use with very young children (ages three to five).

Literature on Questioning Unfair Practices With Regard to Race

We use the book *When Jackie and Hank Met* (Fishman, 2012) again in this chapter. For this activity, the focus is on race rather than cooperating across age. Prior to civil rights legislation that prohibited discrimination on the basis of race, some people used race unfairly to determine who could play baseball in the major leagues. In this activity, students discuss how to recognize when people are using race or ethnicity for unfair practices.

Book: *When Jackie and Hank Met* by Cathy Goldberg Fishman (2012)

As noted previously, the steps for introducing each book to the class include present the story, clarify story concepts through discussion, clarify the features of the desired behaviors through enactments, practice the desired behaviors through real-life applications, respond appropriately to issues of diversity, and provide extension activities to maintain the desired behaviors.

Present the Story

Read the story to and with the class. If students have a hard copy of the book or if they can access the story online, they can follow along as you read aloud. If not, students can simply listen as you read.

Story Synopsis

The story takes place before it became unlawful to discriminate against someone on the basis of race, gender, religion, or place of origin in the United States (Marger, 2015). Two skilled baseball players, Jackie Robinson and Hank Greenberg, navigate structures of racial and ethnic discrimination in professional sports. The story describes how, although Jackie was Black and Hank was Jewish, they each separately experienced varying degrees of prejudice and injustice. As children, they grew up in different communities, but both boys were on the receiving end of verbal and physical aggression based on race and religion. Being Jewish, Hank was able to secure a position on the Detroit Tigers, while Jackie, as a Black man, remained in the separate Negro league baseball until much later, when he became a Brooklyn Dodger. Both men continue to endure insults and backlash from the public, solely due to their racial and religious and cultural differences. The story describes aspects of discrimination the men overcome in other professional arenas during their respective careers. The men form a friendship based on shared experiences and empathy for each other. The story illustrates several examples of discrimination and each character's ability to question unfair practices in his perseverance toward justice.

Discussion

After reading the story aloud with students, discuss what it means if something is unfair. Help students understand it is unfair if you've been appropriate or done the right thing and someone treats you badly. It is also unfair if people are unkind to you just because you are different from them. Have students describe unfair things that happen in their daily lives. Help them understand something isn't unfair just because they don't like it, such as having to go to bed at 8:00 p.m. Remind students that rules sometimes ensure their health and safety (such as getting appropriate amounts of sleep) and are necessary for their well-being.

Use these guidelines to decide what things in the story are unfair and what things in students' lives are fair or unfair. Examples of unfair practices in the story include not allowing Jackie to play in the baseball league with Whites, and the unkind words and harassment Jackie and Hank both endure simply because they are of a different race or religion and ethnicity. An example of something that might be unfair in students' daily lives is if one student always has to go last in a game with peers just because he or she is younger. Another example might be if only the girls in the family get to contribute ideas to the grocery shopping list for the week. On the other hand, the rule saying they must wear a helmet while riding their bicycle is fair because it is necessary to ensure their safety.

Review with students the content of the story *When Jackie and Hank Met*. This is sensitive content, but even with younger students, it's important to be historically accurate with respect to the civil rights movement in the United States. For this activity, emphasize the wise actions of Jackie and some others (for example, Branch Rickey and Hank) who helped resolve unfair practices in baseball and move beyond these difficult conditions. The following are appropriate points to stress for all elementary students (grades K–5).

1. Although highly offended and frightened by taunts from fans and other players, Jackie did not physically fight or counter the taunts with aggression.

2. Jackie was an excellent baseball player, which made it harder for baseball fans to criticize him as an athlete.

3. Jackie countered the unfair practices in both baseball and his time in the army by standing up for what was right, even though it was unpopular at the time.

4. Others (such as Hank and Rickey) stood up for Jackie also and helped support him in this cause.

Challenging and changing unfair practices can be uncomfortable. In the story, Rickey, president of the Brooklyn Dodgers, wants Jackie to play on his major league team instead of in the segregated Negro league. Both Jackie and Rickey knew this would change baseball forever, but it was the right thing to do. Use figure 8.1 (page 176) to help students understand how difficult this was by taking the perspective of the fans, Jackie, and his teammates.

How Did the Fans Feel?	How Did Jackie Feel?	How Did Jackie's Teammates Feel?
They had not seen Black players in the major leagues before.	He had not played with White baseball players before and would be the only one who looked like him on the team.	At first, they may not have liked the change and didn't talk with Jackie or taunt him.
They were angry the managers were making this change.	He was afraid of the angry fans.	They probably wanted good players on their team.
They wanted things to stay like they were before.	He wanted the opportunity to play in the major leagues just like anyone else.	They saw that Jackie was a good player.
They were afraid to have people who looked different from them playing baseball in the major leagues.	He was afraid the fans would hurt him and his family.	They were afraid the fans would ruin the game.
They did not know why they did not want someone who looked different playing baseball in the major leagues.	He did not know why they were angry because he looked different.	Jackie was a good player and teammate.

Figure 8.1: How fans, Jackie, and Jackie's teammates feel.

Visit go.SolutionTree.com/diversityandequity for a free reproducible version of this figure.

Figure 8.1 includes some possible thoughts you might use in your discussion with students. We suggest you initially present a blank chart with the headings from figure 8.1 and elicit statements from students such as those we provide. Some important understandings include the following.

- It is not fair to deny others' rights and opportunities just because they have physical differences.

- Sometimes things society accepts as OK or "just the way it has always been" can be deeply hurtful and unfair. It is everyone's responsibility to change and correct injustice.

- Everyone has either good or bad feelings when things change.

- Change or doing things in a new way can often be a very good experience.

- People should not reject others or call them names simply because they are different or do things in a different way.

- If people are being unkind to you because you are different or because they don't like something you are doing, you should think about what you can do to stop them from hurting you.

- You do not want to fight or call anyone names because that will make the situation worse.

- If someone is threatening you or causing major problems, you should get help from someone such as a teacher or parent.
- You can all take action to prevent or correct unfair practices just like Hank and Jackie.

It's important that students learn to identify when someone is being treated in a hurtful or unfair manner. In Jackie's case, he was subjected to fans teasing and taunting him because he looked different.

Enactments

Remind students of the ways others, such as Hank and Rickey, intervene on Jackie's behalf and act to end the unfair practice of discrimination in baseball. When people are aware of someone being treated in an unfair or hurtful manner, they should participate in the solution. Even though it may be difficult to stand up for others and even themselves, students must be brave, just like Jackie and some of his teammates were, and say or do something if they see injustice or something unfair. Help students think of ways they can be a "Jackie teammate" with the following activity.

Create a chart with three columns titled *Examples*, *What Can I Say?*, and *What Can I Do?*, respectively. In the Examples column, write a situation common to students' daily lives. In the next two columns, identify what students might say in response to the situation and how they might befriend or help someone who is being bullied or rejected. Figure 8.2 shows an example of this activity.

Examples	What Can I Say?	What Can I Do?
Friends are playing a game of kickball, and Alma misses the ball when she tries to kick. The other children make fun of her.	Tell Alma not to worry about making a mistake; it happens to everyone.	Tell the other children not to make fun of people because it hurts their feelings. I can invite Alma to play a different game with me instead.
Samar is a loner; he never seems to play with others at recess. He just walks around by himself.	Introduce myself to Samar, and try to have a friendly conversation with him.	Ask my school principal if we can have a *buddy bench* on the playground. If someone is lonely, he or she can find a friend to talk to on the buddy bench.
Maria is very shy and is embarrassed anytime she has to sing in front of her music class. During a performance, she accidentally sings some wrong words. Everyone hears and laughs and whispers about her.	Smile and tell Maria, "Sometimes I make those kinds of mistakes too." Reassure her that eventually people won't remember it even happened.	Ask Maria if she wants to work together to sing a special duet or create a fun dance together. Help her feel she is not alone, and you can be a good friend.

Figure 8.2: How to be a "Jackie teammate."

Real-Life Applications

Through the story of *When Jackie and Hank Met*, students learn how important it is to question and change an unfair practice, like segregation in baseball. In this story, some people discriminated against Jackie on the basis of his race, whereas some people discriminated against Hank on the basis of his religion or culture (Jewish). It takes all people, not only those the injustice most directly affects, to change the world for the better. In the story, the actions of Jackie, Hank, Rickey, and even the other teammates and fans all had a role to play in altering the course of events.

You can empower students as agents of social change when they take part in questioning practices in their world that may be unfair. They also should learn appropriate ways of enacting change. Take time with the class to identify authentic examples of practices in the real world that may be unfair, unjust, or unsafe. Then identify ways to take action to make a change. This brainstorming session can be as big as international current events or as small as your classroom rules. Although an open brainstorming session might lead students to call into question things they simply don't like (for example, "We don't want to do mathematics for thirty minutes every day!"), remind them that good rules are necessary for their safety and well-being. So, always ensure students ask themselves of their proposed action, "Is this rule necessary for health, safety, and order?" If so, the practice should remain. Figure 8.3 shows examples of brainstorming topics for action. Note these are just examples; students in your class should generate the list that works best for them.

Practice I'd Like to Change	Action I Can Take
Only fourth graders can learn beginning band instruments.	Write a letter to the principal asking if the school can open this opportunity to other grades, maybe through auditions.
Animals in the shelter don't get to go for walks like my dog Albert does.	Volunteer time on weekends to play with and exercise the shelter dogs.
My bedtime is an hour earlier than my sister's, even though I am only a year younger.	Ask for help searching online for information that either supports or disputes my current bedtime.
Energy conservation is important, but my family always leaves lights on when they leave a room, and they leave the water running while brushing their teeth.	Create signs and posters to put around the house to remind my family to turn off lights and water when not in use.

Figure 8.3: What I would like to change.

There are a lot of current issues students may be aware of and wish to express concern about. It is important for you to be unbiased in the discussion and lead students to a productive action to express their concern. The value in the activity is not necessarily to make judgment on the practice in question, but to lead students to ways they can be positive change agents when they perceive something as being unfair.

Diversity Issues in This Story

The introduction of this activity should include an instructional review of segregation and discrimination in the United States. Although labor laws that prevent racial discrimination are widely adopted today, this was not always the case (Marger, 2015). In the past, people accepted the practice to refuse employment and services to non-White citizens. There was a long period of time in U.S. history when some treated people unequally and refused them opportunities based on race, gender, religion, and nationality (Massey & Denton, 1993). These U.S. labor laws protected and enforced segregation, particularly in the South (although similar practices were present throughout the United States); they are sometimes referred to as *Jim Crow laws*. These laws not only enforced segregation and refusal of public accommodations and services based on race but also limited the power to enact civic changes due to voting restrictions. Several unfair practices were enacted during pre–civil rights legislation, including the following.

1. Restrictive voting laws required (1) poll taxes, which most Blacks, who made very little money, were unable to pay; (2) literacy tests, which almost no one was able to pass but were only administered to Blacks; (3) property requirements, which excluded most Blacks who either were not permitted to or could not afford to buy property; and (4) the "grandfather clause," which allowed only those whose grandfathers had voted to cast ballots. This was restrictive to Blacks and immigrants whose grandparents had been enslaved or unable to vote because they were not U.S. citizens (Anderson, 2019).

2. Public accommodations such as parks, libraries, beaches, restaurants, museums, and transportation were segregated by race. One of the most familiar historical events associated with this law was that of Rosa Parks refusing to vacate her seat on a public bus for a White person. Parks's actions were in protest to many years of widely accepted discriminatory practices in public accommodations (Anderson, 2019).

3. Educational statutes established that children should attend racially segregated schools. Only White children attended White schools. In 1954, Oliver Brown, the parent of a Black student, who had lost discrimination suits in lower courts, took the case to the U.S. Supreme Court in the landmark case *Brown v. Board of Education*. In that case, the court found educational

segregation practices violate the U.S. Equal Protection Clause (Fourteenth Amendment to the U.S. Constitution) and thus, American schools were desegregated on the basis of race. At the age of six, Ruby Bridges became the first child to integrate U.S. public schools in 1960 (Anderson, 2019).

After summarizing a few of the unfair practices encoded into law during the post-reconstruction period, help put these practices into context for students by explicitly describing ways they or their family and friends may have been impacted if they were living during those years. Some examples might include the following.

- You could not make a friend in school who was a different race.
- If you weren't White, your family would only be allowed to live in certain places and could not move freely if they decided to do so.
- Certain jobs may have been off limits if you were not White. Even if you were a very talented teacher, singer, actor, or athlete, your opportunities for employment would be limited or denied.
- If you weren't White and you wanted to go to the movies or out to eat, you would need to find a specific place that allowed patrons of your race.
- If you weren't White and you decided you would like to challenge these unjust laws, you may not even be able to vote in elections to make your voice heard.

Help students understand although the U.S. government no longer formally recognizes restrictive laws from the post-reconstructive period, aspects of injustice can and still do occur today. It is important to identify unfair practices, even and especially when they are formalized into laws—and appropriately challenge those practices so everyone can lead more fair and equitable lives.

Extended Literature Activities

Use these literature activities to further ascertain students' understanding of the story and desired social-emotional learning skills. Students use their own words to retell the story and specify appropriate ways to respond. You also could use the annotated book list in the section Books on Questioning Unfair Practices (page 192) to assign more relevant readings to individuals or groups. For each book, we suggest general elementary reading levels.

Retell the Story

Because the story was read and retold in a previous activity, it may only be necessary to recap the most salient points in the story, particularly relative unfair practices. Consider having students participate in a "baseball retelling" similar to the popular reading activity called popcorn reading. In *popcorn reading*, one student reads a small portion aloud and then yells "Popcorn!" and chooses a classmate to continue reading, sometimes tossing a ball or another small object to that student. In this example, start with one student providing a detail they recall from the story and then yelling, "Baseball!" and choosing or perhaps tossing a small ball to a classmate to provide an additional story detail. Continue throughout the class until all students identify all relevant details.

Extend the Story: Is It Fair or Unfair?

Review the statements in figure 8.4 from the story *When Jackie and Hank Met*. Ask students to identify each statement as either a fair or an unfair practice. Remember, something is not unfair simply because it is *different*. To be *unfair* means the opportunities, outcomes, or consequences are disadvantageous through no fault of the individual.

Is It Fair or Unfair?	
Jackie and Hank grew up in different parts of the country.	Fair or unfair?
Jackie attended church, and Hank went to synagogue.	Fair or unfair?
Some of Jackie's neighbors threw rocks at him just because he was Black.	Fair or unfair?
Some of Hank's neighbors threw rocks at him just because he was Jewish.	Fair or unfair?
Jews, Blacks, Irish, Native Americans, and many other groups were denied the freedom to join certain clubs or live in certain neighborhoods.	Fair or unfair?

Figure 8.4: Is it fair or unfair?

Visit **go.SolutionTree.com/diversityandequity** *for a free reproducible version of this figure.*

Additional Readings

There are a number of books you can use to supplement the content of the activity about questioning unfair practices. Use the following list to supplement, extend, and maintain the skills and dispositions from the activities in this chapter.

Passage to Freedom: The Sugihara Story by Ken Mochizuki (2010; Elementary)

This is a story told from the perspective of a five-year-old Japanese boy living in Lithuania during World War II. The boy's father serves as a consul with the authority to issue visas to foreigners seeking entry to the country.

At a time when many Jewish families sought refuge from the violence of World War II, Chiune Sugihara's military officers refused to permit him to issue visas to Jews. Sugihara knows this practice of denying those seeking refuge is wrong, so he consults with his family, who all agree Sugihara must do what's right. Even after his superiors tell him to stop writing visas for the Jewish refugees, Sugihara continues, possibly saving many lives. Ultimately, Sugihara's family is forced to leave Lithuania, but as their train pulls away from the station, the young boy sees many Jewish refugees and promises to remember that, although his father disobeyed orders, it was the right thing to do to help the Jewish people.

La Frontera: El Viaje Con Papá (My Journey With Papa) by Deborah Mills and Alfredo Alva (2018; Upper Elementary)

This story is based on the real-life events of Alfredo Alva who, along with his father, immigrated to Texas from Mexico without papers. Back in Mexico, Alfredo's father and grandfather work in forestry and must make a five-mile journey each day, which ultimately becomes too burdensome for Alfredo's aging grandfather. Alfredo's family experiences hunger and is suffering a lack of resources. Alfredo and his father make the journey to the United States in search of a better life. Throughout the story, the plight of immigrants comes into focus, allowing the reader to understand another perspective regarding why some choose to undertake such a difficult and often dangerous trip.

Action Project: Small Actions Make a Big Difference

For real-life applications, students identify examples of unfair practices and some appropriate actions to take in response to those practices. Just as students need guidance on how to identify if something is fair or unfair, they also need practice in identifying appropriate actions to take in response. Sometimes, taking action seems too big or intimidating to address. Do people need to make major changes and shifts in society for it to be worthwhile? Tell students even little things, like speaking up in class or during a family discussion, can be important. Maybe traveling to a different city or country makes a difference in how students understand other people. Or perhaps they can share with other neighborhood children or classmates what they learn from a book about bullying. Little actions can make a big difference.

To conclude this activity, the class might make a group journal that identifies small actions students have either made themselves or simply noticed others do during their everyday activities. This journal could become part of the class morning routine. Consider using a large notebook or binder students can choose to write in as they enter the classroom each day. They may choose to write things like, *My family donated our furniture to a shelter because we got new furniture; I asked my parents if my brothers and I could take turns with the chores instead of always being the one to do certain tasks*; or *I suggested my church youth group organize a food drive to provide meals to people in need.* Students can share items anonymously or write their name next to them. If you have time to discuss as a group, you might choose to end the school day by sharing the actions students have either taken themselves or noticed others take. Use this time to remind students actions don't need to be large and time-consuming. It's often the little things that matter.

Questioning Unfair Practices With Regard to Poverty

One way to examine social justice emerges from the intersection of unfair practices with issues like structural or economic inequity (poverty). First, it is important to note poverty and economic inequalities are pervasive in the United States, with greater than 20 percent of families living below or near the poverty line (DeNavas-Walt & Proctor, 2015; Heberle, Kaplan-Levy, Neuspiel, & Carter, 2018), and economic disparities may be more extreme than since before the Great Depression (Mistry et al., 2016).

Undoubtedly, poverty is a glaringly present condition that warrants discussion and a more critical understanding for everyone. However, among adults, class-based bias presents through dispositional explanations of poverty (for example, "poor people are lazy"), lack of empathy, and psychologically distancing oneself from the plight of the poor with weakened support of policies and programs that help those in need (Kraus, Piff, Mendoza-Denton, Rheinschmidt, & Keltner, 2012; Mistry et al., 2016). And although people see issues of systemic economic inequality as broad and complex, and perhaps difficult to address with young students, there is some evidence to suggest that they are not only aware of these issues but also quite capable of talking about them (Heberle & Carter, 2020). In fact, young students can express, in age-appropriate terms, an understanding of economic inequality in the world that surrounds them.

Some middle-class children echo adult explanations of poverty as personal deficiencies (for example, laziness) as a reason for economic hardships (Weinger, 2000). Similarly, a sample of middle-class children from a study identifies somewhat simplified explanations, such as having no job or a bad job, or mismanaging money (Sigelman, 2012). But missing from much of the literature on children's understanding of economic disparities is the viewpoint of children who come from lower-income families themselves. One study by Heberle and colleagues (2018) uses interviews and thematic analysis to discern how these children conceptualize the causes and consequences of poverty. Thirty children, ages six through nine, identified themselves as economically disadvantaged and participated in the study. Emergent in the data are overarching patterns of explanation and consequence descriptions, such as material resource deprivation of the poor, personal competence of people who are not living in poverty, and incompetence of people living in poverty, as well as ideas that portray those living in poverty as honorable and honest.

Clearly these themes illustrate children living in poverty echo some of the middle-class conceptions (for example, "people who are not living in poverty are more competent or less lazy than people who are") but also diverge in the sense that economically disadvantaged children tend to attribute positive traits, such as honor and honesty, with economically disadvantaged people, whereas children not living in poverty may not. Interestingly, in this study, some children also note people need money to get a job (Heberle et al., 2018). This idea (that it takes money to make money) suggests a potentially more nuanced evaluation of the plight of poverty than is commonly seen among many children and adults alike.

It is clear children do not lack the ability to identify those who are economically disadvantaged, but do perhaps need more instruction and understanding of the structures and causes of poverty. As Mistry and colleagues (2016) note, "class-based attitudes and beliefs have their roots in childhood, but there is limited evidence of the efficacy of intervention efforts aimed at reducing class-based bias and stereotypic reasoning among children" (p. 781). Further, these authors note, "for attitudinal change to occur, children need to be engaged in explicit discussions of social and societal issues" (Mistry et al., 2016, p. 782). Certainly, using authentic children's literature as a means of contextualizing discussions to broaden and deepen students' understanding of issues of economic disparity is one means to achieve those objectives. There are a number of books you can use to address these themes, many of which we include in other sections of this book (for example, *Each Kindness* by Woodson, 2012). Books that explore the act of questioning unfair practices and the principles that underlie social justice issues are available for children of all ages, and we present one such example here.

Literature on Questioning Unfair Practices With Regard to Poverty

Individuals from low-socioeconomic backgrounds are often underserved in many social, environmental, and educational ways. This activity presents stories on how students can recognize these unfair conditions and serve as their own advocates to rectify them.

Book: *The Streets Are Free* by Kurusa (1995)

As noted previously, the steps for introducing each book to the class include present the story, clarify story concepts through discussion, clarify the features of the desired behaviors through enactments, practice the desired behaviors through real-life applications, respond appropriately to issues of diversity, and provide extension activities to maintain the desired behaviors.

Present the Story

Read the story to and with the class. If students have a hard copy of the book or if they can access the story online, they can follow along as you read aloud. If not, students can simply listen as you read.

Story Synopsis

The story is set in Venezuela, depicting a once lush and expansive natural habitat that becomes industrialized into the densely crowded barrio of San José. Carlitos, Cheo, and Camila, along with other children from the community, struggle to find open spaces for outdoor play, so they often find themselves playing in the streets. Motorists and other community members find the street play obstructive and yell at the children, whose common refrain is "The streets are free!" With the guidance of the town librarian, the children write a list of items they need to develop a playground in an empty lot near the base of the mountain. They take their plans to city hall to request the playground be built so they no longer need to use the streets for play. After some opposition from city hall, the mayor makes promises to the children and uses the opportunity for a political photo op, but he never follows through on the promises. The children, the librarian, and the families grow tired of waiting for the mayor's promises to materialize. They organize a town meeting of their own and engage in a long, vociferous discussion and debate about the playground. Ultimately, everyone brings their own materials, time, and labor to the project, and the playground manifests from idea to reality. The people of the community build the playground for the enjoyment of all.

Discussion

After reading the story, select one or more concepts to explore further through class discussion. You may broach several themes with the class, and some of them may even lend connections to interdisciplinary content (such as social studies, geography, and history). Ask students to respond individually or in small groups to the following questions.

1. "What did the children in this story want? Was it a fair request to make?" (They wanted a playground. Yes, it's a fair request to make because they had nowhere else to play and exercise besides the city streets.)

2. "How did the mayor and other representatives respond to the needs of the community members (the children)? How should they have responded?" (They reluctantly agreed to build the playground. They used the opportunity to get positive publicity by doing a ribbon-cutting ceremony, but never followed up with any action.)

3. "Who was treated unfairly in this story? How so?" (The children and the community members were treated unfairly. The mayor did not listen to the children, and they were under threat of being arrested unjustly. The community members were treated unfairly because the city officials who made promises to them ignored their needs.)

4. "Besides the inaction of the city representatives, what were some other things that made it difficult for the children to get their playground built?" (The children's families lacked time to attend to the needs of the children because they had to work. The children needed to rely on the guidance of the librarian because of their relative inexperience with systems of government.)

5. "What did the children and the residents of the community ultimately decide to do about their problem?" (They organized a meeting of community members to decide how they could take collective action to build a playground for the children. After they listened and debated, they all contributed time, materials, and labor to the effort. Together, they built the playground for themselves and others to enjoy.)

6. "*Barrio* is a word for a small urban neighborhood or area of a city. In this story, was the barrio of San José well-funded and resourced, or was it an area of greater economic need? How do you know?" (Poverty and a lack of resources affected the barrio of San José. We can infer this because there was nowhere for the children to play other than the streets. The book illustrations show very crowded areas of housing in disrepair and garbage in the streets, and the community did not have very much money, materials, or time.)

7. "How do issues like limited money and resources affect urban areas and people?" (In urban areas, there are more people with greater needs in a smaller geographical area. This means there are fewer resources to go around. The people need to work more hours for less pay, and ultimately have less free time to devote to pursuits outside work. Faced with residents of great need and

fewer resources, city officials often fail to deliver on promises made to the community.)

8. "How does the loss of habitat affect natural landscapes, wildlife, or the people living in those areas?" (When people and buildings encroached on the forests and lush landscapes, the tiger tracks slowly disappeared. This means wildlife was driven off or killed in the process of industrialization. As the city became more densely populated, the children also lacked space to play and run around.)

9. "Money is one resource to draw on to make changes. What are some other resources that don't involve money?" (Other resources include time, community organization, and donated materials.)

Enactments

Return to the part of the story in which the children return to the library steps, dejected after their parents are too busy to go with them to city hall. In this part of the story, the librarian guides the children through the steps of problem solving by asking them questions like, "What do you want to tell the mayor?" "Do you know where (you want the playground)?" "Do you know what (the playground) should look like?" "Have you tried going (to city hall) alone?" and so on. Here, the librarian is teaching the children to use their own agency to make changes in their community.

When faced with initial opposition, people often might feel helpless, but usually, they are not. The children learn the action steps to make the change they want to see in their community. Provide small groups of students with a copy of figure 8.5 (page 188), and ask them to act out the steps they would take to solve each problem.

Real-Life Applications

In this story, the children identified an unfair practice in their community (the lack of space and equipment for children to play safely). In the neighborhoods, communities, states, and countries around the world, examples abound of resistant and persistent problems in need of change. Review local, state, national, and world news for current events to serve as the basis for discussion and action planning for your students.

For example, you might use current events related to health, safety, climate, economic, or social justice to illustrate how to apply actions for change to broader communities and issues. Encourage students to either individually or in groups select one of the current events to discuss. Brainstorm possible solutions, resources, and action steps to help address the identified dilemma.

Scenario	What Is My Idea for a Solution?	What Resources Do I Need?	What Can I Do on My Own?	Who Can I Ask for Help?
The regularly scheduled end-of-the-year school festival is cancelled this year because of budget cuts.				
My best friend's birthday party is scheduled during a time I will be out of town, but I really want to celebrate with my friend.				
Our school store is closing because the teacher who is in charge of the store is moving to a new city.				
Arthur is a very talented basketball player. Although he has been playing for many years, the coaches won't allow him to play at the middle school instead of the elementary school. He wants to play with other players who will challenge him.				

Figure 8.5: Scenarios for student problem solving.

*Visit **go.SolutionTree.com/diversityandequity** for a free reproducible version of this figure.*

Diversity Issues in This Story

Although the author does not explicitly state it, she implies the children's community, the barrio of San José, is a lower-socioeconomic area (Kurusa, 1995). For example, there is garbage in the streets and overcrowding. These can be indicators of poverty. Like many adults, children might also struggle to understand and sensitively discuss issues related to socioeconomics. However, poverty is a pervasive experience for many youngsters, so it is worthy of them to directly address it in the curriculum. In the United States, approximately 15 million children live in homes where the income is below the federal poverty line (Wight, Chau, & Aratani, 2011). The description of this community is similar to many children's experiences in U.S. communities. Opening the class to a sensitive discussion of the topic can be reassuring to many children who may feel isolated or embarrassed by their family's circumstances.

Discuss with students how common it is for families to struggle financially. Remind them that although many people experience economic hardships, it is unfair to treat them badly for circumstances they cannot control. Direct students back to the story and ask more in-depth questions such as the following.

- "How did we know this is a community with economic hardship?" (There was no place to play. The library was a converted house.)

- "What are some reasons this community might struggle financially?" (There are a lot of residents and relatively few resources and little space.)

- "Is it fair that the children have no place to play due to the economic hardship of the area? Why?" (No, because those are issues beyond the children's control.)

- "Especially in times of hardship, is it better only to focus on oneself, or is it a good idea to work together collectively to better the circumstances for the whole community?" (Although it may be tempting only to "look out for number one," it is crucial that communities band together to support one another. Together, people can accomplish more than one individual can alone.)

It's important to teach children to be kind and understanding of others and support one another through crises. Communities can be a source of strength, and everyone should support them collectively.

Extended Literature Activities

Use these literature activities to further ascertain students' understanding of the story and desired social-emotional learning skills. Students use their own words to retell the story and specify appropriate ways to respond. You also could use the annotated book list in the section Books on Questioning Unfair Practices (page 192) to assign more relevant readings to individuals or groups. For each book, we suggest general elementary reading levels.

Retell the Story

In small groups, encourage students to tell the story in their own words. Encourage them to consider important aspects of the story including how the children initially searched for many places to play before finding space in the streets; the children went to government officials to solicit action; officials made promises to the children they didn't keep; initially, the families were too busy to help the children; and ultimately, it took the efforts of the entire community to make the playground a reality.

Extend the Story: A Living History

Implied in the story is the effect of industrialization on the environment and natural habitat (for example, in the opening parts of the story and illustrations, it is clear increasing levels of manufacturing and urbanization result in loss of forest plus unbuilt areas of the landscape). The loss of habitat represents fewer natural resources and is one common manifestation of poverty. Ask students to identify how the loss of natural habitat might impact not only the people but also the animals and climate in the area. Engage the class in a discussion on the environmental impacts of industrialization. You can link this discussion to social studies units or other studies in the curriculum.

You may wish to structure this extension as an opportunity to create a *living history* of your community. Students can interview an older friend or family member to obtain a written or recorded description of what life was like in their community long ago. Have the interviews highlight how the economy and natural landscapes may have changed over the years. Students will learn important historical details, and family members and friends can be active partners in learning as well. Some suggested interview questions include the following.

- How long have you lived in this community, city, or area?
- What is your earliest memory of a major change in the area?
- How was this area different economically than it is now?
- Have there been any major changes to the landscape in your time? If so, what were they?

Additional Readings

Explore additional readings about economic hardship, poverty, hunger, and homelessness. The more you expose children to literature that addresses these important topics, the less taboo the issues become. Help children lessen the stigma and shame surrounding poverty by sharing some of the high-quality children's literature with them.

Last Stop on Market Street by Matt de la Peña (2015; Elementary)

In this story, CJ notices things about his life and his community that are different from other children's. He asks his grandmother about the world in which they live, about why he doesn't have things many of his friends have (for example, a car and access to technology). His grandmother answers each question directly and sensitively and helps CJ see beauty in his world.

Fly Away Home by Eve Bunting (1991; Elementary)

This story explores the unique challenges of homelessness. A widowed father and his son, who have no other place to live, find themselves staying in the airport and working together to navigate the logistics of this arrangement. They move from place to place within the airport, always careful to not let others see or discover them. The boy is aware he will soon have to start school and has anxiety over how he will be able to, given their inadequate housing. The two begin to feel hope as they watch a trapped bird make its way to freedom.

The Lunch Thief by Anne C. Bromley (2010; Upper Elementary)

The Lunch Thief extends the discussion of poverty and hunger by examining why some people do things in response that are wrong (for example, stealing) when the need is too great to bear. In this story, Kevin is caught stealing lunches, but later readers discover he is a victim of wildfires and has lost his home. In an effort to survive, Kevin resorts to stealing lunches. Rafael takes notice and invites Kevin to share his lunch, so he does not have to steal.

Action Project: Our Library

In this story, the community children came together to make their vision of an open play area a reality. Along the way, they encountered a number of obstacles, but their collective vision was more powerful than the bureaucratic barriers that slowed them down. For this action project, have students visualize themselves from the perspective of the librarian. He helped the children harness their vision and guided their steps toward the desired outcome. Apply these ideas to another project or activity for the class.

Begin by identifying an objective the class would like to materialize. You might use ideas from the entries in the journal students used for the action project Small Actions Make a Big Difference (page 182). Or you might provide a new idea based on the needs of your community. One example might be to develop an accessible library for all students' use in the school or a book donation to a community center (or other organization or group in need). Place students in small groups and encourage them to "be the librarian." They should engage in similar questioning and problem-solving techniques the librarian used in the story. For example, students could ask themselves, "What kinds of books do we need to collect?" "How can we purchase or secure these book donations?" and "Once we collect the books, where will we keep them so everyone can access them?" Again, refer to the part of the story that details how the librarian helped the children make a plan for their playground, and apply those same approaches to your class project.

After each group develops action steps for the project, ask group members to take responsibility for one of the steps. For example, to develop an accessible library, one group can identify book selections and categorize them. One group can call, email, or write letters to area businesses and other agencies to solicit book donations or monetary donations. One group can look for a physical space for the library and create writing procedures for book checkouts, and so on. In this way, each student has a role to play and can feel agency and ownership of the accomplishments of the class.

Books on Questioning Unfair Practices

Figure 8.6 offers a list of books featured in this chapter that include aspects of questioning unfair practices. As time permits, read these books in class and discuss the themes as we note in the previous activities. Encourage students to read these books independently, when appropriate, and share their observations with you and the rest of the class.

Title	Author	Story Summary
Elementary		
Each Kindness	Jacqueline Woodson (2012)	A young girl is from a family of a lower-socioeconomic status and living under the poverty line. Students in the class learn to be kind and understanding of others' hardships.
Fly Away Home	Eve Bunting (1991)	A homeless boy and his father living in an airport find hope through watching a trapped bird make its way to freedom.
Last Stop on Market Street	Matt de la Peña (2015)	This is the story of an African American boy and his grandmother, which addresses socioeconomic differences between the boy and his friends.
Passage to Freedom: The Sugihara Story	Ken Mochizuki (2010)	In this story of a young Japanese boy and his family during World War II, the father helps Jewish refugees flee to safety.
When Jackie and Hank Met	Cathy Goldberg Fishman (2012)	In this story, African American baseball player Jackie Robinson and Jewish baseball player Hank Greenberg experience many common hardships due to a lack of acceptance of differences during the 1940s and 1950s.
Upper Elementary		
La Frontera: El Viaje Con Papá (My Journey With Papa)	Deborah Mills and Alfredo Alva (2018)	A young Mexican boy and his father make the journey to immigrate from Mexico to Texas.
The Lunch Thief	Anne C. Bromley (2010)	A young boy who is homeless steals lunches to survive. Another student gains understanding and shares his lunch.
The Streets Are Free	Kurusa (1995)	Venezuelan children living in poverty work together to create a community park.

Figure 8.6: Books on questioning unfair practices.

Visit **go.SolutionTree.com/diversityandequity** *for a free reproducible version of this figure.*

Conclusion

In a letter from Birmingham Jail (April 16, 1963), Martin Luther King Jr. wrote, "Injustice anywhere is a threat to justice everywhere" (The National Civil Rights Museum, n.d.). This quote provides a compelling rationale for all of us to take an active role in the fairness and justice of our collective society. When you see or become aware of something that is unjust, you should take action to correct the injustice. You can begin to teach students how to turn citizenship into action by questioning unfair practices. Elementary-aged students often identify certain events as unfair. By teaching students the meaning of fairness and practicing the accurate evaluation of fair or unfair practices, you set the stage for them to take action on important matters. Once we, as citizens, identify situations or events as unfair or unjust, it is our obligation as citizens to act. Engaging students in this process can build a repertoire of social responsibility that serves them well throughout their lifespan.

Chapter Reflections

Individually or with a collaborative group, review and discuss the following questions to reflect on your learning in this chapter.

1. Do you have a responsibility to identify injustice and then act to correct it? Why or why not?

2. Does silence or tacit inaction on matters of injustice make you complicit in the unjust event? Why might an individual choose silence or inaction? How does this affect those most adversely impacted by the injustice?

3. Why is it important to be able to accurately discern the difference between something that is unfair or unjust and something that you simply don't like or don't approve of?

4. If you misidentify something as unfair or unjust and attempt to act on it, what might be the outcome?

5. In addition to questioning unfair practices, what are other ways to be a responsible and active citizen?

Epilogue

Let's revisit Gwen Cartledge's fifth-grade experience. Her teacher, Ms. Conner, did affirm Gwen, comforting her and telling her she was glad to have Gwen in her class. She also told Gwen she discussed the event with Jimmy, who said he moved away because Gwen was a girl, not because of her race. Over a period of a few days, Gwen observed that the fifth-grade boys, like Jimmy, tended to have a toxic attitude toward all girls in the class, and Jimmy was actually one of the nicest boys, who played freely with everyone, including Gwen.

Nevertheless, to her credit, Ms. Conner saw this as a teachable moment. She decided it was important to talk about race and perhaps make everyone feel comfortable, especially Gwen. Ms. Conner decided to read a book about the African American experience. Unfortunately, authentic books written about the African American experience for elementary students mostly began to emerge in the late 1960s and early 1970s, more than a decade after Gwen's elementary schooling, and Ms. Conner knew little about sparse existing literature for this population (for example, Langston Hughes or Paul Laurence Dunbar). So, she resorted to one that was fairly popular among White Americans, *Uncle Tom's Cabin* by Harriet Beecher Stowe, originally published in 1852 (Harriet Beecher Stowe Center, n.d.). Each day after lunch recess, right before social studies, Ms. Conner read portions of the book to the class. The class enjoyed the readings, listening intently and relishing the pleasurable change from their typical academic activities. Gwen especially enjoyed these readings, even though she often found many portions of the story disturbing, occasionally bringing her to tears.

Ms. Conner discussed the readings with the class. Although engaging and apparently well intentioned, these discussions often led to misinformation and distortions. On one occasion, for example, Ms. Conner told the class that African Americans (people used the term *Negroes* until the late 1960s, nearly a decade later than Gwen's schooling) were so angry about the treatment they received during slavery, when they came north, they would fight any White person they met on the street. Gwen was shocked when she heard this statement because it was never part of her experience or observation of African Americans interacting with Whites in her community.

We feature this story to illustrate a few key points relative to this book. First, social-emotional learning is a pervasive need for all students, but conditions of racial and cultural diversity have some unique implications. As this story illustrates, Ms. Conner was confronted with the situation of not just soothing feelings and helping her students be nicer to one another but also, and more important, helping them develop these skills across race. Fortunately, in this situation, Jimmy was not rejecting Gwen because of race, but it was still problematic because Gwen perceived race as the cause. If Ms. Conner chose to ignore or dismiss this event, Gwen could easily have spent the rest of the school year, and perhaps her remaining schooling, misperceiving and misjudging much of her classmates' behavior. Additionally, Jimmy and other students might learn how others can misinterpret typically harmless acts and realize that certain conditions warrant special precautions.

It is good for students to learn that diversity can be a means for enrichment and reward, but everyone has a responsibility in bringing about healthy, enjoyable, diverse environments. Students from the dominant group should learn the importance and specifics of how to welcome diverse classmates, and students from diverse backgrounds should acquire the interpersonal skills they need to develop positive relationships with their non-diverse peers.

In addition, culturally diverse books are important for all children to become successful global citizens. They need to not only learn about and appreciate the differences but also see themselves reflected and valued in these books. Ms. Conner was wise to look for a book about Black America. Although *Uncle Tom's Cabin* was not terribly affirming, Gwen enjoyed it because it was one of the few books that addressed the lives of her people. She wanted to read many more books about Blacks but the offerings in her school and local library were extremely sparse. Gwen's parents provided a few books, one of which she fell in love with—the poems and stories of Paul Laurence Dunbar—but the number of available books was quite limited. She also remembered reading the stories and poems of writers such as Langston Hughes that appeared in the Black newspapers and magazines to which her parents subscribed. Gwen found these writings about the lives of Blacks extremely enjoyable and affirming.

Even though the number of authentic books about culturally diverse populations has increased in recent years, there is still a tremendous need for more such books. Authorities on children's literature point out that the shelf life for many culturally diverse books is extremely short (Fleming et al., 2016). That is, many very good culturally diverse books for children are too soon out of print. Educators need to stock their classrooms, libraries, and homes with these books, and be sure these books are available and accessible to all students.

Gwen had another thought about Ms. Conner's class. Although her classmates were all White, they came from different ethnic and religious backgrounds (for example, German, Russian, Italian, Irish, Jewish, Hungarian, and so on). Instead of simply singling out Gwen's background for reading and discussion, Ms. Conner could have used that opportunity to read and discuss books about various other groups, both represented and not represented in the class.

Finally, an extremely important point is teachers must present information about diversity factually, honestly, and positively. In an attempt to address a perceived problem, during the class discussions, Ms. Conner often resorted to misinformation or stereotypes such as the hostile, angry African American eager to attack the innocent White person without provocation. Stereotypes, which may be taken from "a kernel of truth and distorted beyond reality" (Green, n.d.), are very damaging and counterproductive. You must avoid stereotypes attributed to all groups, especially minority groups, ranging from extremely negative ones such as savages or wild individuals (for example, African or Native Americans) to mythical ones such as model minorities (for example, Asian Americans; Chow, 2017). These negative and misleading stereotypes can be long lasting, greatly shaping people's attitudes, policies, and actions toward others (Green, n.d.).

You must be rigorous in presenting only accurate facts and present information positively. People can make negative statements about any group, and no one group is superior to another. The United States is a *pluralistic society*, which means there is a dominant culture. Members of the dominant culture expect those of other smaller cultures to adhere to the dominant culture as well as identify with their smaller culture. For example, in the United States, most people in the dominant culture speak English, but individuals may also speak a language from their smaller culture, such as Spanish. Many people have come to recognize the value of being fluent in more than one language, so society at large as well as individuals within their own cultural group encourage people from various smaller cultures to continue to embrace and share aspects of their culture (for example, food, dance, music, and history). Difference from the dominant culture does not automatically mean inferior or deviant. People should not denigrate or subjugate any one group but celebrate and embrace the other.

Finally, we contend that in developing social-emotional skills within a culturally diverse context, applied activities have a much greater effect than simply reading about and discussing those skills. This is our rationale for practicing and applying suggestions in the activities throughout this book. Educators and policymakers have rightly begun to question the usefulness of didactic experiences alone in bringing about desired social change (Brooks, 2020).

Depending on how teachers present it, such instruction could possibly have a negative rather than positive effect. McKeown and colleagues (2017) argue teachers should structure their classrooms, so students continue to have positive diverse interactions on a sustained basis.

In Gwen's case with Ms. Conner, for example, despite the less-than-ideal book and Ms. Conner's use of negative stereotypes, Ms. Conner did try to foster a positive racial environment, so Gwen had a good fifth-grade experience. Ms. Conner ensured Gwen not only was accepted by her classmates but also each day got to play small- and large-group games with her classmates as well as participate in small-group academic activities. By the middle of the school year, Gwen and her classmates were quite comfortable with each other.

Positive, culturally diverse schooling can provide the foundation to foster and manage diverse relationships people experience throughout schooling and in later life. The ease with which people interact with others with differences facilitates their personal success, their ability to traverse domestic and global environments, and their ability to contribute to as well as receive from the larger society. With many more resources and much greater diversity awareness, we contend teachers need to be deliberate in teaching for diverse contexts so elementary-aged children not only relate to but also perform on a sustained basis the social-emotional skills they need in a diverse society. Social-emotional learning is for helping young people master interpersonal relationships and enhance their own self-regard. However, equally important social-emotional learning within culturally diverse contexts provides the building blocks for the critical components people need for successful lifelong living in a pluralistic and diverse community, country, and world.

References and Resources

Adam, H., Barratt-Pugh, C., & Haig, Y. (2017). Book collections in long day care: Do they reflect diversity? *Australasian Journal of Early Childhood, 42*(2), 88–96.

American Association of Physical Anthropologists (AAPA). (2019). *AAPA statement on race and racism.* Accessed at https://physanth.org/about/position-statements/aapa-statement-race-and-racism-2019 on October 7, 2021.

American Psychological Association (APA) Dictionary of Psychology. (n.d.). *Self-assertion.* Accessed at https://dictionary.apa.org/self-assertion on October 7, 2021.

American Speech-Language-Hearing Association (ASHA). (1993). *Definitions of communication disorders and variations.* Accessed at www.asha.org/policy/rp1993-00208 on June 21, 2021.

Anderson, C. (2019). *One person, no vote: How voter suppression is destroying our democracy.* New York: Bloomsbury Publishing.

Armitage, C. J., & Rowe, R. (2011). Testing multiple means of self-affirmation. *British Journal of Psychology, 102*(3), 535–545.

Avnur, O. (2014). *Virtues of a great warrior: An adventure about finding the ancient secret of martial arts and also something greater.* Author.

Barrie, J. M. (1904). *Peter Pan; or the boy who wouldn't grow up* [Play]. London: Hodder and Stoughton.

Beaty, D. (2013). *Knock, knock: My dad's dream for me.* New York: Little, Brown.

Billingsley, B. S., Bettini, E. A., & Williams, T. O. (2019). Teacher racial/ethnic diversity: Distribution of special and general educators of color across schools. *Remedial and Special Education, 40*(4), 199–212. Accessed at https://journals.sagepub.com/doi/10.1177/0741932517733047 on June 21, 2021.

Binfet, J. T., Gadermann, A. M., & Schonert-Reichl, K. A. (2016). Measuring kindness at school: Psychometric properties of a school kindness scale for children and adolescents. *Psychology in the Schools, 53*(2), 111–126.

Bishop, R. S. (2007). *Free within ourselves: The development of African American children's literature.* Westport, CT: Greenwood Press.

Blume, J. (2014). *Iggie's house.* New York: Atheneum Books for Young Readers.

Boelts, M. (2007). *Those shoes.* Cambridge, MA: Candlewick Press.

Bromley, A. C. (2010). *The lunch thief.* Gardiner, ME: Tilbury House.

Brooks, D. (2020, December 31). *2020 taught us how to fix this.* The New York Times. Accessed at https://nytimes.com/2020/12/31/opinion/social-change-bias-training.html on August 23, 2021.

Brown, K., & Brown, J. (2019). *I am perfectly designed.* New York: Holt.

Bruchac, J. (1993). *The first strawberries: A Cherokee story.* New York: Dial Books for Young Readers.

Bruchac, J. (1994). *A boy called Slow: The true story of Sitting Bull.* New York: Philomel Books.

Bruchac, J. (1998). *Children of the longhouse.* New York: Puffin Books.

Bruchac, J. (1999). *The Trail of Tears.* New York: Golden Books.

Bruchac, J. (2003). *The warriors.* Plain City, OH: Darby Creek.

Bruchac, J. (2005). *Code talker: A novel about the Navajo Marines of World War Two.* New York: Dial Books for Young Readers.

Bruchac, J. (2019). *Pushing up the sky: Seven Native American plays for children.* New York: Puffin Books.

Bruchac, J., & Bruchac, J. (2003). *How chipmunk got his stripes.* New York: Puffin Books.

Bruchac, J., & Bruchac, J. (2008). *The girl who helped thunder and other Native American folktales.* New York: Sterling.

Budiman, A. (2020). *Key findings about U.S. immigrants.* Accessed at www.pewresearch.org/fact-tank/2020/08/20/key-findings-about-u-s-immigrants on June 21, 2021.

Bunting, E. (1991). *Fly away home.* New York: Clarion Books.

Byers, G. (2018). *I am enough.* New York: Balzer and Bray.

Campbell, S. B., Leezenbaum, N. B., Schmidt, E. N., Day, T. N., & Brownell, C. A. (2015). Concern for another's distress in toddlers at high and low genetic risk for autism spectrum disorder. *Journal of Autism Developmental Disorders, 45*(11), 3594–3605.

Campoy, F. I., & Howell, T. (2016). *Maybe something beautiful: How art transformed a neighborhood.* Boston: Houghton Mifflin Harcourt.

Captivating History. (2018). *Trail of tears: A captivating guide to the forced removals of Cherokee, Muscogee Creek, Seminole, Chickasaw and Choctaw nations.* Author.

Cartledge, G., Bennett, J. B., Gallant, D. J., Ramnath, R., & Keesey, S. (2015). Effects of culturally relevant materials on the reading performance of second-grade African Americans with reading/special education risk. *Multiple Voices for Ethnically Diverse Exceptional Learners, 15*(1), 22–43.

Cartledge, G., Gardner, R., III, & Ford, D. Y. (2009). *Diverse learners with exceptionalities: Culturally responsive teaching in the inclusive classroom.* Upper Saddle River, NJ: Pearson.

Cartledge, G., Keesey, S., Bennett, J. G., Ramnath, R., & Council, M. R., III. (2015). Culturally relevant literature: What matters most to primary-age urban learners. *Reading & Writing Quarterly: Overcoming Learning Difficulties, 32*(5), 399–426. Accessed at https://eric.ed.gov/fulltext/ED576988.pdf on June 21, 2021.

Cartledge, G., & Kiarie, M. W. (2001). Learning social skills through literature for children and adolescents. *TEACHING Exceptional Children, 34*(2), 40–47.

Cartledge, G., & Kleefeld, J. (2009). *Taking part: Introducing social skills to children, preK–grade 3* (2nd ed.). Champaign, IL: Research Press.

Cartledge, G., & Kleefeld, J. (2010). *Working together: Building children's social skills through folktales, grades 3–6* (2nd ed.). Champaign, IL: Research Press.

Cartledge, G., & Milburn, J. F. (1995). *Teaching social skills to children and youth: Innovative approaches* (3rd ed.). Boston: Allyn and Bacon.

Cartledge, G., & Milburn, J. F. (1996). *Cultural diversity and social skills instruction: Understanding ethnic and gender differences.* Champaign, IL: Research Press.

Carver-Thomas, D. (2018). *Diversifying the teaching profession: How to recruit and retain teachers of color* [Report]. Palo Alto, CA: Learning Policy Institute.

Chang, A. (2018, August 27). *We can draw school zones to make classrooms less segregated: This is how well your district does.* Accessed at www.vox.com/2018/1/8/16822374/school-segregation-gerrymander-map on October 10, 2021.

Children's Defense Fund. (2021). *The state of America's children 2020.* Accessed at www.childrensdefense.org/wp-content/uploads/2021/04/The-State-of-Americas-Children-2021.pdf on August 31, 2021.

Choi, J., Johnson, D. W., & Johnson, R. (2011). The roots of social dominance: Aggression, prosocial behavior, and social interdependence. *The Journal of Educational Research, 104*(6), 442–454.

Choi, Y. (2001). *The name jar.* New York: Knopf.

Chow, K. (2017, April 19). 'Model minority' myth again used as a racial wedge between Asians and Blacks. *NPR.* Accessed at https://npr.org/sections/codeswitch/2017/04/19/524571669/model-minority-myth-again-used-as-a-racial-wedge-between-asians-and-blacks on August 23, 2021.

Cilluffo, A., & Cohn, D. (2019). 6 demographic trends shaping the U.S. and the world in 2019. *Pew Research Center.* Accessed at www.pewresearch.org/fact-tank/2019/04/11/6-demographic-trends-shaping-the-u-s-and-the-world-in-2019 on October 7, 2021.

Cohn, D., & Caumont, A. (2016). 10 demographic trends shaping the U.S. and the world in 2016. *Pew Research Center.* Accessed at www.pewresearch.org/fact-tank/2016/03/31/10-demographic-trends-that-are-shaping-the-u-s-and-the-world on October 7, 2021.

Coles, R. (1992, Spring). Interview: Celebrate values. *Teaching Tolerance, 1,* 18–22.

Constitution of the United States. (n.d.). *First amendment.* Accessed at https://constitution.congress.gov/constitution/amendment-1 on June 21, 2021.

Cook, J. (2012). *Teamwork isn't my thing, and I don't like to share!* Boys Town, NE: Boys Town Press.

Cooley, R. (2004). New kids on the block: Fifth graders use Judy Blume's novel *Iggie's House* to think about racism, anti-racism, and the importance of acting for justice. *Rethinking Schools, 19*(2). Accessed at https://rethinkingschools.org/articles/new-kids-on-the-block on June 21, 2021.

Cornelissen, C. (1998). *Soft rain: A story of the Cherokee Trail of Tears*. New York: Delacorte Press.

Covell, K., Howe, R. B., & McNeil, J. K. (2008). 'If there's a dead rat, don't leave it.' Young children's understanding of their citizenship rights and responsibilities. *Cambridge Journal of Education, 38*(3), 321–339.

Covell, K., Howe, R. B., & Polegato, J. L. (2011). Children's human rights education as a counter to social disadvantage: A case study from England. *Educational Research, 53*(2), 193–206.

Craig, A. B., Brown, E., Upright, J., & DeRosier, M. E. (2016). Enhancing children's social emotional functioning through virtual game-based delivery of social skills training. *Journal of Child and Family Studies, 25*(3), 959–968.

Davis, A. N., Martin-Cuellar, A., & Luce, H. (2019). Life events and prosocial behaviors among young adults: Considering the roles of perspective taking and empathic concern. *The Journal of Genetic Psychology, 180*(4–5), 205–216.

Daywalt, D. (2013). *The day the crayons quit*. New York: Philomel Books.

DeGerolamo, A. (2020). *The benefits of knowing a second language* [Blog post]. Accessed at www.niche.com/blog/the-benefits-of-knowing-a-second-language on June 21, 2021.

De La Peña, M. (2015). *Last stop on Market Street*. New York: Putnam's Sons.

Demi. (1996). *The empty pot*. New York: Holt.

DeNavas-Walt, C., & Proctor, B. D. (2015). *Income and poverty in the United States: 2014: Current population reports*. Washington, DC: U.S. Government Printing Office.

Derman-Sparks, L., Edwards, J. O., & Goins, C. M. (2020). *Anti-bias education for young children and ourselves* (2nd ed.). Washington, DC: National Association for the Education of Young Children.

Dolan, E. M. (1987). *Aladdin and the magic lamp*. St Louis, MO: Milliken.

Domitrovich, C. E., Durlak, J. A., Staley, K. C., & Weissberg, R. P. (2017). Social-emotional competence: An essential factor for promoting positive adjustment and reducing risk in school children. *Child Development, 88*(2), 408–416.

Donoghue, C., & Raia-Hawrylak, A. (2016). Moving beyond the emphasis on bullying: A generalized approach to peer aggression in high school. *Children & Schools, 38*(1), 30–39.

Draper, S. M. (2012). *Out of my mind*. New York: Atheneum Books for Young Readers.

Dunkerly-Bean, J., Bean, T. W., Sunday, K., & Summers, R. (2017). Poverty is two coins: Young children explore social justice through reading and art. *The Reading Teacher, 70*(6), 679–688.

Durlak, J. A., Domitrovich, C. E., Weissberg, R. P., & Gullotta, T. P. (Eds.). (2015). *Handbook of social and emotional learning: Research and practice*. New York: Guilford Press.

Elenbaas, L., Rizzo, M. T., & Killen, M. (2020). A developmental-science perspective on social inequality. *Current Directions in Psychological Science, 29*(6), 610–616.

Elya, S. M. (2006). *Home at last.* New York: Lee & Low Books.

Essien, I. (2019). Pathologizing culture in early childhood education: Illuminating microaggressions from the narratives of the parents of Black children. *Western Journal of Black Studies, 43*(1–2), 9–21.

Estes, E. (2004). *The hundred dresses.* Orlando, FL: Clarion Books.

Fishman, C. G. (2012). *When Jackie and Hank met.* Singapore: Marshall Cavendish Children.

Fleming, J., Catapano, S., Thompson, C. M., & Carrillo, S. R. (2016). *More mirrors in the classroom: Using urban children's literature to increase literacy.* Lanham, MD: Rowman & Littlefield.

Flynn, J. E. (2012). Critical pedagogy with the oppressed and the oppressors: Middle school students discuss racism and White privilege. *Middle Grades Research Journal, 7*(2), 95–110.

Flynn, J. E. (2017). Speaking up and speaking out? Long-term impact of critical multicultural pedagogy. *Multicultural Perspectives, 19*(4), 207–214.

Frey, W. H. (2020, July 1). *The nation is diversifying even faster than predicted, according to new census data.* Accessed at www.brookings.edu/research/new-census-data-shows-the-nation-is-diversifying-even-faster-than-predicted on October 7, 2021.

Garcia, G. (2017). *Listening with my heart: A story of kindness and self-compassion.* Austin, TX: Skinned Knee.

Garcia, E. (2020, February 12). Schools are still segregated, and Black children are paying a price. *Economic Policy Institute,* 1–6. Accessed at www.epi.org/publication/schools-are-still-segregated-and-black-children-are-paying-a-price on October 7, 2021.

Gates, M., & Gates, R. (2018). *Yoga friends: A pose-by-pose partner adventure for kids.* Boulder, CO: Sounds True.

Gilani-Williams, F. (2017). *Yaffa and Fatima: Shalom, salaam.* Minneapolis, MN: Kar-Ben.

Glaser, L. (2004). *Mrs. Greenberg's messy Hanukkah.* Morton Grove, IL: Whitman.

Glossop, J. (2013). *The kids book of world religions.* Toronto, ON: Kids Can Press.

Green, L. (n.d.). Stereotypes: Negative racial stereotypes and their effect on attitudes toward African-Americans. *Ferris State University.* Accessed at www.ferris.edu/htmls/news/jimcrow/links/essays/vcu.htm on August 23, 2021.

Gresham, F. M. (2018). *Effective interventions for social-emotional learning.* New York: Guilford Press.

Hakovirta, M., & Kallio, J. (2015). Children's perceptions of poverty. *Child Indicators Research, 9*(2), 317–334.

Hannah-Jones, N. (2019, July 12). *It was never about busing.* Accessed at https://www.nytimes.com/2019/07/12/opinion/sunday/it-was-never-about-busing.html on November 18, 2021.

Harriet Beecher Stowe Center. (n.d.). *A moral battle cry for freedom.* Accessed at www.harrietbeecherstowecenter.org/harriet-beecher-stowe/uncle-toms-cabin on October 7, 2021.

Harrison, V. (2017). *Little leaders: Bold women in Black history.* New York: Little, Brown.

Harrison, V. (2018). *Dream big, little one.* New York: Little, Brown.

Harrison, V. (2019). *Little legends: Exceptional men in Black history.* New York: Little, Brown.

Heberle, A. E., & Carter, A. S. (2020). Young children's stereotype endorsement about people in poverty: Age and economic status effects. *Children and Youth Services Review, 108*(C).

Heberle, A. E., Kaplan-Levy, S. A., Neuspiel, J. M., & Carter, A. S. (2018). Young children's reasoning about the effects of poverty on people experiencing it: A qualitative thematic analysis. *Children and Youth Services Review, 86,* 188–199.

Henderson, D. L., & May, J. P. (2005). *Exploring culturally diverse literature for children and adolescents: Learning to listen in new ways.* Boston: Pearson.

Herrera, L. J. P., & Kidwell, T. (2018, Winter). Literature circles 2.0: Updating a classic strategy for the 21st century. *21st Century Learning & Multicultural Education, 25*(2), 17–21.

Heward, W. L. (2017). *Exceptional children: An introduction to special education* (11th ed.). Boston: Pearson.

Heyes, S. B. (2020). Just banter? Friendship, teasing and experimental aggression in adolescent peer networks. *Developmental Science, 23*(3), 1–8.

Hoffman, M. (2007). *Amazing Grace.* New York: Frances Lincoln.

Hoglund, W. L. G., & Hosan, N. E. (2013). The context of ethnicity: Peer victimization and adjustment problems in early adolescence. *The Journal of Early Adolescence, 33*(5), 585–609.

Holub, J. (2017). *This little trailblazer: A girl power primer.* New York: Little Simon.

Hughett, K., Kohler, F. W., & Raschke, D. (2013). The effects of a buddy skills package on preschool children's social interactions and play. *Topics in Early Childhood Special Education, 32*(4), 246–254.

Huitt, W. (2007). Maslow's hierarchy of needs. *Educational Psychology Interactive.* Valdosta, GA: Valdosta State University. Accessed at www.edpsycinteractive.org/topics/regsys/maslow.html on October 10, 2021.

Isadora, R. (1991). *Ben's trumpet.* New York: Greenwillow Books.

Isadora, R. (1995). *Over the green hills.* New York: Trumpet Club.

Jocius, R., & Shealy, S. (2017). Critical book clubs: Reimagining literature reading and response. *The Reading Teacher, 71*(6), 691–702.

Jung, S., & Sainato, D. M. (2013). Teaching play skills to young children with autism. *Journal of Intellectual & Developmental Disability, 38*(1), 74–90.

Juvonen, J., Kogachi, K., & Graham, S. (2018). When and how do students benefit from ethnic diversity in middle school? *Child Development, 89*(4), 1268–1282.

Keats, E. J. (1975). *Louie*. New York: Viking.

Kepner, T., & Wagner, J. (2020, November 18). Kim Ng has been ready for years. *The New York Times*. Accessed at www.nytimes.com/2020/11/18/sports/baseball/kim-ng-miami-marlins.html?campaign_id=37&emc=edit_rr_20201121&instance_id=24343&nl=race%2Frelated&regi_id=30421208&segment_id=45139&te=1&user_id=d124616e7ec8d35d888b2c33fcc93d67 on June 21, 2021.

Khan, H. (2018). *Amina's voice*. New York: Salaam Reads.

Khan, H. (2019). *Under my hijab*. New York: Lee & Low Books.

Khan, H. (2021). *Crescent moons and pointed minarets: A Muslim book of shapes*. San Francisco: Chronicle Books.

Kimmel, E. A. (1989). *Hershel and the Hanukkah goblins*. New York: Holiday House.

Kourlas, G. (2019, November 28). After Misty comes Marie: Breaking barriers in 'The Nutcracker.' *The New York Times*. Accessed at www.nytimes.com/2019/11/28/arts/dance/nutcracker-Marie.html on June 21, 2021.

Kraus, M. W., Piff, P. K., Mendoza-Denton, R., Rheinschmidt, M. L., & Keltner, D. (2012). Social class, solipsism, and contextualism: How the rich are different from the poor. *Psychological Review, 119*(3), 546–572.

Kurusa. (1995). *The streets are free* (Rev. North American ed.). New York: Annick Press.

Kyle, Z. (2016, August 9). Boise family reconnects after five years. *Idaho Statesman*. Accessed at www.idahostatesman.com/news/local/community/boise/article94520602.html on August 18, 2021.

Lê, M. (2018). *Drawn together*. Los Angeles: Disney-Hyperion.

Lewis, J. P. (2016). *The Navajo code talkers*. North Mankato, MN: Creative Editions.

Lionni, L. (1963). *Swimmy*. New York: Pantheon.

Literature Circles Resource Center (LCRC). (n.d.). *Overview of literature circles*. Accessed at www.litcircles.org/Overview/overview.html on October 7, 2021.

Lord, C. (2007). *Rules*. Recorded Books: Audible.com.

Love, J. (2018). *Julián is a mermaid*. Somerville, MA: Candlewick Press.

Ludwig, T. (2013). *The invisible boy*. New York: Knopf.

Lussier, K. (2019). Of Maslow, motive, and managers: The hierarchy of needs in American business, 1960–1985. *Journal of the History of the Behavioral Sciences, 55*(4), 319–341.

Lyons, K. S. (2018). *A girl named Misty: The true story of Misty Copeland*. New York: Scholastic.

Malti, T., Chaparro, M. P., Zuffiano, A., & Colasante, T. (2016). School-based interventions to promote empathy-related responding in children and adolescents: A developmental analysis. *Journal of Clinical Child & Adolescent Psychology, 45*(6), 718–731.

Marger, M. N. (2015). *Race and ethnic relations* (10th ed.). Stamford, CT: Cengage Learning.

Marohn, K. (2016, February 22). Fact check: How Somali names are chosen. *St. Cloud Times.* Accessed at www.sctimes.com/story/news/local/immigration/2016/02/21/fact-check-how-somali-names-chosen/80422864 on October 7, 2021.

Martin, R. (1992). *The rough-face girl.* New York: Putnam's Sons.

Martinez, A. C. (1991). *The woman who outshone the sun: The legend of Lucia Zenteno.* New York: Lee & Low Books.

Martinez-Neal, J. (2018). *Alma, and how she got her name.* Somerville, MA: Candlewick Press.

Maslow, A. (1954). *Motivation and personality.* New York: Harper.

Massey, D. S., & Denton, N. A. (1993). *American apartheid: Segregation and the making of the underclass.* Cambridge, MA: Harvard University Press.

McClain-Muhammad, L. (2019a). *I need you to know: The ABC's of Black girl magic.* Author.

McClain-Muhammad, L. (2019b). *I need you to know: The ABC's of a young king's greatness.* Author.

McIntyre, L. L., Blacher, J., & Baker, B. L. (2006). The transition to school: Adaptation in young children with and without intellectual disability. *Journal of Intellectual Disability Research, 50,* 349–361.

McKeown, S., Williams, A., & Pauker, K. (2017). Stories that move them: Changing children's behavior toward diverse peers. *Journal of Community & Applied Social Psychology, 27*(5), 381–387.

McLaughlin, M., & Rank, M. R. (2018). Estimating the economic cost of childhood poverty in the United States. *Social Work Research, 42*(2), 73–83.

Medina, M. (2015). *Mango, abuela, and me.* Somerville, MA: Candlewick Press.

Microaggression. (n.d.). In *Merriam-Webster dictionary* online. Accessed at www.merriam-webster.com/dictionary/microaggression on August 24, 2021.

Mills, D., & Alfredo, A. (2018). *La frontera: El viaje con papá (My journey with papa).* Cambridge, MA: Barefoot Books.

Mironenko, I. A., & Sorokin, P. S. (2018). Seeking for the definition of "culture": Current concerns and their implications—A comment on Gustav Jahoda's article "Critical reflections on some recent definitions of 'culture.'" *Integrative Psychological & Behavioral Science, 52*(2), 331–340.

Mistry, R. S., Nenadal, L., Griffin, K. M., Zimmerman, F. J., Cochran, H. A., Thomas, C.-A., et al. (2016). Children's reasoning about poverty, economic mobility, and helping behavior: Results of a curriculum intervention in the early school years. *Journal of Social Issues, 72*(4), 760–788.

Mize, J. (1995). Coaching preschool children in social skills: A cognitive-social learning curriculum. In G. Cartledge & J. F. Milburn (Eds.), *Teaching social skills to children and youth: Innovative approaches* (3rd ed., pp. 199–236). Boston: Allyn and Bacon.

Mochizuki, K. (2010). *Passage to freedom: The Sugihara story*. Washington, DC: National Geographic.

Morales, Y. (2018). *Dreamers*. New York: Porter Books.

National Center for Education Statistics (NCES). (2019). *Common Core of Data (CCD), State Nonfiscal Survey of Public Elementary and Secondary Education 2000–01 and 2015–16; and National Elementary and Secondary Enrollment Projection Model, 1972 through 2017*. U.S. Department of Education. Accessed at https://nces.ed.gov/ccd/pub_snf_report.asp on October 7, 2021.

National Civil Rights Museum. (n.d.). *Justice*. Accessed at https://mlk50.civilrightsmuseum.org/justice on October 7, 2021.

Newport, F. (2017). *2017 update on Americans and religion*. Accessed at https://news.gallup.com/poll/224642/2017-update-americans-religion.aspx on June 21, 2021.

Noguera, P. A., & Alicea, J. A. (2020). Structural racism and the urban geography of education. *Phi Delta Kappan, 102*(3), 51–56.

Norris, D. (2020). *What marketers should know about changing demographics*. Accessed at https://environicsanalytics.com/en-ca/resources/blogs/ea-blog/2020/02/28/canada-2020-and-beyond on October 7, 2021.

Palacio, R. J. (2012). *Wonder*. New York: Knopf.

Palmer, S. B., Rutland, A., & Cameron, L. (2015). The development of bystander intentions and social-moral reasoning about intergroup verbal aggression. *British Journal of Developmental Psychology, 33*(4), 419–433.

Park, L. S. (2008). *Bee-bim bop!* New York: Clarion Books.

Parr, T. (2001). *It's okay to be different*. Boston: Little, Brown.

Pauketat, J. V. T., Moons, W. G., Chen, J. M., Mackie, D. M., & Sherman, D. K. (2016). Self-affirmation and affective forecasting: Affirmation reduces the anticipated impact of negative events. *Motivation & Emotion, 40*, 750–759.

PBS News Hour. (2020, January 8). *Children of color projected to be the majority of U.S. youth this year*. Accessed at www.pbs.org/newshour/nation/children-of-color-projected-to-be-majority-of-u-s-youth-this-year on October 7, 2021.

Pearlman, R. (2018). *Pink is for boys*. Philadelphia: Running Press Kids.

Penfold, A., & Kaufman, S. (2019). *All are welcome*. New York: Bloomsbury Children's Books.

Pew Research Center. (2020). *What census calls us*. Accessed at www.pewresearch.org/interactives/what-census-calls-us on June 21, 2021.

Pfister, M. (1995). *The rainbow fish*. New York: NorthSouth Books.

Poushter, J., & Fetterolf, J. (2019). How people around the world view diversity in their countries. *Pew Research Center.* Accessed at www.pewresearch.org/global/2019/04/22/how-people-around-the-world-view-diversity-in-their-countries on October 7, 2021.

Powell, M. D., & Ladd, L. D. (2010). Bullying: A review of the literature and implications for family therapists. *The American Journal of Family Therapy, 38*(3), 189–206.

Rattigan, J. K. (1993). *Dumpling soup.* Boston: Little, Brown.

Readable. (n.d.). *The Spache readability formula.* Accessed at https://readable.com/readability/spache-readability-formula on October 7, 2021.

Rey, H. A., & Rey, M. (2012). *Happy Hanukkah, Curious George.* Boston: Houghton Mifflin Harcourt.

Rey, H. A., Rey, M., & Hapka, C. (2017). *Merry Christmas, Curious George.* Boston: Clarion Books.

Rey, H. A., Rey, M., & Khan, H. (2016). *It's Ramadan, Curious George.* Boston: Houghton Mifflin Harcourt.

Reynoso, N. (2020). *Be bold! Be brave! 11 Latinas who made U.S. history.* Los Angeles: Con Todo Press.

Rice, L. (2014, December 4). *Why does a woman always play Peter Pan?* Accessed at https://people.com/celebrity/why-does-a-woman-always-play-peter-pan on October 7, 2021.

Risser, S. D. (2013). Relational aggression and academic performance in elementary school. *Psychology in the Schools, 50*(1), 13–26.

Roberts, S. (2010, August 25). New life in U.S. no longer means new name. *The New York Times.* Accessed at www.nytimes.com/2010/08/26/nyregion/26names.html on June 21, 2021.

Robinson-Ervin, P., Cartledge, G., Musti-Rao, S., Gibson Jr., L., & Keyes, S. E. (2016). Social skills instruction for urban learners with emotional and behavioral disorders: A culturally responsive and computer-based intervention. *Behavioral Disorders, 41*(4), 209–225.

Rockliff, M. (2016). *Chik chak shabbat.* Somerville, MA: Candlewick Press.

Ross, S. W., & Horner, R. H. (2013). Bully prevention in positive behavior support: Preliminary evaluation of third-, fourth-, and fifth-grade attitudes toward bullying. *Journal of Emotional and Behavioral Disorders, 22*(4), 225–236.

Sang, S. A., & Nelson, J. A. (2017). The effects of siblings on children's social skills and perspective taking. *Infant and Child Development, 26,* 1–10.

Scholastic. (2015, December 10). *Last stop on Market Street by Matt de la Peña, illustrated by Christian Robinson* [Video file]. Accessed at https://youtube.com/watch?v=0-m6mIZY8aI on August 23, 2021.

Shakespeare, W. (2011). *Romeo and Juliet* (Reprint ed.). B. A. Mowat & P. Werstine (Eds.). Folger Shakespeare Library. New York: Simon & Schuster. (Original work published 1597)

Sharma, S. A., & Christ, T. (2017). Five steps toward successful culturally relevant text selection and integration. *The Reading Teacher, 71*(3), 295–307.

Shriberg, D., & Desai, P. (2014). Bridging social justice and children's rights to enhance school psychology scholarship and practice. *Psychology in the Schools, 51*(1), 3–14.

Sigelman, C. K. (2012). Rich man, poor man: Developmental differences in attributions and perceptions. *Journal of Experimental Child Psychology, 113*(3), 415–429.

Sokol, N., Bussey, K., & Rapee, R. M. (2016). Teachers' perspectives on effective responses to overt bullying. *British Educational Research Journal, 42*(5), 851–870.

Spitzer, B., & Aronson, J. (2015). Minding and mending the gap: Social psychological interventions to reduce educational disparities. *British Journal of Educational Psychology, 85*(1), 1–18.

Sridhar, D., & Vaughn, S. (2000). Bibliotherapy for all: Enhancing reading comprehension, self-concept, and behavior. *TEACHING Exceptional Children, 33*(2), 74–82.

Steele, C. M. (2010). *Whistling Vivaldi: And other clues to how stereotypes affect us.* New York: Norton.

Stell, A. J., & Farsides, T. (2016). Brief loving-kindness meditation reduces racial bias, mediated by positive other-regarding emotion. *Motivation and Emotion, 40*(1), 140–147.

Steptoe, J. (1969). *Stevie.* New York: HarperCollins.

Steptoe, J. (1987). *Mufaro's beautiful daughters: An African tale.* New York: Lothrop, Lee & Shepard Books.

Surat, M. (1989). *Angel child, dragon child.* Milwaukee, WI: Scholastic Paperbacks.

Tarpley, N. A. (2001). *I love my hair!* Boston: Little, Brown Books for Young Readers.

Tatum, B. D. (2017). *"Why are all the Black kids sitting together in the cafeteria?": And other conversations about race.* New York: Basic Books.

Taylor, R. D., Oberle, E., Durlak, J. A., & Weissberg, R. P. (2017). Promoting positive youth development through school-based social and emotional learning interventions: A meta-analysis of follow-up effects. *Child Development, 88*(4), 1156–1171.

TEDx Talks. (2016a, April 28). *Brynn Welch: Missing adventures—Diversity and children's literature* [Video file]. Accessed at https://youtube.com/watch?v=Yq2opVinciA on August 23, 2021.

TEDx Talks. (2016b, April 28). *Grace Lin: The windows and mirrors of your child's bookshelf* [Video file]. Accessed at https://youtube.com/watch?v=_wQ8wiV3FVo on August 23, 2021.

Templeton, A. (2016). Evolution and notions of human race. In J. Losos & R. Lenski (Eds.), *How evolution shapes our lives: Essays on biology and society* (pp. 346–361). Princeton; Oxford: Princeton University Press.

Thomas, J. C. (2000). *I have heard of a land.* New York: HarperCollins.

Thompkins-Bigelow, J. (2019). *Mommy's khimar.* New York: Scholastic.

Thompkins-Bigelow, J. (2020). *Your name is a song.* Seattle, WA: Innovation Press.

Thorn, T. (2019). *It feels good to be yourself: A book about gender identity.* New York: Holt.

Thornberg, R. (2008). 'It's not fair!'—Voicing pupils' criticisms of school rules. *Children & Society, 22*(6), 418–428.

Todd, B. K., Fischer, R. A., Di Costa, S., Roestorf, A., Harbour, K., Hardiman, P., et al. (2018). Sex differences in children's toy preferences: A systematic review, meta-regression, and meta-analysis. *Infant and Child Development, 27*(2), 1–29.

Tov-Nachlieli, I. S., Shnabel, N., Aydin, A. L., & Ullrich, J. (2018). Agents of prosociality: Agency affirmation promotes mutual prosocial tendencies and behavior among conflicting groups. *Political Psychology, 39*(2), 445–463.

Trew, J. L., & Alden, L. E. (2015). Kindness reduces avoidance goals in socially anxious individuals. *Motivation and Emotion, 39*(6), 892–907.

UCLA Williams Institute. (2011). *How many people are lesbian, gay, bisexual, and transgender.* Accessed at https://williamsinstitute.law.ucla.edu/publications/how-many-people-lgbt on June 21, 2021.

United States Census Bureau. (2019). *Quick facts United States.* Accessed at www.census.gov/quickfacts/fact/table/US/PST045219 on June 21, 2021.

Venegas, E. M. (2019). "We listened to each other": Socioemotional growth in literature circles. *The Reading Teacher, 73*(2), 149–159.

Walton, J. (2016). *Introducing Teddy: A gentle story about gender and friendship.* New York: Bloomsbury.

Weinger, S. (2000). Economic status: Middle class and poor children's views. *Children & Society, 14*(2), 135–146.

Wells, A. S., Fox, L., & Cordova-Cobo, D. (2016). *How racially diverse schools and classrooms can benefit all students.* Accessed at https://tcf.org/content/report/how-racially-diverse-schools-and-classrooms-can-benefit-all-students/?session=1 on June 21, 2021.

Wight, V. R., Chau, M., & Aratani, Y. (2011, March). *Who are America's poor children? The official story.* New York: National Center for Children in Poverty. Accessed at http://nccp.org/wp-content/uploads/2020/05/text_1001.pdf on August 23, 2021.

Wiley, R. J. (1985). *Tchaikovsky's ballets: Swan Lake, Sleeping Beauty, Nutcracker.* Oxfordshire: Clarendon Press.

Woodson, J. (2001). *The other side.* New York: Putnam's.

Woodson, J. (2012). *Each kindness.* New York: Paulsen Books.

Woodson, J. (2018). *The day you begin.* New York: Paulsen Books.

Yu, S. Y., Ostrosky, M. M., & Fowler, S. A. (2014). The relationship between preschoolers' attitudes and play behaviors toward classmates with disabilities. *Topics in Early Childhood Special Education, 35*(1), 40–51.

Zentall, S. S., Kuester, D. A., & Craig, B. A. (2011). Social behavior in cooperative groups: Students at risk for ADHD and their peers. *The Journal of Educational Research, 104*(1), 28–41.

Zolotow, C. (1991). *The quarreling book*. New York: HarperCollins.

Index

A

ability differences, affirming others with
   about, 49–50
   additional readings, 55–56
   extended literature activities, 54–56
   literature on affirming others with ability differences, 50–56
action projects
   celebrate us, 66–67
   celebrating firsts, 92–93
   cooperation coach, 166
   cooperative hands, 156–157
   field trip, 49
   getting to know you, 82
   more about tribal nations, 145
   our library, 191–192
   our special guest, 133
   peer buddies, 56
   personalities, 49
   small actions make a big difference, 182–183
   special centers for immigrants or refugees, 114–115
   what's in a name, 106–107
advocacy, 171–172
affirming others
   with ability differences, 49–50
   ability differences, literature on affirming others with, 50–56
   about, 37, 39
   affirming self and others, 81
   being kind and affirming others, 39–42
   books on, 67–68
   chapter reflections, 69
   conclusion, 69
   from different religious or cultural groups, 57–58
   different religious or cultural groups, literature on affirming others from, 58–66
   in poverty, 42
   poverty, literature on affirming others in, 42–49
   self-confidence and, 72
affirming self. *See* self-affirmation
age groups, playing and working cooperatively across
   about, 150–151
   additional readings, 156
   extended literature activities, 155–157
   literature on playing and working cooperatively across age groups, 151–157
All Are Welcome (Penfold and Kaufman), 55, 67, 94, 133, 146
Alma, and How She Got Her Name (Martinez-Neal), 105, 116
Alva, A., 47, 68, 182, 192
Amazing Grace (Hoffman)
   and affirming self with regard to gender differences, 83–93
   and affirming self with regard to race, 72, 73–79
Amina's Voice (Khan), 66, 68
Angel Child, Dragon Child (Surat)
   and conflict management, 29
   and playing and working across racial and ethnic groups, 158–164, 167
   and responding to physical aggression, 123–131
asking for help, 18–19
asserting self. *See* self-assertion
assertive statements, 127–128

assessments and social-emotional learning, 21
auditory cues, 19
authority figures and conflict management, 128–129
Avnur, O., 156, 167

B

Barrie, J., 73, 84
baseball retelling, 181
Be Bold! Be Brave! 11 Latina Who Made U.S. History (Reynoso), 94
Beaty, D., 106, 116
Bee-Bim Bop! (Park), 105, 116
belonging, 37
Ben's Trumpet (Isadora), 114, 116
Bishop, R., 26–27
Blume, J., 172
Boelts, M., 48, 68, 132, 146
Boy Called Slow: The True Story of Sitting Bull, A (Bruchac), 146
Bromley, A., 48, 68, 191, 192
Brown, J., 81–82, 94
Brown, K., 81–82, 94
Bruchac, J.
    Boy Called Slow: The True Story of Sitting Bull, A (Bruchac), 146
    Children of the Longhouse (Bruchac), 146
    First Strawberries, The (Bruchac), 134–143
    Girl Who Helped Thunder and Other Native American Folktales, The (Bruchac and Bruchac), 146
    How Chipmunk Got His Stripes (Bruchac and Bruchac), 144, 146
    Pushing Up the Sky: Seven Native American Plays for Children (Bruchac), 146
    Trail of Tears, The (Bruchac), 146
    Warriors, The (Bruchac), 146
bullying. *See also* responding to aggression
    assertive statements and, 127
    peer intervention and, 123
    peer responses to, 129
    planful ignoring, 127
    self-assertion and, 97
    three understandings of, 121–122

Bunting, E., 48, 68, 191, 192
Byers, G., 80, 94

C

Campoy, F., 165, 167
Cartledge, G., 25
Chik Chak Shabbat (Rockliff), 65, 67
Children of the Longhouse (Bruchac), 146
Choi, J., 150
Choi, Y. *See Name Jar, The* (Choi)
classroom book clubs, 34–35
Coles, R., 26
communication disorders, 50, 53–54
conflict management
    about, 119
    enactments, 127–128
    interpersonal skills, 19
    responding to aggression, 122
    self-assertion and, 97
Cook, J., 166, 167
Cooley, R., 172
cooperation, 150. *See also* playing and working cooperatively with others
Cornelissen, C., 145
counting clubs, 142
Crescent Moons and Pointed Minarets (Khan), 65, 67
cultural principles, 25
culture. *See* ethnic and cultural differences
culture, definition of, 25
cyber aggression, 134. *See also* responding to aggression

D

Day the Crayons Quit, The (Daywalt), 132, 146
Day You Begin, The (Woodson), 68, 92, 94
Daywalt, D., 132, 146
De La Peña, M., 33, 47, 67, 190, 192
Demi, 116
Desai, P., 171
developing social-emotional skills in young children. *See* social-emotional skills
direct instruction, 14
disability and diversity, 2. *See also* ability differences, affirming others with

discussion of story concepts
  Amazing Grace (Hoffman), 74–75, 84–85
  Angel Child, Dragon Child (Surat), 124–126, 159–161
  Dreamers (Morales), 108–109
  Each Kindness (Woodson), 43–44
  First Strawberries, The (Bruchac), 135–138
  Louie (Keats), 51–52
  model for using literature for social-emotional learning, 31–32
  Mrs. Greenberg's Messy Hanukkah (Glaser), 61–62
  Name Jar, The (Choi), 99–100
  Streets Are Free, The (Kurusa), 185–187
  Under My Hijab (Khan), 59–60
  When Jackie and Hank Met (Fishman), 152–153, 174–177
diverse and culturally relevant children's literature
  about, 25–27
  chapter reflections, 36
  conclusion, 36
  literature formats for social-emotional learning, 33–34
  model for using literature for social-emotional learning, 30–33
  selection for social-emotional learning, 27–30
  social-emotional learning and, 11
  student engagement with books, 34–35
diversity
  changes in, 1–2
  peer victimization and, 121
  range of, 2
  teaching workforce and, 7
diversity issues in this story
  Amazing Grace (Hoffman), 79, 89
  Angel Child, Dragon Child (Surat), 130–131, 164
  Dreamers (Morales), 111–112
  Each Kindness (Woodson), 45–46
  First Strawberries, The (Bruchac), 142–143
  Louie (Keats), 53–54
  model for using literature for social-emotional learning, 33
  Mrs. Greenberg's Messy Hanukkah (Glaser), 63
  Name Jar, The (Choi), 103–104
  Streets Are Free, The (Kurusa), 188
  Under My Hijab (Khan), 63
  When Jackie and Hank Met (Fishman), 154–155, 179–180
Draper, S., 56, 68
Drawn Together (Lê), 67, 114, 116, 156, 167
Dream Big, Little One (Harrison), 81, 94
Dreamers (Morales)
  and affirming others, 67
  and self-assertion across immigrant and migrant groups, 107–112
Dumpling Soup (Rattigan), 106, 116

E

Each Kindness (Woodson)
  and affirming others in poverty, 42–46
  model for using literature for social-emotional learning, 31–33
  and questioning unfair practices, 192
Elya, S., 48, 68, 113, 116
emotional regulation and social-emotional learning, 2
empathy
  about, 14
  being kind and affirming others, 39–42
  social awareness and, 20–21
  social-emotional learning and, 2
Empty Pot, The (Demi), 116
enactments
  Amazing Grace (Hoffman), 75–77, 85–86
  Angel Child, Dragon Child (Surat), 126–129, 161
  Dreamers (Morales), 109
  Each Kindness (Woodson), 44
  First Strawberries, The (Bruchac), 138–141
  Louie (Keats), 52
  model for using literature for social-emotional learning and, 32

Mrs. Greenberg's Messy Hanukkah (Glaser), 62
Name Jar, The (Choi), 100–101
Streets Are Free, The (Kurusa), 187
When Jackie and Hank Met (Fishman), 153, 177
Estes, E., 49, 68
ethnic and cultural differences
    additional readings, 105–106, 165–166
    asserting self with regard to ethnic and cultural differences, 98
    extended literature activities, 104–107, 164–166
    literature on asserting self with regard to ethnic and cultural differences, 98–107
    literature on playing and working cooperatively across racial and ethnic groups, 158–166
    playing and working cooperatively across racial and ethnic groups, 158
etiquette rules, 170. *See also* rules
extended literature activities
    for affirming others from different religious or cultural groups, 63–67
    for affirming others in poverty, 46–49
    for affirming others with ability differences, 54–56
    for affirming self with regard to gender differences, 89–93
    for affirming self with regard to race, 80–82
    for asserting self across immigrant and migrant groups, 113–115
    for asserting self with regard to ethnic and cultural differences, 104–107
    model for using literature for social-emotional learning and, 33
    for playing and working cooperatively across age groups, 155–157
    for playing and working cooperatively across racial and ethnic groups, 164–166
    for questioning unfair practices with regard to poverty, 189–192
    for questioning unfair practices with regard to race, 180–183
    for responding to physical aggression, 131–133
    for responding to verbal aggression, 143–145
extending the story
    affirming myself, 80
    affirming self, 90
    I am Unhei, 104–105
    if Maya came to my class, 46–47
    is it fair or unfair?, 181
    kind words for Louie, 54
    living history, 190
    Louie and the puppet play, 54–55
    more about Hoa, 131–132
    my web design, 144
    personal stories, 155–156
    welcome to my Ramadan, Hanukkah, or Christmas celebration, 64
eye contact, 16

F

facial expressions, 19
fairness. *See also* questioning unfair practices
    about, 169–172
    playing and working cooperatively with others, 150
feelings, 15, 21
First Strawberries, The (Bruchac), 134–143
Fishman, C. *See When Jackie and Hank Met* (Fishman)
Fly Away Home (Bunting), 48, 68, 191, 192
Flynn, J., 173
Frontera: El Viaje Con Papá, La (My Journey With Papa) (Mills and Alva), 47, 68, 182, 192

G

Garcia, G., 68, 114, 116
Gates, M., 165, 167
Gates, R., 165, 167
gender, affirming self with regard to
    about, 82–83
    additional readings, 90–92
    extended literature activities, 89–93

literature on affirming self with regard to gender differences, 83–93
occupations and gender activity, 84
Gilani-Williams, F., 65, 67
Girl Named Misty: The True Story of Misty Copeland, A (Lyons), 81, 93, 94
Girl Who Helped Thunder and Other Native American Folktales, The (Bruchac and Bruchac), 146
Glaser, L., 60–63
Glossop, J., 66, 68
group activities, 18

H

Hapka, C., 65, 67
Happy Hanukkah, Curious George (Rey and Rey), 64, 67
Harrison, V.
　Dream Big, Little One (Harrison), 81, 94
　Little Leaders: Bold Women in Black History (Harrison), 82, 94
　Little Legends: Exceptional Men in Black History (Harrison), 82, 94
helping, interpersonal skills, 18
Hershel and the Hanukkah Goblins (Kimmel), 65, 67
hierarchical play, 151. *See also* playing and working cooperatively with others
Hoffman, M. *See Amazing Grace* (Hoffman)
Holub, J., 91, 94
Home at Last (Elya), 48, 68, 113, 116
hostile situations, 20
How Chipmunk Got His Stripes (Bruchac and Bruchac), 144, 146
Howell, T., 165, 167
Hundred Dresses, The (Estes), 49, 68

I

I Am Enough (Byers), 80, 94
I Am Perfectly Designed (Brown and Brown), 81–82, 94
I Have Heard of a Land (Thomas), 113–114, 116
I Love My Hair! (Tarpley), 28, 94

I Need You to Know: The ABC's of a Young King's Greatness (McClain-Muhammad), 91, 94
I Need You to Know: The ABC's of Black Girl Magic (McClain-Muhammad), 90, 94
identity threat, 71
Iggie's House (Blume), 172
immigrant and migrant groups, asserting self across
　about, 107
　additional readings, 113–114
　extended literature activities, 113–115
　literature on asserting self across immigrant and migrant groups, 107–115
　and responding to physical aggression, 129–130
international rescue centers, 114–115
interpersonal skills
　about, 16–17
　asking for help, 18–19
　conflict management, 19
　group activities, 17–18
　helping, 18
　positive statements to others, making, 17
　rules of play, 18
　sharing, 17
　social-emotional learning, 16–19
Introducing Teddy: A Gentle Story About Gender and Friendship (Walton), 92, 94
introduction
　about diversity, 1–2
　conclusion, 8–9
　how to use this book, 6–8
　purpose of this book, 2–3
　what's in this book, 3–6
Invisible Boy, The (Ludwig), 55, 68, 132, 146
Isadora, R.
　Ben's Trumpet (Isadora), 114, 116
　Over the Green Hills (Isadora), 68
It Feels Good to Be Yourself: A Book About Gender Identity (Thorn), 92, 94
It's Okay to Be Different (Parr), 90, 94
It's Ramadan, Curious George (Rey, Rey, and Khan), 64, 67

J

Julián Is a Mermaid (Love), 92, 94

K

Kaufman, S., 55, 67, 94, 133, 146
Keats, E., 50–54
Khan, H.
    Amina's Voice (Khan), 66, 68
    Crescent Moons and Pointed Minarets (Khan), 65, 67
    It's Ramadan, Curious George (Rey, Rey, and Khan), 64, 67
    Under My Hijab (Khan), 58–60, 62–63
Kiarie, M., 25
Kids Book of World Religions, The (Glossop), 66, 68
Kimmel, E., 65, 67
kindness, 39–42
King, M., 193
Knock, Knock: My Dad's Dream for Me (Beaty), 106, 116
Kurusa. See *Streets Are Free, The* (Kurusa)

L

language, 111, 112
Last Stop on Market Street (De La Peña), 33, 47, 67, 190, 192
lateral play, 151. See also playing and working cooperatively with others
Lê, M., 67, 114, 116, 156, 167
Listening With My Heart (Garcia), 68, 114, 116
literature circles, 34–35
Little Leaders: Bold Women in Black History (Harrison), 82, 94
Little Legends: Exceptional Men in Black History (Harrison), 82, 94
Louie (Keats), 50–54
Love, J., 92, 94
Ludwig, T., 55, 68, 132, 146
Lunch Thief, The (Bromley), 48, 68, 191, 192
Lyons, K., 81, 93, 94

M

Mango, Abuela, and Me (Medina), 114, 116
Martin, R., 144, 146
Martinez, A., 56, 68, 146
Martinez-Neal, J., 105, 116
Maslow's hierarchy of needs, 37
Maybe Something Beautiful (Campoy and Howell), 165, 167
McClain-Muhammad, L.
    I Need You to Know: The ABC's of a Young King's Greatness (McClain-Muhammad), 91, 94
    I Need You to Know: The ABC's of Black Girl Magic (McClain-Muhammad), 90, 94
Medina, M., 114, 116
Merry Christmas, Curious George (Rey, Rey, and Hapka), 65, 67
microaggressions, 20, 123, 172
migrants. See immigrant and migrant groups, asserting self across
Mills, D., 47, 68, 182, 192
Mistry, R., 184
Mochizuki, K., 181–182, 192
model for using literature for social-emotional learning
    about, 30–31
    discussion of story concepts, 31–32
    diversity, responding to, 33
    enactments and, 32
    extension activities and, 33
    presenting the story, 31
    real-life applications, 32
Mommy's Khimar (Thompkins-Bigelow), 65, 67
Morales, Y. See *Dreamers* (Morales)
Mrs. Greenberg's Messy Hanukkah (Glaser), 60–63
Mufaro's Beautiful Daughters: An African Tale (Steptoe), 146

N

Name Jar, The (Choi)
    and asserting self with regard to ethnic and cultural differences, 98–104
    and responding to aggression, 132, 146

names
    and asserting self with regard to ethnic and cultural differences, 99
    names and meanings, 101–103
nonverbal aggression, 133. *See also* responding to aggression
nonverbal cues, 19

O

older students, use of term, 8
Other Side, The (Woodson), 114, 116
Out of My Mind (Draper), 56, 68
Over the Green Hills (Isadora), 68

P

Palacio, R., 56, 68
paralanguage, 19
Park, L., 105, 116
Parr, T., 90, 94
Passage to Freedom: The Sugihara Story (Mochizuki), 181–182, 192
Pearlman, R., 92, 94
peer buddies, 56
peer victimization, 121
Penfold, A., 55, 67, 94, 133, 146
perspective taking, 40
Peter Pan (Barrie), 73, 84
physical aggression, responding to
    about, 121, 122–123
    additional readings, 132–133
    extended literature activities, 131–133
    literature on responding to physical aggression, 123–133
physical gestures, 19
Pink Is for Boys (Pearlman), 92, 94
planful ignoring, 127
playing and working cooperatively with others
    about, 120, 149–150
    and age groups, 150–151
    age groups, literature on playing and working cooperatively across, 151–157
    books on, 166–167
    chapter reflections, 168
    conclusion, 167
    and racial and ethnic groups, 158
    racial and ethnic groups, literature on playing and working cooperatively across, 158–166
pluralistic society, 197
popcorn reading, 181
positive self-statements, 15
positive statements to others, making, 17. *See also* affirming others
poverty, affirming others in
    about, 42
    additional readings, 47–49
    extended literature activities, 46–49
    literature on affirming others in poverty, 42–49
poverty, questioning unfair practices with regard to
    about, 183–184
    additional readings, 190–191
    extended literature activities, 189–192
    literature on questioning unfair practices with regard to poverty, 184–192
presenting the story
    Amazing Grace (Hoffman), 73, 83–84
    Angel Child, Dragon Child (Surat), 123, 158
    Dreamers (Morales), 107
    Each Kindness (Woodson), 43
    First Strawberries, The (Bruchac), 134
    Louie (Keats), 50
    model for using literature for social-emotional learning, 31
    Mrs. Greenberg's Messy Hanukkah (Glaser), 60
    Name Jar, The (Choi), 98
    Streets Are Free, The (Kurusa), 185
    Under My Hijab (Khan), 58
    When Jackie and Hank Met (Fishman), 151, 174
primary students, use of term, 8
prosocial behaviors, 14, 21, 39, 40, 41, 150
protecting rules, 170. *See also* rules
psychological aggression, 133. *See also* responding to aggression
psychological pain, 121
Pushing Up the Sky: Seven Native American Plays for Children (Bruchac), 146

Q

questioning unfair practices
    about, 120, 169–172
    books on, 192
    chapter reflections, 193
    conclusion, 193
    poverty, literature on questioning unfair practices with regard to, 184–192
    poverty and, 183–184
    race, literature on questioning unfair practices with regard to, 173–183
    race and, 172–173

R

race
    diversity and, 2
    use of term, 79
race, affirming self with regard to
    about, 72–73
    additional readings, 80–82
    extended literature activities, 80–82
    literature on affirming self with regard to race, 72–82
race, playing and working cooperatively across racial and ethnic groups
    about, 158
    additional readings, 165–166
    extended literature activities, 164–166
    literature on playing and working cooperatively across racial and ethnic groups, 158–166
race, questioning unfair practices with regard to
    about, 172–173
    additional readings, 181–182
    extended literature activities, 180–183
    literature on questioning unfair practices with regard to race, 173–183
racial bias, 41
racial segregation, 119
Rattigan, J., 106, 116
real-life applications
    Amazing Grace (Hoffman), 77–79, 88–89
    Angel Child, Dragon Child (Surat), 129–130, 162–163
    Dreamers (Morales), 109, 111
    Each Kindness (Woodson), 44–45
    First Strawberries, The (Bruchac), 141–142
    Louie (Keats), 52–53
    model for using literature for social-emotional learning, 32
    Mrs. Greenberg's Messy Hanukkah (Glaser), 62
    Name Jar, The (Choi), 101–103
    Streets Are Free, The (Kurusa), 187
    Under My Hijab (Khan), 62
    When Jackie and Hank Met (Fishman), 153–154, 178–179
refugees, 112, 129–130
relational aggression, 83, 133. *See also* responding to aggression
relational rules, 170. *See also* rules
relationships
    culturally diverse children's literature and, 26
    social-emotional learning and, 2
religious and cultural groups, affirming others from
    about, 57–58
    additional readings, 64–66
    extended literature activities, 63–67
    literature on affirming others from different religious or cultural groups, 58–66
religious symbols, 66
respecting and accepting differences, 16
responding to aggression
    about, 119, 121–122
    books on, 145, 146
    chapter reflections, 147
    conclusion, 145, 147
    physical aggression, 122–123
    physical aggression, literature on responding to, 123–133
    verbal aggression, 133–134
    verbal aggression, literature on responding to, 134–145
retelling the story
    Amazing Grace (Hoffman), 80, 90

Angel Child, Dragon Child (Surat), 131, 165
Dreamers (Morales), 113
Each Kindness (Woodson), 46
First Strawberries, The (Bruchac), 143
literature on affirming others from different religious or cultural groups, 63
Louie (Keats), 54
Name Jar, The (Choi), 104
Streets Are Free, The (Kurusa), 189–190
When Jackie and Hank Met (Fishman), 155, 181
Rey, H.
  Happy Hanukkah, Curious George (Rey and Rey), 64, 67
  It's Ramadan, Curious George (Rey, Rey, and Khan), 64, 67
  Merry Christmas, Curious George (Rey, Rey, and Hapka), 65, 67
Rey, M.
  Happy Hanukkah, Curious George (Rey and Rey), 64, 67
  It's Ramadan, Curious George (Rey, Rey, and Khan), 64, 67
  Merry Christmas, Curious George (Rey, Rey, and Hapka), 65, 67
Reynoso, N., 94
Rockliff, M., 65, 67
Rough-Face Girl, The (Martin), 144, 146
rules, 18, 150, 170–171

S

segregation, 119, 179
self-actualization, 37
self-affirmation
  about, 71–72
  affirming others and self and asserting self and, 37–38
  books on, 93, 94
  chapter reflections, 95
  conclusion, 93
  culturally diverse children's literature and, 26
  gender differences, affirming self with regard to, 82–83, 87
  gender differences, literature on affirming self with regard to, 83–93
  race, affirming self with regard to, 72–73
  race, literature on affirming self with regard to, 73–82
  what's in this book, 4
self-affirmation theory, 71
self-assertion
  about, 97
  affirming others and self and asserting self and, 38
  books on, 115, 116
  chapter reflections, 117
  conclusion, 115–116
  ethnic and cultural differences, asserting self with regard to, 98
  ethnic and cultural differences, literature on asserting self with regard to, 98–107
  immigrant and migrant groups, asserting self across, 107
  immigrant and migrant groups, literature on asserting self across, 107–115
  responding assertively, 110
  speaking assertively, 16
self-confidence, 72, 97
self-esteem, 37
self-related skills
  about, 14–15
  feelings, expressing, 15
  positive self-statements, 15
  respecting and accepting differences, 16
  social-emotional learning and, 15–16
  speaking assertively, 15–16
  temper, control of, 16
sharing, 17
Shriberg, D., 171
social aggression, 133. *See also* responding to aggression
social awareness
  about, 19–20
  empathy and, 20–21
  hostile situations, 20
  social-emotional learning and, 19–21
social competence, 3, 5, 19, 25

social justice, 171, 183
social-emotional learning
    impact of, 2
    literature formats for social-emotional learning, 33–34
    literature selection for social-emotional learning, 27–30
    model for using literature for social-emotional learning, 30–33
    social competence and, 25
social-emotional skills
    about, 13–14
    chapter reflections, 23
    conclusion, 23
    diverse and culturally relevant children's literature and, 11
    interpersonal skills, 16–19
    presence or absence of, 21–22
    self-related skills and, 15–16
    social awareness and, 19–21
    tracking individual social-emotional skills checklist, 22
socioeconomic status, 2
Soft Rain: A Story of the Cherokee Trail of Tears (Cornelissen), 145
spatial relations, 19
Steele, C., 71
Steptoe, J.
    Mufaro's Beautiful Daughters: An African Tale (Steptoe), 146
    Stevie (Steptoe), 156, 167
stereotypes, 197
Stevie (Steptoe), 156, 167
story synopsis
    Amazing Grace (Hoffman), 73–74
    Angel Child, Dragon Child (Surat), 124, 158–159
    Dreamers (Morales), 107–108
    Each Kindness (Woodson), 43
    First Strawberries, The (Bruchac), 134
    Louie (Keats), 50–51
    Mrs. Greenberg's Messy Hanukkah (Glaser), 61
    Name Jar, The (Choi), 99
    Streets Are Free, The (Kurusa), 185
    Under My Hijab (Khan), 58–59
    When Jackie and Hank Met (Fishman), 151–152, 174

Stowe, H., 195, 196
Streets Are Free, The (Kurusa)
    and affirming others, 48, 68
    and questioning unfair practices, 185–189, 192
structuring rules, 170. *See also* rules
student aggression, 121–122
Surat, M. *See Angel Child, Dragon Child* (Surat)

T

Tarpley, N., 28, 94
Teamwork Isn't My Thing, and I Don't Like to Share! (Cook), 166, 167
temper, control, 16
This Little Trailblazer: A Girl Power Primer (Holub), 91, 94
Thomas, J., 113–114, 116
Thompkins-Bigelow, J.
    Mommy's Khimar (Thompkins-Bigelow), 65, 67
    Your Name Is a Song (Thompkins-Bigelow), 105, 116
Thorn, T., 92, 94
Thornberg, R., 170
Those Shoes (Boelts), 48, 68, 132, 146
Trail of Tears, The (Bruchac), 146

U

Uncle Tom's Cabin (Stowe), 195, 196
Under My Hijab (Khan), 58–60, 62–63
upper elementary students, use of term, 8

V

verbal aggression, responding to
    about, 133–134
    additional readings, 144–145
    extended literature activities, 143–145
    literature on responding to aggression, 134–145
verbal statements, 19
violence or physical aggression, 29. *See also* responding to aggression
Virtues of a Great Warrior (Avnur), 156, 167
vocal tone, 19

W

Walton, J., 92, 94
Warriors, The (Bruchac), 146
When Jackie and Hank Met (Fishman)
    and playing and working cooperatively, 151–155, 158, 167
    and questioning unfair practices, 174–180, 192
Woman Who Outshone the Sun, The (Martinez), 56, 68, 146
Wonder (Palacio), 56, 68
Woodson, J.
    Day You Begin, The (Woodson), 68, 92, 94
    Each Kindness (Woodson), 31–33, 42–46, 192
    Other Side, The (Woodson), 114, 116

Y

Yaffa and Fatima: Shalom, Salaam (Gilani-Williams), 65, 67
Yoga Friends (Gates and Gates), 165, 167
younger students, use of term, 8
Your Name Is a Song (Thompkins-Bigelow), 105, 116

Change Starts With Me
Madeleine Rogin
Effectively educate elementary students on race and racism. Grounded in real-world examples, this accessible, insightful guide tackles topics like White silence, the scientific origin of skin color, and societal fears of being perceived as a racist.
BKG034

The Metacognitive Student
Richard K. Cohen, Deanne Kildare Opatosky, James Savage, Susan Olsen Stevens, and Edward P. Darrah
What if there was one strategy you could use to support students academically, socially, and emotionally? It exists—and it's simple, straightforward, and practical. Dive deep into structured SELf-questioning and learn how to empower students to develop into strong, healthy, and confident thinkers.
BKF954

Trauma-Sensitive Instruction
John F. Eller and Tom Hierck
Confidently and meaningfully support your trauma-impacted students with this accessible resource. The authors draw from their personal and professional experiences with trauma, mental health, and school culture to provide real insight into what you can do now to help learners build resilience and achieve at high levels.
BKF847

Building Blocks for Social-Emotional Learning
Tracey A. Hulen and Ann-Bailey Lipsett
Support the growth of your students with meaningful, effective social-emotional learning. You'll engage in deep reflection and discover ways to refine instruction, lesson planning, and assessment; promote whole-child development; and foster a productive learning environment for all.
BKG019

Solution Tree | Press

a division of Solution Tree

Visit SolutionTree.com or call 800.733.6786 to order.

Wait! Your professional development journey doesn't have to end with the last pages of this book.

We realize improving student learning doesn't happen overnight. And your school or district shouldn't be left to puzzle out all the details of this process alone.

No matter where you are on the journey, we're committed to helping you get to the next stage.

Take advantage of everything from **custom workshops** to **keynote presentations** and **interactive web and video conferencing**. We can even help you develop an action plan tailored to fit your specific needs.

Let's get the conversation started.

Call 888.763.9045 today.

SolutionTree.com